A World History of Rubber

A World History of Rubber

Empire, Industry, and the Everyday

Stephen L. Harp

This edition first published 2016
© 2016 John Wiley & Sons, Inc

Registered Office
John Wiley & Sons, Ltd, The Atrium, Southern Gate, Chichester, West Sussex, PO19 8SQ, UK

Editorial Offices
350 Main Street, Malden, MA 02148-5020, USA
9600 Garsington Road, Oxford, OX4 2DQ, UK
The Atrium, Southern Gate, Chichester, West Sussex, PO19 8SQ, UK

For details of our global editorial offices, for customer services, and for information about how to apply for permission to reuse the copyright material in this book please see our website at www.wiley.com/wiley-blackwell.

The right of Stephen L. Harp to be identified as the author of this work has been asserted in accordance with the UK Copyright, Designs and Patents Act 1988.

Wiley also publishes its books in a variety of electronic formats. Some content that appears in print may not be available in electronic books.

Designations used by companies to distinguish their products are often claimed as trademarks. All brand names and product names used in this book are trade names, service marks, trademarks or registered trademarks of their respective owners. The publisher is not associated with any product or vendor mentioned in this book.

Limit of Liability/Disclaimer of Warranty: While the publisher and author have used their best efforts in preparing this book, they make no representations or warranties with respect to the accuracy or completeness of the contents of this book and specifically disclaim any implied warranties of merchantability or fitness for a particular purpose. It is sold on the understanding that the publisher is not engaged in rendering professional services and neither the publisher nor the author shall be liable for damages arising herefrom. If professional advice or other expert assistance is required, the services of a competent professional should be sought.

Library of Congress Cataloging-in-Publication Data

Harp, Stephen L., author.
  A world history of rubber : empire, industry, and the everyday / Stephen L. Harp.
    pages   cm
  Includes bibliographical references and index.
  ISBN 978-1-118-93423-4 (cloth) – ISBN 978-1-118-93422-7 (paperback)
1. Rubber industry and trade–History.   2. Labor and globalization.
3. Globalization–Social aspects.   I. Title.
  HD9161.A2H37 2016
  338.4'76782–dc23

                                                              2015021086
A catalogue record for this book is available from the British Library.

Cover image: Firestone World's Fair brochure, 1934. Century of Progress records, Special Collections, University of Illinois at Chicago Library.

Set in 9.5/11.5pt Meridien by SPi Global, Pondicherry, India

1   2016

For my parents,
Sara and Larry Gotshall
Greg and Barb Harp

Contents

Contents

Acknowledgments

Ironically, it took me a long time to write this short book. Over many years, I have incurred considerable intellectual debts. I am very grateful to the following archives and libraries for their assistance: the Archives for Traditional Music and the Kinsey Institute at Indiana University, the Bibliothèque Nationale de France, the British Library, the British National Archives, the Centre des Archives d'Outre-Mer in Aix-en-Provence, the Guildhall Library of the City of London, the Hartman Center for Sales, Advertising, and Marketing History at Duke University, the Hoover Institution at Stanford University, the Herbert Hoover Presidential Library, the National Archives II in College Park, Maryland, the National Library of Vietnam in Hanoi, the New York Public Library, the Ohio Historical Society, the Smithsonian Institution Museum of American History, the University of Akron Archives, the University of Illinois at Chicago Library Special Collections Department, the Wellcome Library in London, and the Western Reserve Historical Society in Cleveland.

I am lucky to have received financial help from the following institutions to collect materials and to present ideas: the Ecole des Hautes Etudes en Sciences Sociales, the Hoover Presidential Library, the National Endowment for the Humanities, the Miller Humanities Center at the University of Akron, the University of Akron Faculty Research Committee, and the Watson Institute at Brown University.

Many people helped me find sources, sent materials, assisted research, responded to my queries, wrote letters, listened to my ideas in both formal and informal contexts, and read drafts. I could not be more grateful to Leah Alanni, Don Appleby, Dominique Avon, John Ball, Lisa Bansen-Harp, Shelley Baranowski, Nathaniel Bassett, TJ Boisseau, Connie Bouchard, George Boudreau, Victoria Brownfield, Kevin Callahan, Ian Campbell, Alain Chatriot, Marie Chessel, William Gervaise

Clarence-Smith, Bill Cohen, Lizabeth Cohen, Mark Cole, Sarah Curtis, Andrew Davidson, Mary Lee Eggart, Victoria de Grazia, Michael Dove, Vic Fleischer, Tannya Forcone, Anne Foster, Patrick Friedenson, Ellen Furlough, Michael Graham, Kolleen Guy, Marie Harp, Sarah Harp, Carol Harrison, Gerhard Haupt, Lisa Heineman, Matthew Hilton, Walter Hixson, Craig Holbert, Kirk Hoppe, Daniel Hovatter, Eric Jennings, Xu Jianchu, Kevin Kern, Julia Kirk, Kyle Liston, John Merriman, Emily Osborn, Sally Osborn, Steve Paschen, Jeremy Popkin, Megan Powley, Becky Pulju, Dionna Richardson, Kym Rohrbach, Janet Sturgeon, Anne Sudrow, Steve Toth, Mike Vann, Martin Wainwright, Victoria White, Wade Wilcox, Greg Wilson, and the anonymous readers for the Press.

I owe particular thanks to my students who read every word and offered excellent suggestions for improvement. As I work with them, I hope constantly to measure up to the standard set by my former professors, especially Carl Caldwell, Bill Cohen, Janina Traxler, and David Waas.

All of the above people and institutions deserve preventive absolution for my many sins of omission in this book. As a short introduction to a huge topic, it is aimed at general readers and students. The book is not comprehensive. As I hope to illustrate, the dynamics of this particular global commodity chain are far too diffuse for me or anyone else to "cover" everything thoroughly, at least not in a single volume that anyone would actually want to read. Instead, I want to show how we might use the history of one thing—in this case rubber—to think about the connected lives of the diverse people who produced, handled, sold, consumed, and profited from it.

Stephen L. Harp
Akron, Ohio

Timeline

Before 1493—Centuries before Europeans "discover" rubber, Native Americans collect latex and fashion into usable products.

1493–96—Columbus sees and describes rubber.

1839—American Charles Goodyear invents the process of vulcanization by heating and adding sulfur to the latex during production, rendering noticeably more stable manufactured rubber that neither melts on hot days nor cracks on cold ones.

1844—Goodyear patents vulcanization in the United States; and Thomas Hancock later does so in Britain.

1851—The Crystal Palace Exhibition (the first world's fair) takes place in London. Goodyear and others regularly introduce manufactured rubber goods to visitors at world's fairs as a form of advertising.

1861–65—The US Civil War creates a market for various rubber goods, notably those useful for protection against rain.

1870—Benjamin Franklin Goodrich founds B. F. Goodrich in Akron, Ohio.

1871—The Continental Caoutchouc und Gutta-Percha Compagnie trust is founded in Hanover, Germany.

1876—Briton Henry Wickham ships hevea seeds from Brazil to Kew Gardens in Britain. The resulting seedlings are then taken to botanical gardens, then plantations, in Southeast Asia.

1885—The Conference of Berlin recognizes the Congo Free State of King Leopold of Belgium, thus enabling the abusive exploitation of Congolese expected to collect ivory and rubber.

1888—John Dunlop invents the pneumatic tire for safety bicycles, increasing demand for rubber.

1889—Edouard and André Michelin found Michelin et Compagnie in Clermont-Ferrand, France.

Rudyard Kipling's poem "The White Man's Burden" appears; in it he appeals to white American men to fulfill their duty to build an empire in the Philippines and beyond.

Joseph Conrad's *Heart of Darkness* published. Long part of the canon of British literature, the novella reveals how even critics of the exploitation of the Congo accepted widespread European notions of white superiority.

1892—Several small rubber companies combine to form US Rubber, a trust, in Naugatuck, Connecticut.

1895—Michelin introduces the pneumatic tire for automobiles, further increasing demand for rubber.

1898—F. A. Seiberling founds Goodyear Tire and Rubber Company in Akron, Ohio; by the 1910s it is the world's largest tire producer.

1900—Harvey S. Firestone, Sr. founds Firestone Tire and Rubber Company in Akron, Ohio.

—Michelin introduces the (red) tourist guide to hotels and garages, meant to encourage automobile travel.

1908—King Leopold II signs the Congo over to the Belgian Government after an international campaign exposes the abuses in ivory and rubber collection in the African colony.

Henry Ford produces the first Model T, which remains in production until 1927, exponentially stoking demand for rubber tires in the United States.

1910—Dunlop and US Rubber begin acquiring rubber plantations in Southeast Asia.

The British Empire replaces the use of contract labor from India on Southeast Asian plantations with the kangani system of recruitment.

1913—The first shipment of liquid latex makes its way from Southeast Asia to the United States. These shipments of liquid latex eventually enable the production of new latex rubber products, notably latex gloves, latex condoms, household goods, paint, and foam rubber, in the United States and Europe.

1914—World War I—the Great War—begins in Europe, ultimately revealing the use of a high number of rubber-tire-shod heavy trucks during war.

The French army requisitions Renault taxicabs from Paris in order to haul men to the Battle of the Marne, symbolically emphasizing the need for automobiles in wartime and thus for their tires.

1915—The Rubber Manufacturers' Association, a trade association and lobbying group for the major tire and rubber producers, is founded in the United States.

1916—William O'Neil founds General Tire and Rubber Company in Akron, Ohio.

Rubber-tire-clad trucks famously prove their mettle in the Battle of Verdun on the well-known "sacred way," able to supply troops at Verdun when trains cannot do so.

1917—The United States enters World War I on the side of Britain and France.

Goodyear acquires its first plantation in the Dutch East Indies.

1918—World War I ends.

1919—A global economic recession begins shortly after the war, during demobilization, sending rubber prices plummeting.

1920—Tire workers go on strike in Clermont-Ferrand. Michelin blames the work stoppage on Kabyles (Algerian Berbers) and Spanish immigrants and fires them.

1921—Secretary Herbert Hoover's Department of Commerce creates a Rubber Division charged with assisting American rubber manufacturers in world markets.

F. A. Seiberling loses Goodyear to his financiers and founds the Seiberling Rubber Company in Akron, Ohio.

1922—Britain introduces the Stevenson Restriction Scheme in British colonies, thereby reducing rubber production and driving up the price of rubber.

1925—The IG Farben trust is created by combining Bayer and other companies in Frankfurt am Main, Germany. IG Farben undertakes the ultimately successful development of a viable synthetic rubber called Buna.

The price of rubber reaches $1.23 per pound as a result of the Stevenson Restriction Scheme.

1925–26—Michelin establishes Dâu Tiêng and Phú Riêng plantations in French Indochina in order to ensure its access to rubber as the price of rubber continues to climb.

1926—Firestone acquires 1 million acres of land for a plantation in Liberia in order to ensure access to rubber at favorable prices.

While working for B. F. Goodrich, Waldo Semon invents marketable plasticized polyvinyl chloride (PVC), a critical development in the evolution of plastics.

1927—With financial support from Harvey Firestone and Henry Ford, Thomas Edison founds the Edison Botanic Research Corporation in order to experiment with, and then to grow, natural rubber in the Americas.

1928—The Stevenson Restriction Scheme collapses as Dutch rubber producers, notably smallholders, ramp up production and manage to undercut British price controls.

Herbert Hoover is elected President of the United States, partly as a result of his success as Secretary of Commerce in the 1920s in helping American manufacturers, including tire producers.

1929—The Great Depression begins in the United States and soon rubber prices crash and plantations retrench.

1931—The International Colonial Exposition (world's fair) takes place in Paris, where displays describe rubber plantations in French Indochina and point out their benefits for France.

Shojiro Ishibashi founds Bridgestone Tire Company in Kurume, Japan, a small company that would later rival the major tire producers.

1933—The Nazis seize power in Germany and begin organizing for war, including the production of synthetic (Buna) rubber.

The Rubbermaid brand appears in the United States and rubber products are on their way to becoming omnipresent in American kitchens and bathrooms.

1933–34—The World's Fair takes place in Chicago. After deciding against a live exhibit of its Liberian workers, Firestone mounts a large display of its Liberian plantation. Goodyear opts to offer fairgoers blimp rides.

1934—In a second effort to stabilize rubber prices, Britain, France, and the Netherlands agree to found the International Rubber Regulation Committee (IRRC), a successor to the Stevenson Restriction Scheme.

1936—Labor strikes, particularly at Goodyear, immobilize the US rubber industry and lead to the unionization of rubber workers.

1937—IG Farben's synthetic Buna rubber wins a prize at the Paris World's Fair.

The Japanese invade China, the massacre of Nanjing serving as a preview of World War II, both in terms of the brutality of the conflict and Japan's military ambitions in Asia.

1939—World War II begins in Europe when Germany invades Poland.

1941—Germany invades the Soviet Union; both German and Soviet armies use synthetic rubber on what becomes Europe's eastern front.

Construction begins on the Buna synthetic rubber plant at the Auschwitz-Monowitz concentration camp.

Japan attacks the US Pacific Fleet at Pearl Harbor in Hawaii; the United States declares war on Japan and Germany.

1942—Japan invades Southeast Asia and imposes the Greater East Asia Co-Prosperity Sphere.

1945—Germany and Japan surrender and World War II ends.

Vietnam and Indonesia declare independence as France and the Netherlands began efforts to rebuild after the destruction of the war at home and to reassert their authority in their colonies.

1947–49—Dutch "Police Actions" in Indonesia attempt to end nationalist and communist resistance to the re-establishment of Dutch rule as plantations become important symbols of imperialism.

1948–60—The British "Emergency" in Malaya against communist insurgents sees isolated rubber plantations serve frequently as important sites of conflict.

1949—Indonesia gains independence from the Netherlands.

1950–53—The Korean War extends the struggle against communism, directly involving US and allied forces, and quickly driving up rubber prices.

1954—North Vietnamese forces defeat the French at Dien Bien Phu, resulting in an increasingly direct American influence and presence in Vietnam.

1957—Malaya gains independence from Britain.

1963—Sabah and Sarawak join Malaya to create the combined new nation-state of Malaysia.

1964—The US Congress passes the Gulf of Tonkin Resolution, essentially authorizing US military participation in the Vietnam War.

1965—The Suharto coup in Indonesia displaces the leftist President Sukarno with a right-wing dictatorship generally more favorable to foreign plantation owners.

1973—Direct US military involvement ends in Vietnam.

During the Yom Kippur War between Israel and Arab states, the latter stops oil shipments, leading to increases in the price of oil, and thus higher prices for synthetic rubber.

1975—North Vietnamese forces re-unify Vietnam and seize the foreign-owned rubber plantations.

1986—B. F. Goodrich and Uniroyal (the former US Rubber) tire divisions merge into Uniroyal Goodrich.

1987—Continental acquires General Tire and Rubber.

1988—Bridgestone acquires Firestone Tire and Rubber.

1990—Michelin acquires Uniroyal Goodrich, leaving Goodyear as the only US-based major tire manufacturer.

1992—Bridgestone's Firestone subsidiary signs agreement with Liberian warlord Charles Taylor to pay taxes to the rebel leader, thereby assisting in the establishment of his dictatorship in that country.

2009—The US Congress passes and President Barack Obama signs the Lily Ledbetter Fair Pay Act, named for the former Goodyear manager who suffered decades of wage discrimination at Goodyear because she was a woman.

2014—Rapidly falling oil prices once again (as in the 1980s and after the economic crisis in 2008) make synthetic rubber more competitive and undermine the profitability of rubber plantations.

Global Rubber and Tire Companies

Major Companies

Name	Date of Founding	Early Head-quarters	Founder
Bridgestone Tire Company	1931	Kurume, then Tokyo, Japan	Shojiro Ishibashi
Continental Caoutchouc und Gutta-Percha Compagnie	1871	Hanover, Germany	As a trust
Dunlop Rubber	1889	Dublin, then Birmingham, UK	John Boyd Dunlop
Firestone Tire and Rubber	1900	Akron, Ohio, USA	Harvey S. Firestone, Sr.
General Tire and Rubber	1915	Akron, Ohio, USA	William F. O'Neil
B. F. Goodrich	1870	Akron, Ohio, USA	Benjamin Franklin Goodrich
Goodyear Tire and Rubber	1898	Akron, Ohio, USA	F.A. Seiberling
Michelin	1889	Clermont-Ferrand, France	Edouard and André Michelin
US Rubber	1892	Naugatuck, Connecticut, USA	As a trust

Others

In addition to the largest concerns, hundreds of smaller rubber and tire companies existed from the nineteenth century onward and some are still in operation. As with the large companies, some of the smaller ones produced both tires and rubber goods, a few only tires, and others only rubber goods. Although economies of scale and marketing muscle favored the major producers in the tire industry, companies manufacturing various rubber goods had relatively low capital requirements, so many appeared and disappeared. Small rubber firms that combined as trusts, in the form of US Rubber in the United States and Continental in Germany, managed to achieve economies of scale that were difficult for smaller companies that remained independent.

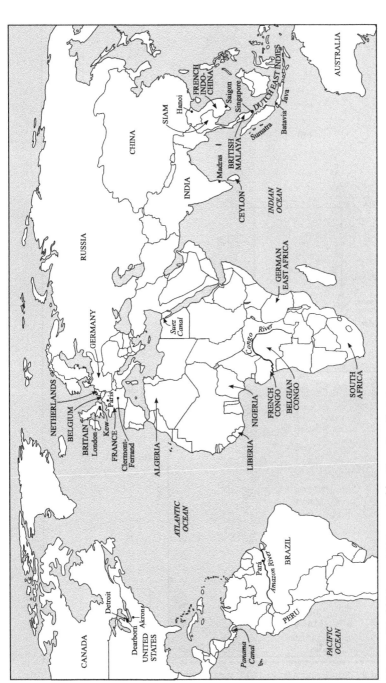

Map 1 World Map, c. 1914, created by Mary Lee Eggart.

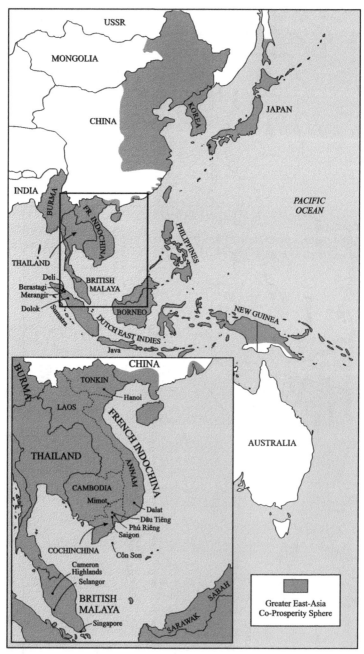

Map 2 Southeast Asia in 1942, created by Mary Lee Eggart.

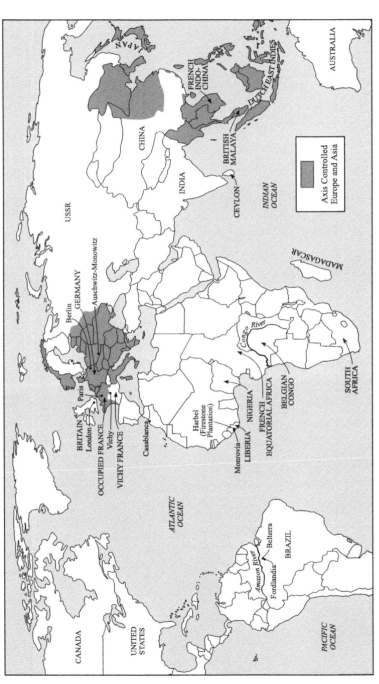

Map 3 World Map, 1942, created by Mary Lee Eggart.

Introduction: Why Rubber?

Let us retrace the trans-global path of the rubber produced by a cup of latex, the milky liquid that comes out of rubber trees, from seed to usable product in the early 1920s.

The seed from which the rubber tree would grow crosses the Atlantic Ocean, traveling from the Amazon River Basin to Great Britain. Then, as a seedling, the tree makes the trip from Great Britain, across the Indian Ocean, to Singapore. From there the seedling makes its way to a small hole in the ground on a rubber plantation, on land that had been cleared by Chinese migrant laborers, in what is today Malaysia. As the planted tree grows, it is cared for by Tamil-speaking migrant laborers from southeastern India, one of whom eventually taps the adult tree to extract the latex. In the morning a young woman delicately cuts away some of the tree's bark so that latex can seep into a cup attached to the tree. Later in the day, she returns and empties the cup of latex in a bucket, which she hauls to the processing warehouse. In large bins, the latex coagulates. Fellow workers slice the somewhat hardened, white substance into thin crepe sheets and hang them up to dry. Once the crepe sheets of latex are fully dried, the same workers pack them for shipment.

All along, Tamil-speaking overseers ensure that the laborers work at a brisk pace. The overseers' boss, a British plantation assistant, is supervised himself by a British plantation manager. The entire plantation belongs to shareholders back in Britain and beyond.

Placed in the hold of the ship by ethnic Chinese longshoremen (shipping containers did not exist before the late 1950s), our rubber

A World History of Rubber: Empire, Industry, and the Everyday, First Edition.
Stephen L. Harp.
© 2016 John Wiley & Sons, Inc. Published 2016 by John Wiley & Sons, Inc.

Figure 0.1 A Plantation Factory. From Firestone, *Rubber: Its History and Development* (Akron, OH: Firestone, 1922), p. 19. Photo reprinted with permission of Archival Services, University Libraries, University of Akron.

Figure 0.2 Crude Rubber in Storage. From Firestone, *Rubber: Its History and Development* (Akron, OH: Firestone, 1922), p. 29. Photo reprinted with permission of Archival Services, University Libraries, University of Akron.

Well before the company acquired its first plantation, Firestone disseminated these images in a book designed to educate college students about the origins and importance of rubber. What are the white men dressed in white doing while the laborers haul in the latex? Can you make out the individual crepe sheets that were bound together to create blocks of rubber sent to Europe and the United States?

travels eastward to the Western Hemisphere, through the newly opened Panama Canal, to the eastern coast of the United States. From the East Coast ports the rubber moves inland by rail to Akron, Ohio, where white workers, very likely from West Virginia, use it to build a tire that goes on to be cured in the "pit" by yet other laborers, including an African American born in the American South. Now, in the form of an automobile tire, the rubber travels by rail even further inland, to Dearborn, Michigan, site of the Ford Motor Company's huge River Rouge plant and its famous assembly line, a veritable pilgrimage site for both American and European industrialists who wanted to see this revolutionary new method of labor in action. The workers mount the new tire as part of the original equipment on a Ford Model T. This particular "Tin Lizzie" is shipped (by rail and then sea) to Southeast Asia, to the island of Sumatra in the Dutch East Indies, in what is today Indonesia. There, a Dutch plantation assistant uses it to run errands, such as picking up the money in town to pay the Javanese laborers on the plantation or going for drinks at the club for white patrons only, where Chinese "boys" serve him—to avoid a collision, or, worse, his Malay-speaking driver often takes the wheel on the early-morning return trips home from a night out. Back at the plantation, the Dutchman's Javanese "housekeeper" awaits his arrival. European wives accompany their husbands to the club; housekeepers, even those who were essentially common-law wives, are not permitted to do so.

Far-fetched as it may seem, the trans-global trajectory of this particular bit of latex was typical. In the early 1920s, most rubber came from trees growing on plantations in Southeast Asia. The seeds had originated in Brazil. Many of the workers who had cleared the land for planting were ethnic Chinese, while most of the tappers were Tamil. The resultant coagulated latex, or rubber, usually ended up in the United States, more specifically in Akron, the "rubber city" of America. The only atypical detail in our proposed journey was the return of a product (the tire on the car) to Southeast Asia. Many Model Ts did in fact find their way back to rubber plantations, where they were prized for the same reasons that American farmers liked the Tin Lizzies: they were easy to fix, reliable, cheap, and could survive on the rough rural roads and even fields. However, the more typical scenario was simply that the car and its tires remained in the United States, where the vast majority of the world's rubber was consumed as part of the "insatiable appetite" of American consumers.[1] More often than not, the "tropical" commodity spent its useful life on North American roads. Similarly, other rubber products, from condoms ("rubbers" in the US) to galoshes (also "rubbers" in the US) to pencil erasers ("rubbers" in the UK), mostly remained in the United States or Europe, the sites of production.

This book recounts the history of rubber as a means to understanding the social and cultural contexts of global production and consumption. During the late nineteenth- and early twentieth-century consumer-oriented industrialization—often called the Second Industrial Revolution—rubber was what sugar and cotton had been to the early, or "first," Industrial Revolution. Just as the violently disciplined organization of slaves' labor on sugar plantations preceded the organization of factory work in Europe, rubber plantations in the colonies generally experienced similar divisions and careful regulation of laborers before European and American tire factories followed suit. Like cotton during the Industrial Revolution, rubber was a global agricultural commodity transformed into increasingly affordable consumer goods. Americans knew about the importance of rubber, particularly during the shortages of it during World War II. Yet ever since those same wartime shortages spurred the development of synthetic rubber, reducing the economic and social importance of natural rubber, the material has largely faded from the collective consciousness. Today there is irony in the fact that early twentieth-century consumers talked about rubber prices and shortages the way that Americans later came obsessively to talk about supplies and prices of oil—the base material needed to make most forms of synthetic rubber after World War II. In fact, the way in which Americans once talked about "our" rubber set a precedent for the way that, in the 1970s and after, they talked about "our" oil supply, regardless of wherever in the world that oil happened to have come out of the ground.

The chapters that follow are an invitation to travel back in time to plantations, to factories, to roadways, and to bedrooms, but not merely to revive early twentieth-century obsessions with rubber. Rather, the global history of rubber reveals the interdependence of imperialism, industrialization, and consumption in the late nineteenth and early twentieth centuries—as well as the five key themes, presented as chapters, of this book.

1 **Race, Migration, and Labor** In the bicycle and automobile crazes of the late nineteenth century, the "wild" rubber gathered in Brazil and the Congo could not meet demand, even as Belgian King Leopold II's minions brutally exploited rubber gatherers in Africa, much as their counterparts did in the Amazon. "Efficient" rubber plantations were established in otherwise "unproductive" and "primeval" jungles in Southeast Asia. In areas of British Malaya (now Malaysia), Sumatra in the Dutch East Indies (now Indonesia),

and French Indochina (now Vietnam and Cambodia), European planters directed Asian migrants, moving hundreds of thousands as contract laborers to huge plantations. On the plantations, a distinct racial hierarchy determined who did what work, how surveillance and discipline regulated that work, who physically struck whom, where workers slept, with whom they slept, and what they ate. A comparable, though by no means identical, racial hierarchy later emerged in the huge European and American factories that transformed plantation rubber into tires. In the United States, African-American workers did the toughest jobs for the lowest pay. They too were migrants (from the Deep South), nominally free but as bound by economic circumstance as many plantation workers. Those same African Americans lived in different neighborhoods from white workers, let alone managers, who were always, like plantation managers and assistants, white men.

Intricate hierarchies within both white and indigenous groups tended to reinforce, at different times, both racial differences and class differences, between locals and Europeans but also within those groups. Asian laborers, or "coolies" to use the language of the time, cleared the jungles, planted trees, tapped them, and did the weeding. Their direct foremen, and those administering beatings, were often of the same ethnic group. Some office help was Asian or mixed race. European assistant managers held the next rank in the hierarchy, with the manager at the pinnacle. Thus were rubber plantations microcosms of a global racial hierarchy in the heyday of European imperialism.

2 Gender on Plantations, in Factories, and Consumption Traditional histories of rubber, like so many older business and economic histories, posited that bold white men ventured out to the "tropics" in order to establish plantations, and then transformed the raw rubber (something all but worthless) into useful and, above all, profitable consumer goods. Women rarely appear in such stories. Yet they were actually present in large numbers as rubber tappers, as domestic laborers, and as sexual partners (whether voluntarily or not) for Asian and European men. And once European women began to appear on plantations, they were blamed for contributing to European racism and the increasing distance between Europeans and Asians. It has been widely assumed that European women condemned European men's liaisons with Asian women and therefore erected a racial barrier that had not existed. In addition, on plantations, as in the empires generally, notions of femininity and masculinity played a central role in the imperial culture and ideology, even when and where women were not physically present. Stories of the founding of plantations see men "penetrating" the "virgin jungle" to "tame nature" and make it "productive." Often in descriptions of Asians, planters feminized "weak" plantation laborers, despite the fact that the latter actually did the strenuous manual labor on plantations. At the same time, plantation workers occasionally portrayed planters as "womanly" for their sexual exploits and their presumed "softness." Clearly, gender hierarchies were in no way simple. The manufacture and consumption of rubber products, from tires to condoms, were also steeped in assumptions about the appropriate roles for women and men in Europe and North America.

3 **Demand and Everyday Consumption** Although plantation workers had very little contact with consumer goods made of rubber, workers across the United States and eventually Europe could increasingly buy tires for their bicycles and cars. However, the dynamics of this seemingly democratic pattern of consumption— even in the United States, where the Model T offered mobility to American workers, in the factory and on the farm—revealed significant class differences. It was the well-off who did much of the driving in the early years of the automobile; for example, the managers of tire companies driving their cars to work in the morning from posh neighborhoods well upwind of the tire factories, workers meanwhile walking into work from company-built neighborhoods downwind of the plants. Advertising, too, reinforced class differences between the middle-class and blue-collar workers, all the while reminding audiences that people of color sat exclusively in the latter camp.

Although a few rubber products besides tires, namely pencil erasers, had been around since the late eighteenth century, it was in the nineteenth and twentieth centuries that they became veritable consumer goods, first in Europe and North America and ultimately globally, initially for the elites and increasingly for the masses. As a stable elastic substance, rubber took myriad forms, seen and unseen, by global consumers. Rubber boots and rubber raincoats may first come to mind, but a host of "hygienic" goods lay not far behind. Condoms, diaphragms, and cervical caps (called "pessaries" at the time) brought rubber into bedrooms. Rubber elastic transformed swim- and sportswear. Rubber sheeting covered food and industrial products, keeping out oxygen and moisture. Rubber soles offered traction, and rubber sandals protected the feet of the rich and the poor. Latex gloves significantly reduced infections from surgery. Latex paints covered walls. Foam rubber replaced Spanish moss in

Model T seats, and soon became a standard material in all sorts of upholstery. Rubber gaskets, hoses, and belts became integral to machinery, from the generators on plantations to tractors on Midwestern farms, to ships, to automobiles, to airplanes. Until the widespread adoption of synthetic rubber and plastics after World War II replaced much of it, industrially processed natural rubber was literally omnipresent in Europe and North America.

4 **World Wars and Nationalism** While nationalism was long a motivation for the establishment and maintenance of empire, the "struggle for rubber" symbolized the acute nationalism of the early twentieth century. Tire-clad trucks, and even taxi cabs, had proven their mettle during World War I. Immediately after the war, Britain, which controlled much of the global supply, attempted to raise prices for raw rubber. Americans responded with a furor, worked to protect "our" rubber supply, experimented with alternative rubber-bearing plants, and, in the case of the Firestone Tire and Rubber Company, established plantations in Liberia. French companies, notably Michelin, created plantations in French Indochina. Germany focused on developing synthetic rubber. Clearly, national economic self-sufficiency (called "autarky" by economic historians) became the name of the game, even if it never actually came to pass. When Japan invaded Southeast Asia, cutting off much of the world's supply in World War II, talk of rubber shortages and a crippled economy reached fever pitch in the United States. Fierce competition over rubber did not cause world war, but it did lay bare for Southeast Asians how vulnerable European powers were.

5 **Resistance and Independence** For many students of history, the success of independence movements and the rapid decline of European empires after World War II often seem surprising. Here we take a longer-term perspective, tracing the resistance that had accompanied the imposition and maintenance of plantations and empire all along. Resistance, sometimes passive, began when locals refused to work on the plantations created in their midst. Labeling them "lazy," plantation managers imported laborers, and regimes of violence ensured the productivity of workers far from home. In the interwar years, as international communism condemned imperialism, working conditions continued to lead to revolts among plantation workers. Combinations of sticks and carrots, reforms and repression, temporarily ended incidents of resistance. However, once the Japanese occupied Southeast Asia, the limits of European control became obvious. By the end of the war, when arms flowed

7

about the world freely, rubber plantations became veritable armed camps, targets of nationalists and some communists seeking independence, and hated symbols of imperialism itself. European plantation owners attempted to reassert control, the European states declaring "police" actions and states of "emergency" for what was, in fact, open warfare. One by one, each with a unique trajectory in the midst of the Cold War, Indonesia, Malaysia, and Vietnam became independent nations, and the rubber plantations therein usually passed to local control, symbolizing national independence.

Global Connections

Although this book explores plantation agriculture, advertising, governments, multinational businesses, and consumer goods from tires to condoms, the commodity of rubber—the chemical properties of rubber, trade figures, and business profits or losses—is not its focus. Rather, the book is a version of what anthropologist Arjun Appardurai dubbed "a social life of things."[2] Here, like the material itself, rubber serves as elastic, stretching to tie together the assumptions people made about themselves and their fellow human beings across the globe. In a sense, the history of rubber allows us to recreate historical links, since obscured, reminding us of the interrelatedness of our world long before anyone used the term "globalization."

Rubber thus allows us to trace the underlying global linkages of the nineteenth and twentieth centuries. That is no mean feat, as there is an irony to the late nineteenth- and twentieth-century world. On the one hand, it was more interconnected than ever, as people and goods moved increasingly quickly, and in greater numbers and quantities, all around the globe. On the other, fundamental connections were hidden by the social and cultural norms of the time, norms that made careful and elaborate distinctions among races—especially between people of color and whites—between women and men, and between middle-class managers and working-class laborers. European empires at home and abroad were above all hierarchical, much as plantations were. European planters saw themselves as undertaking what British imperial writer Rudyard Kipling called "The White Man's Burden" to control and "civilize" people of color, women, and workers.

In the wake of two world wars, as well as evolving nationalisms and independence movements, much has changed. Today we live in a world that appears free and democratic on the surface, but is often quite rigid, even hierarchical, and grossly unequal. By contrast, the early twentieth century, the heyday of empire, was explicitly and openly hierarchical, even racist and elitist. The myriad industrial products made from rubber were not shared equally; neither were the vast profits made on the sale of those products. The people producing them were not paid or treated equally. In fact, colonial subjects in Asia and Africa, and eventually industrial workers in urban sites in North America and Europe, did most of the actual physical labor. It was the well-off, and over time less well-off, Europeans and Americans who enjoyed the fruits of that labor. In this book we will explore how this early form of "globalization" worked, and how it changed over time. Long before European and American businesses moved production offshore in order to exploit nonwestern labor for western consumers, rubber came from South America, Africa, and especially Southeast Asia, and ended up on the automobiles, feet, hands, and even genitalia of European and American consumers. Then as now, consumer lifestyles came with a price tag paid largely by laborers halfway across the globe. In a sense, the history of rubber will reveal the global social inequalities that have long characterized our world.

Notes

1 Richard P. Tucker, *Insatiable Appetite: The United States and the Economic Degradation of the Tropical World* (Berkeley, CA: University of California Press, 2000).
2 Arjun Appadurai, ed. *The Social Life of Things: Commodities in Cultural Perspective* (Cambridge: Cambridge University Press, 1986).

1

Race, Migration, and Labor

Suggested film clip: Goodyear's "Island of Yesterday" (1920)
https://archive.org/details/Islandof1920

These people have lived as they live [now] through generations for thousands of years. While their ancestors were eating with chopsticks or with their fingers, the boiled rice and the curries which have been their diet for centuries, our ancestors were probably tearing apart with their hands and their teeth, raw meat; if they were not as some claim swinging from trees with the monkeys. These people are the product of a dead civilization, or rather an unchanging civilization. We, on the other hand, are advancing by leaps and bounds to the 100% efficiency point in thinking and living.[1]

Thus did Goodyear Tire and Rubber Company introduce rubber plantations to employees in the United States in 1919. While it sounds ridiculous today, this short passage actually says much about North American and European assumptions regarding what was often called a mystical, unchanging, and timeless "East" or "Orient." Although the comment on monkeys can be read as a bizarre swipe at Darwin's theory of evolution, Goodyear's broader point is fundamentally Social Darwinist and imperial. In the perceived competition among "races," "these people" of the "East" had stagnated with a "civilization" either dead or static, while "we" (meaning "Westerners" or, to be more direct, "whites") had moved forward and would continue to progress toward a perfect "efficiency." Here Goodyear briefly laid out a key justification for empire. Europeans (and

A World History of Rubber: Empire, Industry, and the Everyday, First Edition.
Stephen L. Harp.
© 2016 John Wiley & Sons, Inc. Published 2016 by John Wiley & Sons, Inc.

Americans of European descent investing and working in European colonies) could undertake what the French called the "civilizing mission [*mission civilisatrice*]" by making the colonized more efficient and thus more productive.

This chapter explores issues of race and imperialism in colonizers' management of people and land from the late nineteenth century through the first half of the twentieth. For background, it begins with an account of the "wild" rubber "discovered" and exploited in the Amazon and the Congo, especially once nineteenth-century inventors fashioned various useful (and marketable) products out of rubber. Yet, for many Europeans the shocking abuses perpetuated by management on labor in those two mighty river basins did not necessarily point to the exploitative nature of imperialism itself. In their eyes imperialism was not to blame; bad imperialists were. The same line of thinking unfolds when we go on to consider the imposition of British, Dutch, and French rubber plantations in Southeast Asia, where Europeans firmly controlled the land as well as the laborers. Here "pioneering" Europeans were to put "unproductive jungle" to good use. (Today, Americans and European citizens decry comparable actions on the part of Indonesian planters and Brazilian ranchers as abusive labor practices and the wanton destruction of the rainforest.) Simultaneously, the European planters billed their efforts as benevolent, in that they were helping indigenous people by "civilizing" them, lest they continue in their present "lazy" state, with no sense of time or "efficiency" in their (as Goodyear put it) "thinking and living." The chapter concludes with a look at the hierarchies of race on Southeast Asian plantations as well as in European and American factories.

"Wild Rubber" and Early Industry

No one ever used the term "Wild Rubber" until the development of rubber plantations at the end of the nineteenth century. Several trees and other plants that bore harvestable latex grew "in the wild," long before they were cultivated on plantations. The resultant rubber varied widely in both quality and cost of production, depending on the source. Indigenous peoples in the Americas and Africa were well aware of the elastic quality of the "latex" that oozed out of certain plants for many years before the arrival of Europeans. In the late fifteenth and sixteenth centuries, Columbus and other Europeans "discovered" rubber, much as they "discovered" so much of the flora of the Western Hemisphere and sub-Saharan Africa: indigenous people introduced it to them.

11

For centuries, Mesoamerican societies had harvested latex from what later became known as *Castilla elastica*, a tall tree found in what are today southern Mexico and Central America. Latex's most important use, as described by the Spanish, was in fashioning balls for ritual games. Columbus himself saw what we would call a rubber ball, so unusual for a European at the time that there was no Latin or Spanish word to describe the substance of which the ball was made. At Moctezuma II's court in Tenochtitlan (today's Mexico City), Spanish conquistadors watched the complex game, especially marveling at the bouncing ball, so much so that they hauled both players and balls all the way back to Spain to serve as live exhibits for the Spanish court.

There does not appear to have been significant ongoing trade in latex or rubber objects between the Mexica and the Incas or other groups on the South American continent, so it is likely that the inhabitants of the Amazon river basin learned independently of Central American peoples how to tap what Europeans later dubbed rubber trees, including *Hevea brasiliensis*, or simply *hevea*. Tupi-speaking Indians in what is now Brazil called the tree *cahuchu*, literally "wood that weeps," variants of which became the word for "rubber" in several European languages: *caucho* in Spanish, *caoutchouc* in French, and *Kautschuk* in German. Amazonians fashioned coagulated latex into a series of products, notably boots, which were obviously very useful in the tropical rainforest where the *cahuchu* tree thrived. Little by little, over the next two centuries Europeans on scientific expeditions learned more about the mysterious substance, seeing the actual latex-bearing trees, how they were tapped, and how Indians transformed the latex into objects. The Frenchman who first described a rubber tree, Charles Marie de la Condamine, had led an expedition to the equator in order to conduct measurements and verify the shape of the globe, gathering and describing specimens of plants and animals along the way. While in South America, he saw a rubber tree tapped and named the whitish sap-like substance "latex" (Latin for liquid or liqueur) and the smoke-cured result *caoutchouc*.

Although we generally associate the desire to find, name, and control global fauna and flora with the eighteenth-century Enlightenment, it had a much longer history. As early as the fifteenth century, Europeans gathered objects, transported them back to Europe, and tried to figure out commercial uses. The "age of discovery" was fundamentally about profits. Initially, rubber seemed much less profitable than other "discoveries" such as cocoa, tobacco, corn, tomatoes, potatoes, or cinchona bark (from which the anti-malarial drug quinine could be produced, which in turn enabled yet more imperial expansion). However fascinating rubber might have been, well into the eighteenth century the substance was not an industrial commodity. At the end of the century the

Montgolfier brothers in France used a sort of rubber sealant on their hot air balloons, and the British inventor Joseph Priestley used a nub of the substance to erase or "rub out" pencil marks, naming it "India Rubber," a designation that eventually became simply "rubber."

In the nineteenth century, rubber, a product of empire, became a product of industry. In the 1820s, the British chemist Charles Macintosh used coal tar naphtha to dissolve solid rubber (and then apply it to canvas to make effective raincoats, henceforth called "Macintoshes"). When combined with Briton Thomas Hancock's patented "masticator," which could chew up solid balls of cured rubber shipped from South America (later, plantations would produce crepe sheets), the manufacture of rubber products became possible outside rubber-growing regions. Up to this point, the latex had generally been smoke-cured into objects, such as boots or balls, on site in South America, then shipped to Europe or North America. Now, however, solid balls of smoked rubber could be broken down, easily dissolved, and made into objects in the Northern Hemisphere. Like cotton manufacture, which the British empire largely removed from India over time and installed in Britain, the base of rubber manufacture would similarly move from South America to Europe and the United States.

By the late 1830s, American inventor Charles Goodyear had found that the addition of sulfur to heated masticated rubber would keep the resultant rubber products from melting in the heat and cracking in the cold. In traditional histories of the Industrial Revolution, which inevitably focus on Britain, much space is devoted to explaining the strength of the British patent system. Yet, much like British free trade (which was not always free outside Europe, notably in nineteenth-century India and China), the British patent system worked well for British subjects and less well for others. Goodyear got a US patent for the process he had discovered, which he named vulcanization after the Roman god of fire. However, the British did not recognize US patents, and Hancock freely patented the same process in Britain before Goodyear did so. (As a result, Goodyear never made much money from his patent, even though many small nineteenth-century rubber companies paid homage by using Goodyear in their companies' names; tellingly, the eventually huge and profitable American tire firm Goodyear Tire and Rubber Company did not belong to Charles Goodyear or his heirs.)

In 1851 in London, at the first world's fair, the Crystal Palace Exhibition, rubber manufacturers exhibited a host of rubber goods in an effort to build a market. There Thomas Hancock and other British manufacturers showed toys, Macintosh cloaks, capes, pillows, cushions, life preservers, model pontoons, and assorted other rubber products. Charles Goodyear set up a large stand with myriad articles called "Goodyear's

Vulcanite Court. " He displayed walls, furniture, jewelry, household goods, and medical instruments of ebonite (hardened rubber later used for telephone casing and other products before the development of modern plastics). For a comparable rubber exhibit at the first international exposition in Paris in 1855, Goodyear received the cross of the Legion of Honor from French Emperor Napoleon III.

Less noticed at the time were the industrial—as opposed to what we today would call the consumer—uses of rubber. In the steam engines that powered the factories that built weapons, the steamships that carried European troops and indigenous laborers back and forth across empires, and the railway engines that moved men, women, and material in Europe and increasingly in European colonies, rubber was the raw material for a host of industrial parts. Washers, gaskets, buffer and bearing springs, rolling pistons, plug valves, hoses, belts, motor mounts, and other unseen rubber parts became key components of both advanced industry and the imperialism it made possible. Much like the rubbery substance gutta percha, a related natural product that protected transoceanic submarine telegraph cables from water, rubber underlay the expansion of European empires in the nineteenth century. Rubber made empires possible, and empires ensured increased supplies of rubber.

"Wild Rubber" and Empire

The 1880s and 1890s witnessed two developments that in hindsight we often view as separate, but were in fact inextricably tied. First, industrialization intensified after the start of what historians refer to as the Second Industrial Revolution, during which ever more manufactured goods found their way to ever larger numbers of Americans and Europeans who could afford to purchase them. Second, these same years saw the emergence of the era of European empires, as strongly nationalist Europeans scrambled to expand their own country's control of Africa and Asia, where they clashed at times with the colonizers of other European nations. Two key consumer products born of the Second Industrial Revolution were bicycles and, increasingly, automobiles. Both machines needed tires, first solid rubber ones, which required a considerable amount of energy to turn (as on a tricycle today), and then pneumatic ones, which rolled along much more smoothly (as on a bicycle today, with a rubber inner tube and a rubber tire as separate components). In 1888, Briton John Dunlop marketed a pneumatic tire for the safety bicycle, the newer version of the original bicycle, which, rather than a giant wheel in front and a considerably smaller one at the back, had two equally sized wheels that made it much easier to ride. Frenchmen Edouard and André Michelin introduced a pneumatic tire for early automobiles in 1895, with the rubber tube and rubber tire replacing the solid tire. With the global demand for rubber exploding at the end of the nineteenth century, a rapid increase in global production ensued.

While most of the world's rubber came from Brazil, the African rubber trade grew dramatically in the 1890s, with European imperial powers attempting to profit from it. On that continent native species of latex-producing plants included the tree *Funtumia elastica* (sometimes known as Lagos silk rubber) and the woody *Landolphia* vines that grew into the branches of other trees. In some regions, such as the Kongo area of what is today Angola, Africans remained almost entirely in control of trade in rubber.[2] More notoriously, in the Congo river basin, particularly in Belgian King Leopold II's personal domain known as the Congo Free State, state-sponsored companies received land as concessions for exploitation, where they forced Africans to gather rubber. Leopold's men oversaw an armed force of African troops, called the Force Publique, to enforce rubber collection; poorly paid and brutalized by white superiors, they in turn treated local Congolese horribly. Congolese workers who did not meet rubber quotas, in the form of smoked balls of coagulated rubber of the required weights, were whipped. Because intense tapping of the *Landolphia* vine killed it, Congolese men were forced to go deeper and deeper into the forest in order to find enough rubber. Women and children were taken as hostages until the men met the rubber quotas. The Force Publique burned villages to the ground, and Africans abandoned fields to hide and scavenge in the forest. Much like the practice of scalping in the American West, when the Force Publique suppressed so-called rebellions they gathered butchered hands, supposedly only of those who had resisted, although numerous pictures of children, women, and men without their right hand serve as evidence of the indiscriminate maiming of the Congolese. While we have no census data for nineteenth-century Africa, estimates of deaths of indigenous peoples gathering rubber in the Congo Free State range as high as 10 million, a number that does not even include some comparable abuses in the French Congo to the north.[3]

As the stories of the abominable treatment of human beings in Africa at the hands of Leopold and his operatives hit the papers, the atrocities reminded many Americans and Europeans of slavery. While the term "human rights" was not widely used until the mid-twentieth century, the struggle to expose the abuses in the Congo ranks among the great humanitarian movements of the nineteenth century, alongside abolitionism. The Americans George Washington Williams and William Henry Sheppard, and Britons E. D. Morel and Roger Casement, led much of the charge, which ultimately resulted in the Belgian Parliament removing the Congo Free State from Leopold II's direct control. The Congo became a colony of Belgium in 1908. Soon thereafter, Roger Casement, as British envoy in Brazil, would expose similarly horrific abuses of the Indian rubber gatherers (*seringueiros*) in the Amazon at the hands of fellow Brazilians, as well as Portuguese and other Europeans.

Nevertheless, the success of the Congo reform movement lay in what it never jeopardized: imperialism itself. Although Casement would later champion Irish nationalism and thus question English hegemony there, the reformers who led the charge against the Belgians in the Congo did not effectively question the idea of empire or any particular European empire other than Leopold's. Rather, British, Dutch, and French advocates of empire could—and did—comfortably assume that Leopold II and even the Belgians did not understand how to run an efficient and humane empire focused on bringing "civilization" to the "uncivilized," instead of resorting to the brutal exploitation of the colonized in the name of profit. At times, they placed the blame on the indigenous police force in the Congo, or on businessmen traders in Brazil and Peru who failed to stop abuses in the Amazon. In short, the branding of the "bad imperialists" did nothing to undermine the legitimacy of the "good imperialists" bent on undertaking the "civilizing mission."

Joseph Conrad's novella *Heart of Darkness* (1899) relays a fascinating microcosm of widely held assumptions about Africa at the time of its writing, which helps to explain both how the atrocities in the Congo could take place and why their exposure did not fundamentally undermine the commonly held belief that empires brought progress. Much of the action in the story takes place in the Congo, and Conrad is clearly critical of the abuses of company officials and mocks other Europeans for the indiscriminate shooting of Africans. Nevertheless, throughout the narrative he also implies that the crux of the problem was that the Europeans involved in the colonial trade (in the case of the story, that in ivory) had "gone native," as if the atrocities were African, and by extension "primitive," in origin. Like so many other Europeans at the end of the nineteenth century, Conrad assumed that the heat, humidity, tropical diseases, and moral "darkness" of the "Dark Continent" rendered formerly rational European men completely mad. *Heart of Darkness* has long been part of the canon of English literature, so when Nigerian writer Chinua Achebe described Conrad as "racist" in 1975, more than one English professor expressed surprise at the apparent harshness of the charge. Yet, if Achebe's point was to get Europeans and Americans to understand just how thoroughly Conrad reflected widespread European notions of race, which were most certainly racist by our standards, his critique was a resounding success. Those same notions go a long way toward helping us to understand how the Congo Free

State and Leopold II could be so roundly and widely condemned even as imperialism could remain alive and well.

In short, reformers did not doubt that empire was a good thing, if done properly. In the case of rubber, the building of new plantations in Southeast Asian colonies seemed like an effective way to meet the growing demand for rubber. In this endeavor the use of domesticated and transplanted trees would replace the harvest of "wild rubber" and with it the abuses and "inefficiencies" of the Congo and Amazon concerns. The new Southeast Asian plantations would be orderly, efficient, and directly managed by Europeans who claimed to know vastly more about how to run an empire—namely the British, the French, and the Dutch. In Southeast Asia, colonial authorities granted, at very low cost, huge tracts of native land for plantations, much as the American government had granted Native American lands to individual white settlers in the Homestead Acts. Assumed to be uncultivated "wasteland" but often thinly populated areas where local people practiced swidden or "slash and burn" agriculture, such "jungle" forest lands effectively passed from local to European control. Carefully monitored Asians could provide the labor, while white managers and assistants could run the show, ensuring its, and their own, prosperity.

Plantations' Progress: "Rationality and Efficiency"

In the nineteenth century, colonial powers honed systems to encourage the economic exploitation of their empires. Agricultural development was central, and plants moved to and fro across the globe. For example, Clements Markham had already transferred specimens of the cinchona tree from Peru to India so that Britain would have its own source for producing quinine—thus could Britain prevent and treat malaria, further enabling the expansion of its imperial control into tropical, and mosquito-invested, lands. Among the many efforts to gain control over global plant life, the British Royal Botanic Garden at Kew (the largest in the world and a model for botanical gardens everywhere) contracted with several Britons with contacts in Brazil to gather hevea seed. In 1876, Henry Wickham took a shipment of some 70,000 hevea seeds from Brazil to Kew and presented them to the director of the garden, Joseph Dalton Hooker. Kew was literally a hothouse from which plants were disseminated to other, smaller botanical gardens of the empire. In a sense, Kew was the hub, and the smaller gardens the "spokes," of an elaborate system of government-subsidized agricultural science and production.[4] Eventually seeds from Kew resulted in seedlings sent to Asia, some of which ended up at the Singapore Botanical Garden.

And it was in Singapore that botanist H. N. Ridley studied and prop-agated hevea trees. In Brazil, each hevea tree grew in isolation, only about two per acre, a naturally occurring spacing that prevented the tree-to-tree transmission of a microscopic fungus widespread in the country. Ridley found, however, that the hevea trees could grow on plantations in Southeast Asia, where the fungus was not a major threat, ideally spaced some 16 feet apart (later planters would experiment with different spacing), in huge symmetrical grids. He found that latex pro-duction could be maximized if the trees were tapped every other day, along the trunk, moving from top to bottom. Diagonal cuts worked best, with latex flowing downward into a container. Moreover, Ridley claimed that trees could only be tapped on one side at a time (or the tree would die), but that once tappers reached the bottom of one side, they could commence on the top of the trunk on the other side. He also learned that, properly cared for, a tree could begin yielding latex in about six years, after which it could be tapped for about thirty. Ridley thus led an effort to develop a science of the rubber tree, asserting that the hevea was the most economically viable source for the latex needed to make the high-quality rubber that industrialists increasingly demanded. In essence a colonial agricultural extension agent, he promoted rubber trees to planters, insisting on the trees' long-term profitability. By 1899, more than a million seedlings had been planted on the Malay Peninsula. His persistence earned him the nickname "rubber Ridley" and fame among planters.

Hevea trees proved an ideal plantation crop in Southeast Asia. Requiring tropical heat and some 70 inches of rain per year in order to thrive, the trees seemed perfect for the huge tracts of rainforest that colonial governments had been granting planters as virtually free concessions, with long-term leases for coffee, tapioca, sugar, pepper, tea, tobacco, and now rubber cultivation. Colonial governments also offered planters subsidized loans. In European eyes, the "jungle" was essentially vacant land, even in areas where it had long been used for swidden agriculture, in which farmers burned an area of the rainforest, farmed it until the light soil was depleted, then moved to another loca-tion and repeated the process. (As in North America, most lands that Europeans saw as deserted were in fact used, if not intensely farmed, by indigenous populations.) Colonial authorities envisaged ongoing, intensive cultivation as in Europe or as on European coffee, sugar, and tobacco plantations in the Western Hemisphere.

Southeast Asian plantations enjoyed two other advantages. Nearby shipping lanes facilitated the transportation of rubber back to Europe then, during and after World War I when rubber shipments could not go through the Suez Canal, directly to North America. There also were the

Figure 1.1 Tapping Rubber Trees. From Firestone, *Rubber: Its History and Development* (Akron, OH: Firestone, 1922), p. 15. Photo reprinted with permission of Archival Services, University Libraries, University of Akron.

Describe the arrangement of trees. How could symmetrically spaced trees (all planted at the same time and thus the same size) suggest order, efficiency, modernity, progress, and the "West" in an area that had been a "disorderly jungle"?

nearby sources of what advocates inevitably called "cheap, abundant labor," from China, the Indian subcontinent, and Java. By the turn of the century, British planters had imposed rubber plantations on the Malay Peninsula in what is today Malaysia, using Chinese and Tamil laborers, the latter usually of lower caste from the southeastern Indian region then known as the Madras presidency (roughly today's province of Tamil Nadu)—thus hauling people from one part of the British empire to another along a well-established sea route. The Dutch East Indies encouraged international investment, so British, American, and other nationalities joined the Dutch in founding plantations in what is today Indonesia, particularly on the island of Sumatra, notably in the area known as Deli; here most laborers were Javanese and Chinese. As in Malaysia, on Sumatra Chinese people had traded and labored for centuries. Many Chinese plantation laborers came from the Chinese mainland as contract laborers. Planters heavily recruited such workers from the more densely populated Java to work in the Sumatran wilderness. The French followed suit in Indochina, creating plantations in southern Vietnam (the colony of Cochinchina at the time) and Cambodia, employing laborers shipped down from the densely populated northern Vietnamese province of Tonkin.

Relatively quickly, plantation rubber all but replaced "wild rubber" in world markets. In 1900, of the 59,326 tons of rubber produced in the world, only 3 tons originated in Asia. In 1919, of the 465,845 tons produced in the world, 420,046 tons came from Asia, almost all from rubber plantations.[5] Given the costs of clearing, planting, and then awaiting the first harvest, rubber plantations were capital intensive, and big firms signed leases on huge tracts of land. Investors owned most plantations in the form of shares, and many plantations were actually managed not by owners directly but by agency houses, such as the British firm Harrisons & Crosfield. As late as 1956, Harrisons & Crosfield managed some 135,000 acres in Indonesia and 225,000 in Malaysia, employing the staff and overseeing operations.[6] Some of the largest rubber plantations were owned by tire companies, which wanted to ensure a steady supply of affordable rubber, whatever the price fluctuations for the commodity in global markets.

Plantations began huge and grew larger. In 1910, Dunlop acquired 50,000 acres in Malaya and added another 10,000 or so by 1917. Even after World War II, its Malaya plantations remained the single largest private landholding in the entire British Commonwealth.[7] American firms preferred Sumatra because the Dutch encouraged international investment in order to use foreign capital to "develop" the island. In 1910, the American rubber and tire conglomerate US Rubber took over the leases on 88,000 acres in Sumatra and controlled more than 110,000 acres in Sumatra and Malaya in 1926, and 135,000 acres in 1937.[8] In 1917, Goodyear had 16,700 acres, and 54,700 in 1932.[9] By 1927, the French-owned Michelin Tire Company's plantations of Dâu Tiêng and Phú Riêng in southern Vietnam consisted of some 21,750 acres and 13,750 acres, respectively (out of about 417,500 acres of rubber plantations in French Indochina generally) and employed more than 4,000 laborers.[10] The very size of the plantations required corporate bureaucracies that considered plantations rational and efficient, veritable oases of order in the disorderly jungle.

Of course, there was a gap between the much-vaunted "rationality" and "efficiency" that supposedly characterized the plantations and the reality on the ground. Certainly, trees were exactingly spaced in perfect rows, seemingly making an efficient use of land; plantations seemed organized rationally in order to maximize production and eliminate "waste"; and laborers were ordered about to maximize their productivity. However, we are talking here about the costs of production—and the potential for high profits—not necessarily the human costs. Although Europeans worried a great deal about the perils to their health in "the tropics," developing an entire medical subfield of "tropical medicine," it was Asians who died en masse on the colonial plantations. Particularly in the early days of the concerns, during the clearing of the land for planting, laborers' death rates were shockingly high. In 1900 in Sumatra, mortality rates briefly ranged as high as 23.8 percent per annum.[11] In 1926, the mortality rate on the Société Indochinoise des Cultures Tropicales' Budop plantation was 47 percent per annum.[12] Even once tapping began, mortality rates of plantation workers, while falling, seem to have remained close to those of nearby rural populations. Given their demographics, plantation death rates should have been much lower. The sick and weak were filtered out during recruitment; workers were young, in their prime, and overwhelmingly male (thus mortality rates hardly reflect death in childbirth). In essence, imperial notions of race determined longevity, and the deaths of workers and native peoples mattered less to planters than the deaths of whites. "Efficiency," it seems, lay in the eye of the beholder.

Plantation Hierarchies

Like the symmetrically spaced trees on rubber plantations, order reigned in the careful hierarchy from plantation manager, to European assistants, to office clerks and overseers, to the laborers known as "coolies," who actually did the physical work of clearing the forest, planting trees, tapping trees, hauling latex from the trees to processing areas, and constant weeding. Managers could be quite brutal with assistants, seasoned assistants with new assistants, assistants with overseers, and especially overseers with laborers. Pay scales reflected one's place on the totem pole. Managers lived the dream of European plantation staffs, in that they earned enough in salaries and bonuses to retire to an upper-middle-class lifestyle in Europe after their stint in the colonies. On Michelin rubber plantations in the late 1930s, the plantation manager earned about five times more than assistants and about two hundred times more than laborers.[13] Laborers often ended their contracts owing more than when they arrived, which of course served as a strong incentive to re-up. The logic of empire assumed that Asian workers were inferior workers as well as inferior beings "with fewer needs," thus ideologically justifying much lower wages than for Europeans. Symbolically, even walking on the plantation could reveal the overall hierarchy: in the 1920s in Deli, mandors or mandurs (overseers) normally walked two steps behind the European assistants, while laborers walked two steps behind mandors.

Clothing similarly revealed status. Outside their bungalows Europeans were usually dressed in white. White not only reflected the hot sun but

Figure 1.2 Boy on Plantation: "Native Rubber Collector." Photograph (2073) dated July 24, 1915, Goodyear Collection. Photo reprinted with permission of Archival Services, University Libraries, University of Akron.

Figure 1.3 Goodyear President Litchfield Tapping a Rubber Tree. Photograph (Dolok 905b) dated August 23, 1935, Goodyear Collection. Photo reprinted with permission of Archival Services, University Libraries, University of Akron.

What do these two photos tell us about hierarchies on plantations? Presumably the boy in the first image taps rubber trees, as the original caption refers to him as a "native rubber collector." The second image shows CEO Paul W. Litchfield on a visit to one of the Goodyear plantations in Sumatra. Is it relevant that the boy's name does not appear while Litchfield is identified? How would you compare their clothing and headwear? How would you describe Litchfield's stance beside the tree? Does he appear to know how to tap a rubber tree?

Figure 1.4 Goodyear Whites on Wingfoot Plantation. Photograph (42 gc) dated January 15, 1935, Goodyear Collection. Photo reprinted with permission of Archival Services, University Libraries, University of Akron.

Figure 1.5 "A Group of Newly Arrived Javanese Laborers." *Wingfoot Clan* (March 8, 1919): 8, Goodyear Collection. Photo reprinted with permission of Archival Services, University Libraries, University of Akron.

What do these two photos tell us about those employed on Goodyear plantations? Which group was called "labor" and which "staff"? Which were "employees" as opposed to "laborers"? Is it significant that one group crouches while the other stands for a photograph? Can you imagine which received pensions when they retired? How was the hierarchy of the plantation easily visible to all who worked on one?

also reflected a white power structure: it showed who had the power and resources to have others clean the white suits worn everywhere, every day, on the plantation. Among laborers, women wore sarongs while men often wore loincloths or sarongs. As in other imperial contexts, Europeans and

Americans arriving on plantations commented endlessly on naked men (meaning those in loincloths or sarongs, not complete nudity), often suggesting that lack of clothing made Asians more "primitive" or "childlike." Housing, too, mirrored the plantation hierarchy. The manager's house was the largest and generally stood apart from the others. Those of European assistants formed the next level, and they were larger and better built all the time. The size of household staffs reflected one's status on the plantation. Domestic workers had distinctly separate quarters, away from the main house. In the 1930s, an American working in Sumatra marveled at the arrangement:

> a family of two people usually have about five servants in the house. The cook and the house boy do the kitchen work, the boy also cleans the house and runs errands. A house woman takes care of the bedrooms and the laundry, and the chauffeur drives and cares for the car. The gardener is usually kept busy mowing the lawn.... The servants' quarters are in a separate building in the back of the house, but connected to it by a sheltered concrete walk.[14]

Field laborers, by contrast, usually lived in barracks or contiguous huts known as "coolie lines." By the early twentieth century, coolie lines often consisted of a line of twenty 10-foot-by-10-foot rooms, one for each family or for several bachelors. There was a common verandah running along the line, where inhabitants cooked their meals.[15]

Even naming reflected the hierarchy of the plantation. Government reports refer to the full names of managers and European assistants, and usually the first names of overseers. Laborers did not always get the same privilege. As late as 1936, in a long description of a workers' protest in response to the unwarranted beating of a colleague, a work inspector in Cochinchina reported that "folio 14,436 of village 6" apparently bled after "overseer Thanh" hit him. "Folio 13,988" told the inspector that he had received blows with a rattan cane. "Folios 13,985, 13988, 13966, and 13,459" were accused of leading the march and received five days of prison each. Thus, even when charged with breaking the law by encouraging a work stoppage, laborers remained numbers—no doubt those they received when shipped down from Tonkin to work on the plantation.[16]

Male plantation laborers, like African-American men in the United States at the time, were often called "boys" whatever their age, especially when they were domestic help. "Coolie" was more often used for tappers, although they were equally infantilized. Their shorter stature, due to inadequate nutrition, was not the reason. (Contrary to widespread assumptions then, as now, there is no link between "race" and height.

Figure 1.6 Plantation workers' barracks at Goodyear Wingfoot Estates. Photograph (42dw) dated January 15, 1935, Goodyear Collection. Photo reprinted with permission of Archival Services, University Libraries, University of Akron.

Initially, plantations had rudimentary "coolie lines" or barracks, which improved in construction quality over time. This image shows Goodyear laborers' barracks from the 1930s. Even then several had no rooms or partitions, serving instead as huge dormitories for male workers.

Rather, better-fed children tend to grow into taller adults, depending on individual genetic backgrounds.) European men consistently called Asians "little," reinforcing the notion of colonized peoples as "children." Echoing the lines "half-savage and half-child" of Rudyard Kipling's description of the colonized in his famous imperial poem "The White Man's Burden" (1899), one author of a book on rubber plantations described Malaya as

> a land of little brown men…. The country will ere long come to its own as a rich and most valuable asset to the British Empire, even as today she is the very youngest, the latest born, of her children…. They are simple, jungle-bred children, half-savage and half-child. They have much that we cannot, or do not, understand. And they look upon the white man as… a superior being.[17]

"Savage" and "child-like," workers presumably required strong discipline and had no "self-control" without European order. Reminiscent of the ways in which white Americans routinely referred to Native Americans, planters in Southeast Asia repeatedly claimed that the simple "coolies" had a strong penchant for gaming, one that kept them from getting ahead. Like children, "coolies" lived "for the moment," with no thought for the future. Yet, gambling served the interests of planters, who knew how to use it to their advantage. On days off, companies extended lines of credit to workers as the latter gambled; indebtedness bound them to the estate, so that when their contracts came up for renewal, they had little choice but to re-engage. Gambling thus helped to save estates the cost of training new laborers.

Discipline was tight. The workday essentially lasted from sunup to sundown, as elsewhere near the equator, from reveille before 6 a.m. to dismissal by 6 p.m. (workdays were generally shorter by the 1930s). At the morning assembly, overseers took attendance and formed the day's work groups. Trees were tapped early in the morning, when the latex flowed best; gathering and processing were done later. While we usually associate careful attention to time with the steam-powered industrial factory, earlier sugar plantations had already been intricately organized operations with tightly controlled slave workforces—this well before the appearance of British textile mills at the height of the Industrial Revolution. Not only were organization of labor and attention to time necessary to bring in sugar cane, they were also critical for operating the boilers and producing sugar. Similarly, rubber plantations were at least as well regimented as American and European rubber factories, with a more disciplined workforce and far greater surveillance, at least until the 1920s.

Michelin was a European champion of "Taylorism." Named after the American Frederick Winslow Taylor and associated with time–motion studies and the time clock generally, the method of industrial management known as Taylorism defined the importance of the "one best way" of efficient manufacture. It has been argued that Michelin took Taylorism from its French and American factories and applied the technique to its plantations. Yet plantations had Taylorist efficiency before most European factories did. The organization of Michelin plantations mirrored the well-established British, Dutch, and American ones in Malaya and the Dutch East Indies, which were highly disciplined organizations before Michelin began advocating Taylorism in France. Michelin was also a champion of Fordism in Europe, but Henry Ford's implementation of the assembly line was accompanied by the famous $5 day. However intrusive the latter (involving surveillance over home life), it encouraged working-class consumption. Michelin did not fully apply Fordism to its French or American operations. It was completely out of the question in the colonies, where an exploited labor force was not supposed to consume Michelin products. While consumption was partly based on class in Europe (with the well-off consuming and workers producing), it was largely based on race in the colonies (with

Europeans consuming and Asians producing). The $5 day had been designed to reduce worker turnover in Ford factories. Tightly enforced labor contracts fulfilled that role in Southeast Asia.

In return for a small advance on their eventual pay and their passage from southern India to Malaya, from Java to Sumatra, or from northern to southern Vietnam, laborers had signed recruitment contracts, usually for three years, an arrangement akin to indentured servitude. In 1910, the British replaced that practice with the "kangani system," in which a Tamil "kangani" (overseer) recruited Indian laborers, then became their foreman on the plantation. Still, there was strong continuity over time, and among British, Dutch, and French colonies, even after the change. In areas with three-year contracts, laborers who had signed the contract and then refused to work, ran away, or broke other rules could be imprisoned, fined, or have the length of their contracts extended. In a sense, their lives were no longer their own. In British Malaya under the kangani system, kanganis had enhanced power over "their coolies" and could literally "force" their reliability; the fate of the laborers was not necessarily better than before the reform.

In the nineteenth century, European assistants had often managed laborers directly. Over time, however, planters found it more effective to use overseers (kanganis in Tamil, mandors in Malay, caïs in Vietnamese) as go-betweens. Retaliatory attacks on managers and assistants, at least on European ones, were supposed to decline as a result of the institution of overseers, as workers could now direct their anger at fellow Asians. By the 1920s, European assistants often received instructions not to manage the laborers directly, and not to undertake beatings themselves. There were notable exceptions, as on the Michelin plantations into the 1930s, and the colonial government of Indochina repeatedly complained to Paris and the Michelin management in Europe about the inadequacies of its assistants and overseers.

Just as Europeans and Americans at the time distinguished among European "races" (English, Dutch, and French were assumed to be essentially different), they also created typologies of "race" among Asians. British and Dutch planters regularly claimed that "Hindoo" Tamils from southeastern India were the most pliable and peaceable, the easiest to manage. Sometimes Hinduism got the credit, as Tamils were presumed to be always gentle, with insects as well as animals. Muslim Javanese were supposedly "touchy," easily offended, and treacherous. The Chinese were presumed to be very "hard working," no doubt because Chinese labor gangs often cleared forest for the plantations. The Chinese were also "entrepreneurial," as their families had for several centuries been small merchants in Southeast Asia, trading and running many small shops. Come the 1930s the Chinese were often also dubbed "political," as Chinese nationalist and communist movements on the mainland influenced ethnic Chinese in Southeast Asia. In French Indochina, "Annamites" (coastal Vietnamese) were supposed to be "diligent" while the mountain peoples (*montagnards*) were "primitive." In what is today Malaysia and Indonesia, people from Malaya and Sumatra (Malays) were generally assumed to be "lazy" because they did not want to work on European plantations and could not be bound to do so. Of course, different groups did have different historical and cultural experiences. European planters, however, attributed what we would call cultural differences to "race" in much the same way that Europeans and Americans generally threw that word around before World War II.

European assistants needed to learn some rudimentary market Malay (generally not the more complex Javanese) on Sumatra, some Tamil in Malaya, or a bit of Vietnamese in Vietnam, with which to communicate with the overseers, even when the latter in turn gave many of the orders to the actual laborers. There were even phrasebooks for European assistants. The key expressions that one book lists inadvertently reveal much about the dynamics of plantation work for laborers, and the role of overseers. Expressions were blunt and direct:

> Come here!
> Go there!
> Sir, a coolie is dying in the lines. –All right, I will come at once.
> You must send a coolie quickly!
> Each coolie must take a basket.
> Yes, kangani, I know that, but the Assistant Superintendent does not believe it.
> Kangani, look at these boys who are doing nothing!
> Hurry up, run!
> Be quick, it is late!
> Kangani, shout for the coolies to come!
> Stop talking there!
> Take your tools, you lazy fellow!
> Are you a man, or a woman?[18]

Obviously, orders and insults were the most important of the expressions, not to mention apparently oft-needed words to describe a laborer in danger of soon dying. Perhaps the most telling insult, accusing a man of color of being a "woman," allowed the speaker to assert both racial and gender hierarchies at the same time, putting both groups in their presumed places. There is of course no little irony in the fact that those who did most of the actual physical labor on the plantation were the ones consistently labeled as lazy.

Although there were more labor inspectors and increased inspections in the interwar years (largely as a result of the labor inspections required by the newly created League of Nations), these still had severe limitations in reining in abuses.

When Vietnamese laborer and later communist leader Tran Tu Binh complained that "the contract forbids beatings," Michelin overseers proceeded to beat him until he passed out, after which he was shackled and imprisoned for three days. He confided this to the government labor inspector (a post created to deal with reports of abuse and to meet League of Nations requirements) E. Delamarre, who decided to question other shackled laborers as well and reported the abuses on the Michelin plantation to the governor of Cochinchina.[19] Although government officials in the colony complained privately to each other and to Michelin management, the company could afford to ignore local officials. In short, companies were run by Europeans, and European officials handled the European personnel of plantations with kid gloves, even when privately resenting companies' actions. When labor inspector Jean-Pierre Rougni arrived at the Michelin plantation for an inspection, the plantation manager M. Planchon told him that the

administration [of the colony] needed to remember the power of Michelin.... The administrators and labor inspectors have the governor [of the colony of Cochinchina] as their boss. The governor has, above him, the general governor [of all Indochina], and above the general governor is "Michelin and Co. in Paris." Be sure to remember that the Michelin company can ruin a bureaucrat, just as it can sponsor one with whom it is satisfied.

These remarks enraged not only the inspector, but the governor of Cochinchina and the governor general, who reported the outrage to the Ministry of Colonies and received authorization to file criminal charges against Planchon. That did not, however, discredit Planchon in any way with Michelin. He remained in his position as plantation director for seven more years.[20]

Race and Industry in the United States and Europe

Domestically, European and American assumptions about race mirrored those held by the far-off managers of the empires. In rubber factories and their surrounding cities, supposed "natural" differences between and among "races" justified careful distinctions of status. Jobs, pay, housing, and access to public services depended directly on well-established, and repeatedly asserted, notions of race.

29

In the early twentieth century, Akron, Ohio, was to tires what Detroit, Michigan, was to automobiles, the overwhelmingly dominant center of production in both the United States and the world. In Akron, the treatment of laborers resulted above all from perceived notions of racial difference. As the rubber industry grew exponentially in the early twentieth century (resulting in a threefold increase in the population of Akron from about 69,000 to 210,000 inhabitants between the 1910 and 1920 censuses), rubber industry titans faced an acute shortage of workers and undertook repeated recruitment drives. When possible, companies favored Appalachian "whites" over "immigrants" (only in the 1930s and 1940s would Irish and Italian immigrants in the United States be considered fully "white," just as the British had dubbed the Irish and South Asians "black" rather than "white"). Largely poor rural folk from West Virginia, many of the migrants attracted to the rubber factories had no familiarity with trade unionism or the leftist politics associated with recent immigrants from Europe; in the United States at the turn of the century, unions sometimes had socialist and internationalist positions resembling those of their European counterparts, and factory owners believed that poor, rural whites would be less likely to unionize than the ethnic whites from Europe. While clearly not perceived as the equals of the White Anglo-Saxon Protestants (WASPS) who led most of the major rubber companies (the Catholic Irishman William O'Neil founded a much smaller firm, General Tire), these rural migrants were initially politically conservative and as racist in their worldviews as were their employers.

In addition, many African Americans had migrated from the South to the North in search of work. Clearly "free" laborers, meaning that they could legally leave their jobs while contract laborers could not, the former were driven by the same destitution and hope for something better that led Tamil, Javanese, and northern Vietnamese farmers to sign contracts to work on rubber plantations. And just as it did for plantation laborers, racial discrimination severely limited African Americans' options, leaving them few choices but to accept menial jobs and lower pay. Working upstairs in the multistoried tire factories, tire builders were exclusively white until after World War II. Meantime, some African Americans worked in the mill room, where noxious chemicals were mixed with raw rubber, or the hellishly hot "pit," where the tires assembled upstairs were cured, or "vulcanized," in extreme heat. Other African-American rubber workers normally emptied spittoons, swept floors, hauled trash, and cleaned toilets. During the economic crises, especially the Great Depression, African Americans were the first to be laid off and the last to be rehired, regardless of seniority or quality of work. White workers called male African Americans of all ages "boys."

Their jobs were lower in the factory hierarchy, and so was their pay. Needless to say, managerial and executive jobs were out of the question, even for well-educated African Americans, until well after World War II. More symbolically, African-American workers could not eat in the main cafeterias in either the Firestone or Goodyear factories, as cafeterias were segregated. Even entertainment isolated and belittled African-American employees: the Goodyear company's Theatre featured minstrel shows beginning in 1916; upper management clearly approved, as glowing accounts of the shows regularly appeared in the company newsletter.

Of course, it should be noted that racial segregation also reigned outside the workplace. During the rapid expansion of the rubber industry in the 1910s and 1920s, companies struggled to end the rapid turnover of their workers. Both Goodyear and Firestone adopted a host of employee benefits, known as "company welfare" among American historians. The most significant form of company welfare was the creation of whole neighborhoods near rubber factories, where workers could buy their own homes through company purchasing plans. Designed to tie workers to a given company, Goodyear Heights (which had a street named Sumatra, a reminder of the Goodyear plantations there) offered well-built houses with indoor plumbing, central heating, garages, and other conveniences, designed by architects and different from each other (with nineteen different models, they were a cut above the later post–World War II tract housing of Levittown). However, the realty company handling the sales of the homes in Goodyear Heights specifically excluded African Americans, even those employed by Goodyear, as potential buyers. Banned from other neighborhoods as well, many African Americans in Akron lived in poor-quality housing near the Cuyahoga river and the Ohio and Erie canal (thus prone to flooding). The racial hierarchy was clear. White executives and managers lived on the northwest side in neighborhoods like Fairlawn Heights, where the deeds forbad reselling to "any person or persons of African descent or belonging to any other branch of the Ethiopian race"[21] (at the time whites often used the term "Ethopian" to refer to all people of African descent); white workers lived in quality housing in places with names such as Goodyear Heights and Firestone Park near the factories; and African Americans, whether employed in the same factories or not, lived in ramshackle housing, some of it on the flood plain.

Ostensibly free, as compared to plantation laborers, African-American factory workers resisted the status quo only at their own risk. While there is a tendency in the United States to attribute racism to white southerners, like those who migrated from Appalachia to Akron, in fact housing segregation had widespread support. In 1913, William Anderson, the second African American to buy a house in the North

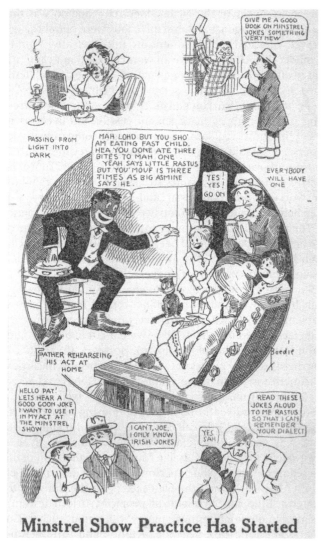

Minstrel Show Practice Has Started

Figure 1.7 "Minstrel Show Practice Has Started." *Wingfoot Clan* (January 13, 1917): 3, Goodyear Collection. Photo reprinted with permission of Archival Services, University Libraries, University of Akron.

How does this image reinforce the idea that there was a global racial hierarchy, at least in the eyes of Goodyear executives, who permitted this cartoon in the company newsletter and opened the Goodyear Theatre to minstrel shows?

Hill neighborhood north of downtown Akron, opened his front door to find 150 people on his doorstep. One of their leaders, Dr. L. B. Clark, made it clear that "we do not want a colored colony on the hill, and that is what they are trying to establish." Clark's language reveals much about some whites' secret fears. He evoked the idea that whites could eventually be *colonized* by blacks as a reason for denying equality to blacks (a sentiment expressed by racists in the United States as late as the election of Barack Obama in 2008: "What if they [blacks] do to us [whites] what we did to them?"). A concerned Akron attorney, F. D. Shannon, told the local *Akron-Beacon Journal* that he would use extralegal means to keep blacks out of North Hill: "We refuse to have them in our midst.... We cannot eject them under the law, but we will do without the law if necessary." The quotation is astonishing from a member of the bar sworn to uphold the law.[22]

Conditions had not improved by the 1920s. Although there were only about 5,000 African Americans out of a population of around 210,000 inhabitants in Akron in 1920, the city had one of the nation's most active Ku Klux Klan (KKK) chapters. Claiming a Summit County membership of more than 50,000 in 1925, the Klan controlled the Akron school board and the city council. "The mayor, the sheriff, county prosecutor, [and] clerk of courts were all reputed to be Klan members."[23] Tellingly, the rubber companies that essentially ran the city of Akron in the 1920s did not condemn the KKK. Many migrants from West Virginia may have joined the Klan, but we have no evidence that they were preponderant. Long ridiculed in the Akron area, West Virginians did serve as a convenient scapegoat much later in the twentieth century, when few Akronites or Americans generally wanted to admit the widespread, endemic racism of early twentieth-century Akron or the United States in general.

A comparable, if different, racial hierarchy existed in Europe. Although Michelin's tour-guide business was headquartered in Paris, its tire production remained in Clermont-Ferrand, in the province of Auvergne in south central France. For the quite conservative Michelin family, the factory's location had the distinct advantage of a large, rural labor force nearby. Some of the workers moved into Michelin housing while others took Michelin buses to and from work, remaining part-time peasant farmers. To a much greater extent than urban labor forces, the inhabitants of Auvergne would presumably be immune to trade unionism and the call of socialist and communist political parties after World War I. During the war, however, Michelin had also hired ethnic Kabyles (Berbers) from the French colony of Algeria as well as a fair number of Spanish immigrants.

Like elsewhere in Europe, the Michelin factories experienced considerable labor agitation just after the war. Beginning on May Day 1920, strikes interrupted production. Michelin asked for, and received help from, local troops to end demonstrations in front of the plant by those workers blocking the entry of others. Like other rubber factory owners in Clermont-Ferrand, Edouard Michelin claimed that it was the Kabyles and the Spanish workers who were responsible for the strikes; Michelin fired them, setting a clear example of what would happen to other workers who agitated for change. Perhaps the Kabyles and the Spanish were disproportionately involved in the strikes, as their ranks were composed largely of single men, who thus may have believed they had less to lose. Nevertheless, they also made for easy scapegoats as outsiders (European settlers of Algeria were citizens at the time, but the indigenous Muslims were colonial subjects—not citizens). Without ties to Auvergne or France, they were easily dismissed as an example to other workers, then deported, garnering much less public sympathy than had workers from Auvergne who had been let go.

Like American tire companies attempting to maintain a stable workforce in the interwar years, Michelin had elaborate benefit schemes that included company-owned housing (for which Kabyles were not eligible) and generous benefits designed to encourage their workers to have big families by paying monthly stipends that increased with the number of children a couple had. Michelin widely advertised its "family allowances" (*allocations familiales*) in pamphlets that both reminded tire buyers of Michelin's concern about the future of the French birthrate, but also pressured other manufacturers to follow suit. In one such pamphlet, "An Experience with Natality," Michelin remarked that France would soon be "a desert or a colony." Noting the declining birthrate among its own employees as among French generally, the company wrote that "if this continues, our factory will slowly become empty or we will have to fill it with foreigners. And since we are no exception, either France will become a desert, or it will become a colony."[24] Apparently readers were supposed to fear France becoming a "colony," potentially one with people of color, or at least southern Europeans, in charge. The notion is fascinating when one remembers that Michelin was a huge investor in rubber plantations in French Indochina. However much French imperialism was supposed to be a "civilizing mission," there was still a tacit omission that imperialism was above all about dominance on the part of the colonizer and submission on the part of the colonized. Needless to say, Michelin did not pay the family allowances to foreigners or Kabyles.

Of course, this is not to suggest that working or living conditions in Europe or the United States and in Southeast Asia, let alone the Congo or the Amazon, were in any way comparable. Instead, it is enough to remember that the dynamics of industrialization and empire building were never "neutral" or exclusively economic, isolated from the cultural assumptions of race—or gender, or class, the subjects of the next two chapters. In Europe, in European settler colonies such as the United States and Canada, and in empires generally, well-off white men controlled the flow of commodities, labor, and the resultant products. There were clearly important lines of distinction, based on pervasive ideas of race—in the empire, in the metropole, and in the settler colonies. Colonizers were often preoccupied with maintaining what they called "white prestige" in the colonies, but, as we shall soon see, this also meant the maintenance of elite white *male* prerogatives at home.

READING

Working and Living on the Mimot Plantation in Cambodia

The following excerpt comes from French Labor Inspector Delamarre's inspection of the Mimot plantation in Cambodia in the wake of the desertion of nearly three hundred laborers. Intended for his superiors in 1927, Inspector Delamarre's report was leaked to the press and appeared in 1928 in *La résurrection* [The Resurrection], a French-language newspaper reporting events in French Indochina.

- What can you glean about working and living conditions on the Mimot rubber plantation?
- How about the gap between what managers said and what actually happened?
- Why does the inspector include laborers' testimonials of hours worked, but then calculate their workdays on the basis of what the plantation management told him?
- Why do you suppose that colonial authorities, charged with maintaining stability, became frustrated with Mimot's management?
- To what extent were their concerns about political stability?
- Can you imagine why colonial administrators demanded that Mimot improve working and living conditions?

When I [Delamarre] asked about work hours, the director of the Mimot plantations told me that the wake-up call took place at 5:30; the departure from the barracks was about 6:00, and that work ended at 11:00, then began again at 12:30 and lasted until 5:00 pm, with coolies taking their midday meal right there.

But the statements of coolies that I gathered were all in agreement in affirming that the working hours are the following: reveille at 3:00 am, assembly at 4:00 am. Because there are one thousand coolies to assemble, it is certain that the departure cannot take place before 4:30; the midday rest does indeed last an hour and a half, but that the coolies cannot return [to the barracks] until nightfall.

Even in accepting the hours indicated by M. d'Ursel [the manager], one gets the following:

From 5:30 to 11:00	5½ hours
From 12:30 to 5 pm	4½ hours
Total	10 hours

In addition to the ten hours, the coolies [must] walk 5 to 6 kilometers [3 miles] from the barracks, it is necessary to add one hour and a half of walking, assuming a pace of 4 kilometers an hour. The coolie thus spends, at work, or en route to the worksite, 11 to 11½ hours....

According to the terms of the contract, the work day for men is paid at the rate of .40 piastres [less than US$.10 in the late 1920s][25] per day for men, and .30 piastres for women. Days of rest and days laid off are not paid, unless there are more than 6 per month.... The coolies who signed up to earn .40 piastres daily did not realize that much of their pay would be withheld to pay for rice, to reimburse the advance [that is, for the cost of transporting them to the plantation], days laid off, and fines, so that they are far from earning 18 piastres each month.

Here is, in fact, what they have earned since their arrival at Mimot, according to the figures taken from the account books of the company. The numbers reflect the situation of the average coolie, not including reductions in pay, absences, or illnesses.... They in fact earn 3 piastres [less than $1] every two weeks. And these 3 piastres are further reduced, down to 2 piastres for most coolies, as a result of the fine applied by order of the [plantation] director.

This fine of 1 piastre has greatly upset the Tonkinois [the contract laborers were from the northern region of Tonkin] because it is applied almost across the board and is excessive. Moreover, it was inflicted on coolies who have neither hats nor raincoats (hats made of latanier [palm] are too expensive and raincoats of woven hatch [*paillotte*] are nowhere to be found at Mimot) and had left their work places during a storm. But it would only be fair if the Mimot company is going to make the coolies work in the rain—and during the rainy season, it will be inevitable—that the company furnishes, at no cost, hats and indigenous raincoats [of woven straw, not rubber], since they are necessities given the nature of the work demanded.

The director of Mimot has understood, and he has ordered hats and coats of woven thatch, which apparently have just arrived, but he is now taking the cost out of the salaries of the coolies.

With a salary of 3 piastres every two weeks and 4 piastres once the advance [for his transport from Tonkin] is reimbursed (which should take about one year), can a coolie buy, on or near the plantation, sufficient food, as well as clothing and indispensable items?

That's the big question, the most important of all, because a coolie with insufficient food will be less resistant to illness, notably malaria, and will be demoralized. The exhortations of overseers will not be enough [to get them to work], leading to frustration and blows.

In this case the work teams have only three solutions, flight, rebellion, or falling victim to disease. In a normal day's work, an agricultural worker uses up about 45 calories per kilo [2.2 lb] of body weight. Since a Vietnamese man [an Annamite] in good health weighs on average 65 kilos [143 lb], it is thus necessary to ensure that those working on plantations receive 2925 calories, 3000 when rounding up, taking into account the fatigue due to the climate and the long work hours. Moreover it is essential that, as part of his food supply, he gets an adequate amount of fresh foods containing necessary vitamins....

The coolies employed on the Mimot plantations receive, from the company, a [rice] ration of one sack of 100 kilos every two weeks, on pay day, for *eight people* [emphasis in the original].

Before 280 coolies deserted in February, the same size sack was given to 10 men; 100 kilos of rice for 10 men over 15 days represents a daily ration of 666 grams of rice, giving 2297 calories. There was thus a deficit of 3000 − 2297 = 703 calories, and, as one will see later, food is rare and expensive at Mimot, so the coolies found themselves insufficiently nourished. They were correct in their claims on this point.

But a coolie is not an agricultural machine fueled by rice; he needs other foods and items of basic necessity. The Mimot company had not considered this question, and M. d'Ursel, whom I questioned about the purchasing power of the salary distributed to his coolies, simply declared to me that they earned enough to buy "disgusting bits of pigswill [*petites cochonneries*]" that they added to their rice.

Coolies unanimously complained about the lack of water. The plateau on which the quarters are established overhangs, above a rather steep grade, a valley where there is, about 60 meters away, a well that supplies all of the water.... The hauling of water is done in the morning and the evening after work, when the coolies have to go get the water they need. But, because it is late when they get back [from work] and because of the long hours they have worked, it is easy to understand that they avoid climbing down and back up the hill.

The coolies, lacking water for washing which they cannot do without going to the well, at the base of the hill, are dirty, suffering in large numbers from scabies, covered with vermin, on their heads as well as their bodies. If morale were better and they had a little more free time, they would make an effort to keep themselves clean, but it is noteworthy that when work teams are put in unfavorable and discouraging conditions, they neglect to keep clean and let themselves fall into a repugnant filthiness, as is the case at Mimot....

[In addition], the cases of dysentery that I documented at Mimot make one wonder whether the water from the well, which is downhill from the quarters and unprotected, is contaminated; to do their business, the numerous coolies in the camp have only holes in the ground on the grade that leads down to the well.[26]

Notes

1 Goodyear, *Wingfoot Clan*, 8, no. 19 (March 8, 1919): 8.
2 Jelmer Vos, "Of Stocks and Barter: John Holt and the Kongo Rubber Trade, 1906–1910," *African Slavery in Latin America and the Caribbean* 19 (2011): 153–175.
3 Adam Hochschild, *King Leopold's Ghost: A Story of Greed, Terror, and Heroism in Colonial Africa* (Boston, MA: Houghton Mifflin, 1998); Catherine Coquéry-Vidrovitch, *Le Congo au temps des grandes compagnies concessionnaires, 1898–1930* (Paris: Mouton, 1972). Ten million is Hochschild's number, now widely repeated, but it is impossible to verify: Guy Vanthemsche, *Belgium and the Congo, 1885–1980*, trans. Alice Cameron and Stephen Windross (Cambridge: Cambridge University Press, 2012), pp. 23–24.
4 Toby Musgrave and Will Musgrave, *An Empire of Plants: People and Plants That Changed the World* (London: Cassell, 2000), p. 149.
5 Roberto Santos, *História econômica da Amazônia, 1800–1920* (Sâo Paulo: T.A. Queiroz, 1980), p. 234.
6 G. C. Allen and Audrey G. Donnithorne, *Western Enterprise in Indonesia and Malaya: A Study in Economic Development* (London: Allen & Unwin, 1962), p. 47.
7 James McMillan, *The Dunlop Story: The Life, Death and Re-Birth of a Multinational* (London: Weidenfeld & Nicolson, 1989), p. 147.
8 Shakila Yacob, "Model of Welfare Capitalism? The United States Rubber Company in Southeast Asia, 1910–1942," *Enterprise and Society* 8, no. 1 (March 2007): 143, 145; Glenn D. Babcock, *A History of the United States Rubber Company: A Case Study in Corporation Management* (Bloomington, IN: Indiana University Graduate School of Business, 1966), p. 87.
9 Ann Laura Stoler, *Capitalism and Confrontation in Sumatra's Plantation Belt, 1870–1979* (New Haven, CT: Yale University Press, 1985), pp. 18–19.
10 *Annuaire du Syndicat des Planteurs de Caoutchouc de l'Indochine* (Saigon, 1926), pp. 83–84; *Annuaire du Syndicat des Planteurs de Caoutchouc de l'Indochine* (Saigon, 1931), pp. 17–33, 55, 85.
11 Stoler, *Capitalism*, p. 34.
12 Eric Panthou, *Les plantations Michelin au Viêt-Nam: Le particularisme des plantations Michelin* (Clermont-Ferrand: Editions "La Galipote," 2013), p. 244.
13 Panthou, *Les plantations*, p. 206.
14 D. W. Peabody, "Three Years on a Rubber Plantation" in uncatalogued Goodyear Plantation file, University of Akron Archives (UAA).
15 Ravindra K. Jain, *South Indians on the Plantation Frontier in Malaya* (New Haven, CT: Yale University Press, 1970), p. 236.
16 Contrôleur de Travail Lespinasse to the Labor Inspectorate, October 14, 1936, forwarded through the governor of Cochinchina and the governor-general of Indochina to the Ministry of the Colonies in Paris, Centre des Archives d'Outre Mer (CAOM) FM INDO NF 2404.
17 Teed Ahpa, *By Jungle Track and Paddy Field to Rubber Plantation and Palm Grove* (Liverpool: H. Young, 1913), p. viii.

18 W. G. B. Wells, *Coolie Tamil as Understood by Labourers on Tea and Rubber Estates, Specially Arranged for Planters and Planting Students* (Colombo: Ceylon Observer, 1915), pp. 9–49.

19 Tran Tu Binh, *The Red Earth: A Vietnamese Memoir of Life on a Colonial Rubber Plantation*, trans. John Spragens, ed. David G. Marr (Athens, OH: Ohio University Center of International Studies, 1985), pp. 36–40.

20 J.-P. Rougni to the Labor Inspectorate, forwarded to the Ministry of the Colonies, 23 December 1932, in CAOM FM INDO NF 2616; Martin Thomas, *Violence and Colonial Order: Police, Workers and Protest in the European Colonial Empires, 1918–1940* (Cambridge: Cambridge University Press, 2012), pp. 145–170; Panthou, *Les plantations*, pp. 265–305.

21 Steve Love and David Giffels, *Wheels of Fortune: The Story of Rubber in Akron* (Akron, OH: University of Akron Press, 1999), p. 54.

22 David Giffels and Steve Love, "Chipping Away at Racism," *Akron Beacon-Journal*, 1 June 1997, reprinting quotations from 1913 newspaper reports.

23 Kevin F. Kern and Greg S. Wilson, *Ohio: A History of the Buckeye State* (Chichester: Wiley-Blackwell, 2014), pp. 361–362.

24 Michelin, "Une expérience de natalité" (Clermont-Ferrand: Michelin, 1926), pp. 3, 11.

25 The exchange rate between the French franc and the piastre was fixed, at 1 piastre = 10 francs. The exchange rate between the US dollar and the French franc fluctuated: Bertrand Blancheton, "French Exchange Rate Management in the mid-1920s: Lessons Drawn from New Evidence," http://repec.org/mmfc03/Blancheton.pdf, accessed February 28, 2014.

26 Delamarre, Rapport, 28 April 1927, National Archives of Cambodia RSC 8218, partly reprinted (without Ursel's name) in *La résurrection* 1 (December 1928), and more recently in the reprint of Félicien Challaye, *Un livre noir du colonialisme: "Souvenirs sur la colonisation"* (Paris: Les Nuits Rouges, 1998 [orig. ed. 1935]), pp. 155–161.

2

Women and Gender on Plantations and in Factories

Suggested film: Régis Wargnier's *Indochine*, 1992

The feature film *Indochine* debuted in 1992. In the United States, it won an Oscar in the category of best foreign-language film, the last time that a French film won the award. It also won the Golden Globe award for best foreign-language film. Catherine Deneuve received an Oscar nomination for her role, and she also won a César for best actress in France, where the film garnered five Césars overall at the famous Cannes international film festival. Clearly, this was an important film that seemed to resonate with critics around the world in the late twentieth century.

Much of the film, a veritable masterpiece, takes place on a rubber plantation, something symbolic of the very essence of French Indochina. Although the plantation scenes were shot in Malaysia, others were filmed in Vietnam, including one at the Imperial Palace, quite a coup for director Régis Wargnier—Hollywood films set in Vietnam had been shot elsewhere, such as the Philippines. As one would expect, the scenery in *Indochine* is absolutely fabulous.

The film itself is fantastic, both in the sense of being fantastically rich in landscape and realistic décor (some 159 minutes' worth), and in the sense of telling a story that is the stuff of pure fantasy. The film portrays the life of a middle-aged woman, Eliane Devries (Catherine Deneuve), who owns and runs a rubber plantation during the interwar years in French Indochina. Devries is a sort of "Modern Woman," a term that Europeans

A World History of Rubber: Empire, Industry, and the Everyday, First Edition.
Stephen L. Harp.
© 2016 John Wiley & Sons, Inc. Published 2016 by John Wiley & Sons, Inc.

and Americans used in the early twentieth century to mean a strong, independent woman.[1] Eliane manages the laborers, in one scene finishing up the beating of a recalcitrant worker. She relies on no man financially. Although her father is still alive, she has curiously (given norms at the time) already taken the reins in running the plantation. Moreover, she controls her own sexuality, accepting or rejecting male lovers as she chooses. The film implies that Eliane Devries is far freer in the colonies than she could have been in France at the time. It suggests that in French Indochina a European woman could move beyond the usual constraints that society places on women; that she could live there, in a sense, in the manner of a European man.

The character of Eliane Devries also reveals how colonial masculine culture regularly feminized Asian men. Referring to Asian men as "small" and "effeminate" in an era when European women were regularly considered "naturally" inferior to European men, European men asserted their "natural" superiority over Asian men. By having Devries order, manage, and even beat "her" male "coolies," the film reminds viewers of the widespread imperial assumption that Europeans were so racially superior that even European women could be superior to Asian men in an elaborate racial, gender, and class hierarchy. Clearly, the implication is that European men must be essentially unassailable in their superiority over Asian men.

Indochine is a perfect point of departure for consideration of women and gender on plantations and in rubber factories. In so many ways, the film depicts a reality that simply did not exist, not in French Indochina, not in British Malaya, not in the Dutch East Indies, and not in Europe or the United States for that matter. In an era, the 1990s, when women continued to struggle to achieve equality, the film's critics clearly liked the heroic tale of a strong European woman in charge of "her coolies" as well as her own sexual life, but Wargnier was taking a good bit of artistic license. He was, like all successful filmmakers, in touch with his time, but he was incorrect historically. This means that we can use *Indochine* and its various historical inaccuracies to explore the actual constraints of women's lives in the period in which it was set, in the colonies and in the metropole, as well as the assumptions about gender on plantations and in factories. The exercise is meant to remind us how grave a mistake it can be to project our own hopes for gender equality onto a past that was fundamentally hierarchical, with men legally in control of women's lives.

In this chapter, then, we need to consider both women's experiences and gender as a category for historical analysis.[2] Historians today normally make a distinction between the history of women on the one hand, and the social construction of gender on the other. In addition to what women could and could not do at any given time, it also is important to analyze the assumptions about masculinity and femininity as applied not only to women, but also to men in society generally. Traditional economic, business, industrial, labor, and agricultural histories have often neglected both women's work and broader notions of gender, however important they were in reality. Here it should become clear that the history of rubber can lead to an exploration of women's lives and the gendering of social reality—both in the colonies and in Europe and the United States. Moreover, this chapter reveals how imperialism represented women as global symbols of class difference; while women of whatever social class in Europe lived middle-class, even aristocratic, lives in the empire, most Asian women on plantations lived lives akin to working-class and poor women in Europe and North America.

Gendering the Jungle and the Plantation

In *Indochine*, Eliane Devries runs a plantation of some 15,000 acres in a fascinating reversal of the usual historical tale of empire, wherein bold men "conquer" and then control natural landscapes inevitably gendered as female. In fact, long before European men established rubber plantations in Southeast Asia, global landscapes were seen as female. From at least the "age of discovery," European exploration was not gender neutral or without sexual imagery. European men "penetrated" the "jungle" or the "bush" as they "thrust" forward, establishing "dominance." Their subjugation of both native peoples and lands, long gendered as female à la "Mother Nature," were "conquests." Areas without permanent settlements were "untouched" or "virgin" lands, "ripe for the taking." Subsequent place names often reinforced such visions of landscape as decidedly female, as in the case of the Grand Tetons (site of a US National Park in Wyoming); "*grands tétons*" means "big boobs" in French, and it was of course French men who named the mountain range.

By the late eighteenth and nineteenth centuries, Europeans increasingly referred to imperial efforts not as "conquests," as had been the case in the sixteenth century, but as "civilizing missions," bringing knowledge and technology to indigenous peoples and, in the case of military action, "pacifying" them. Literary critic and theorist Mary Louise Pratt calls the new focus on scientific knowledge "anti-conquest," because the ever tighter European control of Africa and Asia was instead billed as leading to scientific and cultural progress. In short, eighteenth- and nineteenth-century European scientists contributed to the growth and success of European empires, just as had their predecessors, but did not see themselves as conquerors.[3] Nevertheless, their efforts were every bit as gendered. In his schema of global fauna that remains largely in use today, Swedish scientist Carl Linnaeus named a whole class of animals "mammals," indicating a focus on mammary glands (and thus breasts) likely influenced by the eighteenth-century preoccupation with breast-feeding. Clearly, none of the group's other distinguishing characteristics—hair, three middle-ear bones, and the neo-cortex—had seized contemporaries' imaginations in quite the same way as had breasts.

The establishment of rubber plantations, an effort to "rationalize" rubber production, was not as fundamentally gendered as comparing big mountains to big breasts. Yet, in the wake of Atlantic Revolutions in the late eighteenth and early nineteenth centuries, as many common European men got the right to vote while even the wealthiest of women were specifically excluded from political rights, "nature" was mobilized to explain the difference in what we today call human rights. Just as "natural rights" (such as John Locke's life, liberty, and property—or Thomas Jefferson's life, liberty, and the pursuit of happiness) could be used to justify why adult males should have the right to vote, "women's nature" became an argument for denying the same rights to females. While men were presumably "reasonable," thus capable of reason (and thus "rationalizing" production), women were supposedly "emotional," closer to the sentiments, and thus less capable of "reason." Their "nature" was instead to nurture, the boys they raised going on to become good citizens, the girls to become good wives.

Nineteenth-century notions of male and female "natures" extended from the political realm to the economic. In the imagined "separate spheres" for European women and men, women were to remain in the domestic sphere, meaning inside the home, while men were expected to venture outside the home, to the office or factory, in order to make a living—or even to venture further out into the world in the pursuit of profit and progress. The establishment of "efficient" rubber plantations, then, evoked a man's world outside the home country. In the colonies, European women were not initially allowed on plantations, while men were supposed to work heroically to clear the land and foster the development of "civilization." Men were pioneers who ventured onto the frontier.

In the wider empire as in Europe, the notion of "separate spheres" depended on social class. In Europe, wealthy women were not supposed to work outside the home, but the great majority of European women were working-class or peasant and usually did a considerable amount of manual labor. In rubber factories, middle-class women did not generally work, but working-class women certainly did. That pattern was replicated on plantations, with a colonial/racial divide mirroring the European class divide. European women, deemed to be middle class by virtue of being in the colonies, did not work on plantations. European women who lost their husbands and those married to husbands who lost their jobs were normally sent back to Europe, so that the colonized would not see indigent Europeans, deemed a threat to "white prestige." Asian women, however, worked both as field hands and domestic help.

Asian Women on Plantations

Early in *Indochine*, viewers see both male and female "coolies" going about their work. Here, fiction reflected reality. Although male laborers cleared lands for estates, female laborers also worked on plantations. Women generally earned half to two-thirds what men did. They sometimes tapped rubber trees; they always did weeding and household tasks. Pictures of plantations reveal that women, not men, sometimes had children in tow as they weeded and tapped. In fact, children learned to weed at their mothers' sides, as only adolescents and adults tapped. Like men, women hauled in the latex after tapping, carrying buckets that ranged up to ten gallons in size. Women also worked in the plantation processing facilities, where rubber was coagulated before shipping. Sometimes Asian men, but not women, worked as clerks and secretaries. Given their wages, always a fraction of men's, women obviously cost plantations much less than did male laborers. However, like eighteenth-century sugar plantations in the Americas on which human lives were so expendable—that is, before the abolition of the slave trade—in the early years of rubber plantations women were viewed as a burden because they could became pregnant. Since contract laborers were so "cheap and abundant," to use the expression of the time, there was initially little need among plantation managers to assume that laborers would need to reproduce, becoming a self-sustaining workforce. Planters mostly employed men in the early years.

Among rubber plantation laborers, women were usually a distinct minority. They made up as little as 10 percent of the workforce on Sumatra in the late nineteenth century, though their numbers grew throughout Southeast Asia in the twentieth. In French Indochina a government rule in 1927 stipulated that at least ten percent of laborers on any given plantation should be women, as their presence presumably made it easier to manage the male workforce. In other words, even if still a minority, the figure of ten percent allowed the presence of enough women to cook for and sexually "serve" male laborers. Early planters complained of sodomy (a term that could mean oral or anal sex) among male laborers, a "vice" associated with Chinese workers

Figure 2.1   Woman Tapping Tree. Firestone, *Rubber: Its History and Development* (Akron, OH: Firestone, 1922), p. 17. Photo reprinted with permission of Archival Services, University Libraries, University of Akron.

Plantations rarely had what we would call daycare. Most large plantations held classes for at least partial days, but images reveal that children of all ages often accompanied their mothers, eventually learning to weed and to tap rubber trees at their mothers' sides. In what ways were children's futures determined by their parents' employment on rubber plantations?

because they worked in the exclusively male gangs that cleared the land. Whatever the planters' intentions, the resulting proportion of women to men, combined with women's inadequate wages, led to a sex trade. Young, without resources, and often single, women had even less control over their bodies than did male plantation workers. Like single working-class women in nineteenth-century Europe, women who found themselves on the rubber plantations earned too little for basic necessities. Most were forced into informal prostitution in one way or another, a fact acknowledged among planters. Married women shared rooms with their husbands and any children, but those forced to work for a European assistant sometimes had to sleep in that assistant's room. The situation of unattached women was even worse. On some plantations they were housed in barracks if not pulled to "serve" a European. At other times they were assigned no room at all, as plantation staff assumed they would sleep with (in both senses of that phrase) a male laborer. As a contemporary Dutch critic of plantation practices, J. van den Brand, reported:

> Everyone—the planters most of all—knows that they, the girls I mean, don't have enough to eat. When an estate manager from one of the largest companies took me on a tour of his plantation and showed me the housing of Chinese and Javanese male workers I asked him, where do the unmarried Javanese women live? Reluctantly he finally answered; they have no housing but end up staying anywhere they can.[4]

Planters asserted that Asian women were less moral than Europeans, ignoring a power structure that did not allow women to object. In British Malaya, "the planter need have no apprehensions on the subject of mixing the sexes as the Tamil coolie is most philosophical in this respect—a young unmarried woman not objecting in the least to reside with a family or even to sharing her quarters, if necessary, with quite a number of the opposite sex."[5]

"Possession" of the women sometimes became a flashpoint for conflict among male laborers as well as between European and Asian men. On Sumatra, Chinese and Javanese men fought each other over "their" women. Although European men simply took the women they wanted, such actions led to physical attacks by aggrieved fathers and husbands whose daughters or wives had been summoned to the manager's house and had not returned. Whites, of course, always enjoyed rights to the first "picking." Van den Brand cites one particularly vivid example: an administrator who decked out a small room in his office with a couch, table, mirror, and washing things, and here chose from among the newly arrived women those "who seemed most amiable—as he euphemistically put it."[6]

Sexual exploitation also took place in the barracks, in the fields, and of course in the bungalows of the managers and assistants. Tran Tu Binh described an assistant manager, a former first lieutenant in the army, who "had no wife or children. He did not beat [laborers]. He just raped. He neither spared the young nor had pity on the old.... When his passions rose, he would rape the women workers right out in the forest, right in the work area."[7]

Yet, Europeans' forced sex with contract laborers was not deemed by Europeans as rape. In the early years, before European assistants were allowed to marry, these men regularly selected a "housekeeper" from the ranks of female laborers. Called a *huishoudster* (housekeeper) in the East Indies, a "keep" in Malaya, or a *con gái* (meaning "girl" or "young woman") in French Indochina, the arrangement was not one based on equality or consent. Many female contract laborers were simply assigned to a European assistant; "taking care of" him was thus fulfilling the work contract. The women involved had no choice. This is not to say that there was not tenderness in some such relationships, as well as brutality and violence. Of course, however, the relationships had no legal standing and any resulting children were bastards who remained in Southeast Asia when their European biological fathers returned to Europe. More than one new assistant improved his ability to speak Malay, Tamil, or Vietnamese with the help of his, to use the colonial English slang of the time, "horizontal" or "sleeping" dictionary.

Such sexual arrangements caused relatively little consternation among Europeans in the colonies, as the plantation itself was less about actual separation of different "races" so much as the maintenance of hierarchies of race, as well as gender, in close contact. As in the American South, where a liaison between a white planter and an African-American slave did not cause much problem for the social hierarchy, while the mere suggestion of sex between a white woman and a black man was viewed as a highly dangerous threat to society itself, European planters' sexual relations with Asian laborers simply became a norm of life on a rubber plantation.

Interestingly, in the film *Indochine* an important early scene shows Eliane's aging father gently caressing "his" *con gái*, apparently after sex. In the next scene, Eliane's Vietnamese housekeeper complains in pidgin French that the father's *con gái* does not work, eats too much, and should be sent away. Eliane flatly disagrees, as the young woman makes her father "happy." As in so much of the film, here Wargnier seems simultaneously to be stoking colonial nostalgia and reminding the audience of the sexual norms of empire. Remarkably, he obviously chose not to provoke the audience; viewers learn that Eliane has had many affairs with (European) men passing through, her affair portrayed in the film is with a French navy lieutenant—not a Vietnamese man (unlike in Marguerite Duras's famous *The Lover*).

Given the hundreds of European planters and tens of thousands of laborers, there was no doubt sexual exploitation of men as well—particularly of Asian men and boys by European assistants and managers. In his autobiography, Tran Tu Binh described what he deemed unnatural sexual exploitation in order to criticize Michelin's plantation manager, Soumagnac, a former air force captain:

> Soumagnac was a tall man and quite handsome. He always wore gold-rimmed glasses and spoke with a voice as sweet as sugar. He was dissolute in some bestial fashion. He always had six or seven servants at his bungalow, as drivers, house servants, cooks, secretaries, and the like. Soumagnac selected each person with great care. They had to be handsome, strong, and young before he would take them. Any man who went to work in Soumagnac's bungalow had to spread his buttocks to satisfy the manager's carnal passions.[8]

We do not have another source as confirmation of Soumagnac's rape of laborers, even though French officials' reports corroborate much of the rest of Tran Tu Binh's account. If utterly untrue (even if there is no reason to believe that it is), the description becomes instead a reminder that Vietnamese society could be every bit as homophobic as its European counterparts, since charging Soumagnac with rape of men and boys somehow is meant to make him seem much worse than the run-of-the-mill rapist who preys on women and girls. Whatever his culpability, because of the prevalence of violence on plantations it is not surprising that there was considerable sexual violence as well.

European Women and Racism

The film *Indochine* could easily give one the impression that it was normal to find European women on rubber plantations. Not only does Eliane Devries run the entirety of the concern, her European assistant Raymond is accompanied by his wife, Yvette. In fact, however, there were virtually no European women on early rubber plantations, except in rare cases the manager's wife. As on tobacco plantations, there was often a ban on European assistants marrying in the Dutch East Indies, particularly before their fourth year of service. The agency house Harrisons & Crosfield, which ran so many rubber estates in Malaya and Sumatra, did not allow assistants to marry until their fourth year. In the interwar years, when most such bans were eased, assistants increasingly married and brought their wives from Europe to live with them in their bungalows.

Over time, the racial divide between Europeans and Asians seemed to contemporaries to be getting deeper. Europeans lived apart from Asian laborers, just as they socialized apart; only in the hierarchical world of the workplace did they mingle. Interestingly, European and North American (male) scholars have often blamed the presence of European women in twentieth-century colonies for the deepening gulf between Europeans and Asians in the empire. Arguments vary. Some claim that pressure from European women doomed European men's taking of Asian concubines, thus distancing European men from Asians generally.[9] Others maintain that European men now needed to spend time with their European wives, and that the latter's "honor" needed to be protected from Asian men.[10] Still others baldly assert that European women were far more racist than European men.[11] The cumulative effect of all such arguments has essentially been to lay the responsibility for European racism in the colonies on the arrival there of European women.

In fact, as anthropologist and historian Ann Stoler has argued so persuasively, sexual relations between European men and Asian women, which had never been founded on equality, did not signify less awareness of racial difference. As in the American South, sex initiated by white men with enslaved women did not erase perceived racial differences; it could in fact accentuate racial difference, especially when the opposite, sex between men of color and white women, was so overwhelmingly threatening to white male prestige. The colonies, and plantations in particular, remained a domain controlled by European men, both before the arrival of European women and afterward. Stoler has found evidence that European women's condemnation of planters' sex with local women stemmed from their concern for the plight of Asian women, rather than from the notion that they viewed them as competition for the attentions of European men. Moreover, it was European men who insisted that Asian servants sleep in quarters separate from the bungalows inhabited by European women and their families. It was European men who also assumed that Asians needed to perform domestic labor, so that even European women from more modest backgrounds lived on the plantations as if they were upper middle class. And it was European men who set the rules that usually forbad white women's work in the colonies.[12]

Here again, the appeal of *Indochine* is that it offered critics in 1992 a late twentieth-century idealization of a European woman in the colonies, because Eliane Devries breaks the stereotypes (of a bored woman suspicious of the "natives" who pulls her husband into her European and racist orbit rather than a native Asian one). On one level Eliane is obviously European and seems aristocratic in her airs, but she grew up in Saigon and she speaks Vietnamese. She smokes opium, even in an opium den, in the way that Europeans imagined opium as fundamentally part of a timeless Asia; Eliane herself tells the French lieutenant that the opium trade is timeless, just like "eternal Asia." More important, at one point Eliane tells us quite simply that she is "Asian," while eating tropical fruit (unlike the typical Europeans eating meat and butter out of cans). She is a settler and, given references to her childhood, is probably what we would call a Creole in South America—someone born of European parents living permanently in a colony. In this sense, Eliane is not at all like most European women who actually lived on Southeast Asian plantations—who lived there with their husbands, were not allowed to work, and fully expected to return to Europe—and who ultimately were blamed for European racism in the colonies. Rather, she is more like European settlers in the French colony of Algeria who called themselves "Algerians." Or, more famously, she is like Dutch Boers in South Africa who named their version of Dutch "Afrikaans" and called themselves "Afrikaners," appropriating even the name of the continent as their own. These settlers took control of the space, making it theirs, as if there were no native Algerians or Africans, just as Eliane took control of "eternal Asia," implicitly displacing actual Asians, in this case Vietnamese, who had been there long before the Europeans arrived.

The Colonizing Woman

There was, in fact, one—and only one—woman in French Indochina who resembled *Indochine*'s Eliane Devries. This was Madame de la Souchère, on whom the character of Eliane was partly modeled. Born Janie Bertin in Normandy, she married Charles Rivière de la Souchère, a captain, and arrived in Saigon in 1904. In 1909, the couple purchased a rubber plantation at Long Thành, some 55 kilometers east of Saigon. In 1916, Janie's husband died and she began running the plantation herself, succeeding him in the Indochinese Union of Rubber Planters, later serving as its vice president and then honorary president. In 1922, she received the cross of the Legion of Honor. Eventually becoming overextended, like many planters when the price of rubber plummeted during the Great Depression (to 10 percent of its 1927 value), she watched as her plantation was auctioned off for a fraction of its pre-Depression value. After eventually purchasing a second plantation, Mme. Rivière de la Souchère returned to France before the outbreak of World War II with her adopted Vietnamese children. There she died in 1963.

The life of Madame Rivière de la Souchère became the stuff of legend, so much so that her life story is still recounted in French circles that maintain nostalgia for French Indochina. The only European woman planter (note that the term "planter," like "industrialist," assumed a man, hence the expression "woman planter"), she directed the establishment of the plantation. As she supposedly put it:

> during three years, every day, from sunrise to sunset, with only an hour
> for a nap, in boots,… I sat on a termite hill equipped with an umbrella. My

coolies said [here she indicated that they spoke rudimentary French to her] 'Madame Rubber, not good for you. Rain fall. You go back. Too much sun for you.' I responded, 'my children, the rain and the sun are for everyone.' In explaining her tenacity, Madame de la Souchère noted that she slept 'like my coolies, in a hut, on the bare ground. Not one time in three years of clearing did I go to Saigon. Had I done so, I would not have had the courage to return to the plantation.'[13]

The story is an appealing one, in that Mme. Rivière de la Souchère, the colonizing woman, was not limited by her gender. She was not afraid of "her coolies." She could sleep alongside them without fear of rape. She was their "mother" as well as their manager. Like the well-known Danish author in British Kenya, Karen Blixen (Isak Dinesen), she could manage her estate and "her" workers without oversight by a European man. Like May French Sheldon, the famous American woman who traveled alone in late nineteenth-century Africa bossing around her African porters, Mme. de la Souchère was a sort of colonial feminist, managing men as well as women of color, undertaking responsibilities perceived to be the purview of men.[14] Like these other colonial women, she overcame presumed feminine weakness by exercising power over men of color.

Of course, Mme. Rivière de la Souchère's story was an extraordinary one that did not change the dominant narrative of the delicate nature of European women in "the tropics." To a large extent, the epic tales of her deeds reinforce just how extraordinary she was. Her (husband's) name helped her image; even though noble titles had no legal place in Third Republic France, she could still be seen as a noblewoman managing her estate. More importantly, she managed primarily Asian men, not European ones. In this sense, race had trumped gender in the colonies, where a European woman had passed beyond the usual gender constraints operative in Europe. Her story also reminded all how much whiteness mattered, so much so that it overcame the presumed natural limits of the female sex.

While Eliane Devries was a single woman, not a widow, *Indochine* nevertheless suggests a certain nobility in the name Devries, even if the film's promotional material did not use the more obviously noble spelling of De Vries. Eliane's work clothes (a shirt tucked into riding pants) on the plantation look remarkably like European aristocratic riding gear. Eliane is a veritable parent: she beats one of "her coolies," who tried to desert, but he realizes after her correction that she is his "father" and "mother."[15] She in turn asks him if parents enjoy hitting their children, giving viewers yet another reminder of the colonial infantilizing of the colonized. Finally, like Mme. de la Souchère, she has nothing to fear from "her coolies."

51

When Le Guen, the French lieutenant who later becomes her lover, expresses concern about the manner (presumably sexual) in which male plantation laborers are looking at her, he proclaims that "men should command men." Eliane abruptly dismisses his idea, noting simply that "they are my coolies. I'm their boss." Like her real-life predecessor, the fictional Eliane Devries is the exception that proves the rule: she is such an extraordinary woman that she passes beyond her gender in the colonial context, proving the rule that whiteness matters more than gender.

Gendered Production in the United States and Europe

In the United States and Europe, many women worked in the rubber factories, but here, too, lay important distinctions of class as well as gender. As on the plantations, in the factories men were firmly in control. Although two women briefly served on the Goodrich board of directors in the late nineteenth century, they were as rare as was Mme. de la Souchère among planters, and they also operated in a traditional realm, of widows managing what had been their husbands' assets, in this case company shares. "Mrs. Benjamin Goodrich and Mrs. Alanson Work" were the widows of the company founder and its plant superintendent and vice president.[16] Even they were also exceptions that proved the rule. In the rubber industry, executives were men. Managers were men. Supervisors were men. Normally, men oversaw women, but in those cases where women became what were called "foreladies" (as opposed to the usual "foremen") their charges were exclusively women—as in departments in which women were the only workers, such as in rubber boot, shoe, and heel production. Here their work could be seen as an extension of women's work in textiles and hat making.

Although it is widely assumed in the United States and Europe that women's work only became important during the world wars, for working-class women that was simply not the case—and certainly not so in the rubber industry. In fact, in 1870, 1,851 (47.6 percent) of the 3,886 rubber workers in the United States were women. With the advent of the automobile, however, rubber factories rapidly expanded into tire manufacture. There, where layers of rubber were placed on molds over the top of cotton fibers, women could not always easily lift the uncured tire, so tire building became exclusively men's work. Women's work in rubber factories did not decline, nevertheless; it simply did not grow as fast as men's, so that by 1900, 7,374 (33.7 percent) of the 21,866 rubber workers in the United States were women. In 1930, they numbered 21,276 (26.3 percent) of the 80,811 rubber workers.[17]

During the labor shortages that often plagued the industry in the United States, women workers were an immediate, and inexpensive, solution. In 1912, women workers at Goodrich, who labored mostly in departments producing shoes or industrial products, began earning 10 cents an hour during a ten-hour day, but shifted to piecework once trained; the fastest workers could earn $2 per day and the slower ones as little as 80 or 90 cents a week. Women generally earned much less than men, a differential deemed justified because they did different tasks. During the 1910s, as the rubber industry expanded, women workers made mechanical goods (such as conveyor belts for industry), balloons, and gas masks. At Goodyear in 1920, they also did much of the preparation for tire building.[18] While a few women earned wages approaching men's, most women at Goodyear on average earned much less than men; for example, in 1922, women's minimum wage was $2.40 per day, while men's was $4. The Great Depression worsened the gap. At Goodrich, "the per-hour average wage for women went from 50.7 cents an hour in 1929 to 39 cents an hour in 1932. The per-hour average wages for men also went down, from 81.5 cents per hour to 67 cents an hour over the same period. That meant that in 1929, the women workers at Goodrich made 62.2 percent of what men made, compared to 58.2 percent in 1932."[19]

Thus, well before World War II, when wartime propaganda encouraged women to take jobs in American industry in support of the war effort, women already had jobs in rubber factories. It is perhaps not surprising, then, that their actions undermine yet another widespread assumption about female workers in the nineteenth and twentieth centuries, one often maintained by male union leadership: that women were much more pliable and passive than their male counterparts, and thus less interested in collective action. In fact, although generally excluded from union leadership, women rubber workers repeatedly went on both wildcat strikes and those planned by union leadership. As early as 1913, women participated fully in the ill-fated strike of the Industrial Workers of the World (the IWW, whose members nicknamed the Wobblies) in Akron. Their testimony to the Ohio Senate committee investigating the causes of the strike included complaints about low wages, bad working conditions (women were exposed to the same chemicals as men, most notably benzene), long hours, and sexual harassment.[20]

Certainly, more women joined the ranks of female rubber workers during both of the two world wars, building much of the war materiel that left the factories in Akron and made its way to Europe and Asia. Yet, the most profound impact of World War II was not women entering rubber factories, but African-American women entering the production force in the factories as part of integrated work teams. Before World War II, African-American women in rubber factories worked only in maintenance, especially janitorial service, a seemingly "natural" variant of their work outside their own homes as maids in the homes of others—often the only jobs they could get. Segregation was so thoroughgoing within the rubber companies' workforces before World War II that even company picnics, co-sponsored by companies and the union, the United Rubber Workers, enforced a color barrier; in 1937, the Firestone picnic had separate beauty contests, including one for a white "Miss Firestone" and another for a black "Miss Firestone." Separate was of course not equal. The white winner received a $15 prize, while the African-American winner got only $10. During World War II, however, as rubber companies scrambled to fill their ranks with so many men overseas, they put African-American women into positions in the production of aircraft, surveillance balloons, and assorted war materiel (including the air-filled rubber tanks that helped fool the Germans about the location of the likely location of D-Day landings), working alongside white women,

Figure 2.2   Photo, July 4, 1925, of Centennial parade in Akron. Photo courtesy of the Akron-Summit County Public Library Special Collections Division.

How do you explain the women's auxiliary of the KKK at a time when white women had themselves just been given the right to vote in the United States? Is it surprising that one politically marginalized group was not standing in solidarity with another? Is it fair or appropriate to expect people of color, women, and the less fortunate always to be champions of other oppressed people?

54

sometimes against the latter's wishes.[21] Many of the African-American women, like many white women, were pushed back out of "men's jobs" as men returned to the factories after the war, but wartime integration set a precedent—that women could be productive workers outside the home, even in industrial posts—for the postwar years.

In Europe, where World War I was largely fought, France already had a higher proportion of women in the workforce than Britain or Germany. Among historians, the difference is attributed to the fact that France had a lower birthrate and hence more demand for women's labor, although some who decried the nation's low birthrate argued at the time that it was women's participation in the workforce itself that led to a lower birthrate. The Michelin tire company found itself in a unique position. An extremely vocal advocate of the importance of repopulating France, the company nevertheless relied heavily on women's labor during World War I and continued to do so during the postwar labor shortages (France had the highest proportion of casualties among the major combatant powers during World War I, losing about one of every ten men in their prime). In need of women as workers in its factories, Michelin could hardly fall back on longstanding conservative assumptions that if women simply stayed at home, out of the workforce, they would have more babies and the birthrate would increase.

Instead, the company set an important standard for France and ultimately European countries more generally. During the war, in 1916, Michelin established an early system of family allowances, which consisted of direct payments to couples with multiple children. However, it simultaneously put those women to work. It provided minimal short-term aid to women who decided to stay home and nurse their babies, but they could earn salaries by returning to the workforce after giving birth. The company created and heavily subsidized nurseries, nursery schools, and primary schools near the plant for workers' children. Although Michelin was not the only French company to undertake such initiatives, its system—basically of corporate daycare—was quite comprehensive and ahead of its time. In a series of widely disseminated pamphlets, it called on other employers and the French state, always a major employer in France, to do the same.[22] Michelin thus helped to set a precedent that combined women's work with the easy availability of childcare, a combination taken over by the French state after World War II. Among historians the French system receives at least part of the credit for the postwar baby boom in that country, and has since become a model for European countries, notably very recently Germany, where the population is not currently, without immigration, reproducing itself. Today, France has the highest birthrate in Europe, alongside the Republic of Ireland.

Rubber and Sex in *Indochine*

By the late nineteenth century, rubber was often the material of choice for condoms, diaphragms, cervical caps, as well as some early sex toys, such as dildos; thus, rubber became associated with sex. After World War II, sex toys and latex clothing—increasingly manufactured from synthetic rubber—made rubber an object of sexual fascination, even fetishes. In *Indochine*, a film featuring the production of rubber on a plantation controlled by a woman, director Régis Wargnier found a roundabout way to titillate viewers by linking rubber and sex. In a later scene, the svelte Yvette (Dominique Blanc) dances seductively in a nightclub while singing *La môme caoutchouc*, a title that would translate as the "rubber kid" or "rubber girl." The lyrics could not be more sexually suggestive and seem very much a cultural artifact of the late twentieth century. In fact, the song has a much longer history in film, one that stretches back to the interwar years. It first appeared on the screen in 1932, in the *Coeur de Lilas* [*Heart of Lilac*], starring the famously roguish Jean Gabin (better known for his role in Jean Renoir's *La Grande Illusion*) and the music hall star Fréhel. After Gabin sang of his sexually nimble "rubber girl," the physically imposing Fréhel took charge, declaring herself a "rubber girl" and bellowing the bawdy lines that follow. The scene reveals that the association of rubber and sex predated the creation of rubber sex toys and fetish wear after World War II. *Indochine* repeats the song, reminding viewers of the link. What sexual imagery do you find in the song?

I can tell you, just between us
The rubber kid is yours truly
Oh yes, that's what they call me
Compared to me, taffy
Is as stiff as a board
When we beat the snake, my man,
How I give it back
I fan my feathers for you
I pinch my cheeks
I jump like a marmoset
I run your household,
But I want us to laugh about it
The rubber kid
That's [...] us
When you take hold of my two bazooms
My two big boobs, that's a chore
The rubber kid
When he gets hold of one of you
It gives him biceps
It turns him on
The rubber kid.[23]

READING

Women Workers, Gender, and Beatings

Female plantation laborers were not spared the beatings that were regularly meted out to male laborers. In this inspection report of the Mimot plantation in Cambodia in 1927, Inspector Delamarre reports the abuses perpetrated by the plantation assistant to his superiors. As you read the following excerpt from Delamarre's report on the assistant, Verhelst, ask yourself:

- How might the inclusion of certain of the details have strengthened Delamarre's condemnation of Verhelst?
- Given assumptions at the time about women as the "gentler sex," would Verhelst have seemed more brutal because he beat women as well as men?
- Because he beat a pregnant woman?
- Because the marks could later be verified by a physician?
- Because he beat them personally, instead of having an overseer do it?
- Because he made the man lower his pants, thus humiliating him in front of the women, before his beating?
- How else might Verhelst have been seen as unusually brutal?

In any case, Delamarre's strategy worked: while there is evidence of beatings on plantations throughout the interwar years, for these deeds and many additional ones reported by Delamarre, Verhelst was sent back to Europe.

All of the plantation labor is directed by M. Verhelst, a 23 year-old Belgian, the plantation assistant. The coolies complained of a brutal regime to which they have been subjected.

[Among the incidents,] on a work site situated about 2 and a half kilometers from the village of Dong, the water hauled in containers by a coolie charged with providing laborers with potable water, ran out. Several workers, thirsty, abandoned their work to go drink. They ran into M. Verhelst who was coming from the opposite direction. He led them back to the worksite. After a short inquiry, he released those who had had permission to go drink and kept three women and one man: Nguyên-Thi-Tuong, no. 9, aged 21 years, wife of overseer Nguyên-Van, at this moment in the hospital of Kompongcham to learn nursing [as a medical orderly]; Nguyên-Thi-Liên, no. 1021, a widow aged 30 and six months pregnant; Nguyên-Thi-Nhon, aged 36 years-old and mother of three; and Nguyên-Van-Ty, no. 312, who is single and aged 19.

M. Verhelst [who apparently lacked the vocabulary in Vietnamese] made a sign that they needed to lie down on the ground, which all four did. With a rattan cane, the size of a thumb and with an end wrapped in telegraph wire, he hit each of the women successfully on the bottoms and upper thighs, first the youngest Thi-Tuong, then Thi-Liên, and finally Thi-Nhon. They each received ten strikes.

Then getting to Nguyên-Van-Ty, M. Verhelst signaled with the end of his cane that the former needed to pull down his pants, which he did. He then hit him twenty times on the bottom.... M. Verhelst claimed not to have... struck the women more than 3 times or Nguyên-Van-Ty more than 10. But the medical examination indicated that the women had indeed received ten strikes, confirming their stories, and if, in the case of Nguyên-Van-Ty, the doctor did not find more than ten bruises one and a half centimeters in width, he also noted that the skin was broken in an area 2 centimeters in width and 5 in length, which could correspond to several strikes.

Moreover the water carrier Tao-Van-Chi, no. 261, and the overseer Nguyên-Van-But, no. 283, who witnessed the incident, confirmed the accounts of the aggrieved as to the number of strikes meted out by M. Verhelst. Three of the aggrieved, Nguyên-Van-Ty, Nguyên-Thi-Nhon and Nguyên-Thi-Liên affirmed that, in beating them, M. Verhelst used a cane with an iron tip and that, when hitting them, he held the cane with the iron tip in a such a way that they were lashed by the hilt wrapped in iron wire.

This fact was confirmed by the water carrier Tao-Van-Chi. But M. Verhelst claims to have used a simple large rattan cane, but that he could not show for verification, because he says he lost it.[24]

Notes

1 Mary Louise Roberts, *Civilization without Sexes: Reconstructing Gender in Postwar France, 1917–1927* (Chicago, IL: University of Chicago Press, 1994), esp. pp. 17–87.

2 Joan Wallach Scott, *Gender and the Politics of History* (New York: Columbia University Press, 1988).

3 Mary Louise Pratt, *Imperial Eyes: Travel Writing and Transculturation* (London: Routledge, 1992).

4 J. van den Brand, *Nog eens: De Millionen uit Deli* (Amsterdam: Hoveker & Wormser, 1904), p. 70, cited and translated by Ann Stoler, *Capitalism and Confrontation in Sumatra's Plantation Belt, 1870–1879* (New Haven, CT: Yale University Press, 1985), p 31. Shakila Yacob deems US Rubber's plantations particularly progressive; there the ratio was two-thirds men to one third women: "Model of Welfare Capitalism? The United States Rubber Company in Southeast Asia, 1910–1942," *Enterprise and Society* 8, no. 1 (March 2007): 161.

5 Ravindra K. Jain, *South Indians on the Plantation Frontier in Malaya* (New Haven, CT: Yale University Press, 1970), p. 241, citing a planter.

6 Stoler, *Capitalism*, p. 33, citing Brand, *Nog eens*, p. 53.

7 Tran Tu Binh, *The Red Earth*, p. 34.

8 Tran Tu Binh, *The Red Earth*, p. 61.

9 J. de Vere Allen, "Malayan Civil Service, 1874–1941: Colonial Bureaucracy/ Malayan Elite," *Comparative Studies in Society and History* 12, no. 2 (1970): 169; William B. Cohen, *Rulers of Empire: The French Colonial Service in Africa* (Stanford, CA: Hoover Institution Press, 1971), p. 122.

10 Alain Tirefort, "'Le bon temps': Approche de la société coloniale. Etude de cas: La communauté française en Basse Côte d'Ivoire pendant l'entre-deux-guerres, 1920–1940," (PhD thesis, Centre d'Etudes Africaines/EHESS, 1979), p. 197; Thomas O. Beidelman, *Colonial Evangelism: A Socio-Historical Study of an East African Mission at the Grassroots* (Bloomington, IN: Indiana University Press, 1982), p. 13.

11 Pierre Nora, *Les Français d'Algérie* (Paris: Julliard, 1961), p. 174; Octavio Mannoni, *Prospero and Caliban: The Psychology of Colonization*, trans. Pamela Powesland (New York: Praeger, 1956), p. 115; Lewis H. Gann and Peter Duignan, *Rulers of British Africa, 1870–1914* (London: Croom Helm, 1978), p. 242.

12 Ann Stoler, *Carnal Knowledge and Imperial Power: Race and the Intimate in Colonial Rule* (Berkeley, CA: University of California Press, 2002), pp. 32–34, 50–61.

13 http://belleindochine.free.fr/MmeSouchere.htm, accessed March 2, 2014; H. Célarié, *Promenades en Indochine* (Paris: Editions Baudinière, 1937), p. 221.

14 Patricia M. E. Lorcin, *Historicizing Colonial Nostalgia: European Women's Narratives of Algeria and Kenya, 1900–Present* (New York: Palgrave Macmillan, 2012); and Tracey Jean Boisseau, *White Queen: May French-Sheldon and the Imperial Origins of American Feminist Identity* (Bloomington, IN: Indiana University Press, 2004).

15 This line "you are my father and my mother" seems to have come from a novel by Henri Fauconnier, set on a rubber plantation in Malaya in the interwar years, where in the context of a beating, a laborer says it to a male European: *The Soul of Malaya*, trans. Eric Sutton (Singapore: Archipelago Press, 1983 [1931]), p. 26.

16 Mansel G. Blackford and K. Austin Kerr, *BFGoodrich: Tradition and Transformation, 1870–1995* (Columbus, OH: Ohio State University Press, 1996), pp. 21–23, 41.

17 Department of Commerce and Labor, Bureau of the Census, *Special Reports: Occupations at the Twelfth Census* (Washington, DC: Government Printing Office, 1904); Alba M. Edwards, *Sixteenth Census of the United States: 1940 Population, Comparative Occupation Statistics for the United States, 1870 to 1940* (Washington, DC: Government Printing Office, 1943); Kathleen L. Endres, *Rosie the Rubber Worker: Women Workers in Akron's Rubber Factories during World War II* (Kent, OH: Kent State University Press, 2000), p. 21.

18 Daniel Nelson, *American Rubber Workers and Organized Labor, 1900–1941* (Princeton, NJ: Princeton University Press, 1988), pp. 20–21, 52–53, 88.

19 Endres, *Rosie*, pp. 37, 41.

20 Ibid., p. 26.

21 Nelson, *American Rubber Workers*, p. 223.
22 Stephen L. Harp, *Marketing Michelin: Advertising and Cultural Identity in Twentieth-Century France* (Baltimore, MD: Johns Hopkins University Press, 2001), pp. 126–155.
23 Translation from Kelley Conway, "Flower of the Asphalt: The *Chanteuse Réaliste* in the 1930s French Cinema," in *Soundtrack Available: Essays on Film and Popular Music*, ed. Pamela Robertson Wojcik and Arthur Knight (Durham, NC: Duke University Press, 2001), p. 144. Today, the nickname *la môme* often refers specifically to the famous singer Edith Piaf. The song itself was found at http://www.youtube.com/watch?v=2p-ONIKaOYA, accessed July 19, 2014.
24 Delamarre, Rapport, 28 April 1927, National Archives of Cambodia RSC 8218, partly reprinted (without Verhelst's name) in *La résurrection* and more recently in the reprint of Félicien Challaye, *Un livre noir du colonialisme: "Souvenirs sur la colonisation"* (Paris: Les Nuits Rouges, 1998 [orig. ed. 1935]), pp. 162–165.

3

Demand and Everyday Consumption

Suggested audio recording: Voice of Firestone radio program
http://www.youtube.com/watch?v=86OniBh_Tro

In 1913, Michelin introduced its "lever," a tool for removing Michelin tires from rims. Here the Michelin Man, a persona invented by the company, explains its use:

> We need to think of our overseas clientele, of our friends in the colonies, of those who, in Brazil, in the Sudan, in Australia, as in Canada, only want to drive on Michelins. Do you think that these distant friends run into a nice tire dealer every ten kilometers who is ready to give them lessons in mounting tires? Their mechanics are negroes or coolies. With the lever, today they… repeat the following, "Is good, massa Michelin Man, is good way to mount tires without pinching [them] or pinching fingers. No longer get… kicks in butt. Now have fun all the time!"

Michelin then makes it clear that if even "negroes and coolies" can figure it out, the lever will obviously be quite helpful to European men. The illustration that accompanies the advertisement shows the Michelin Man sitting in a rocking chair with a pith helmet, that ultimate symbol of imperial dominance, atop his head. To his right is a black man changing a tire, to his left a "coolie."[1]

To a large extent, the Michelin advertisement is typical of early twentieth-century efforts to create demand for rubber products. Rubber

A World History of Rubber: Empire, Industry, and the Everyday, First Edition.
Stephen L. Harp.
© 2016 John Wiley & Sons, Inc. Published 2016 by John Wiley & Sons, Inc.

became an object of everyday consumption in Europe and North America at this time. However, it was never simply a commodity fashioned into myriad products. Rather, in an era when mass advertising became big business, purchasers were invited not merely to buy a product, but also to buy a lifestyle and an identity. As suggested above, the tire buyer who bought Michelins and used the Michelin lever could imagine himself a big shot, the equivalent of a well-off white man in the colonies who sat idly by as simple and silly "negroes" and "coolies" did his bidding.

Selling a lifestyle was possible because most rubber, however critical for industry and empire, was largely unseen. Behind the scenes, rubber was a "tool of empire."[2] Largely unnoticed, rubber gaskets and hoses made the steam engines in modern steamships possible, thereby assisting in the movement of troops and weapons to and around empires. New networks of communication relied on rubber and gutta percha. Rubber insulated telegraph, telephone, and electric lines. Gutta percha protected transatlantic telegraph and telephone cables; thus, the prices of rubber and other commodities passed through cables with rubber insulation and gutta percha protection. Machinery and power plants in weapons factories required rubber, and the weapons produced could be used to secure and extend empires. Steam engines and later diesel engines on trains used rubber. Even the rubber truncheons and rubber bullets sometimes employed against striking workers required rubber. Very rarely did any of these uses appear in ads. Instead, advertising encouraged Europeans and Americans to craft class, gender, and racial identities in consumerist dreamscapes by buying rubber goods.

This chapter has two objectives: to consider everyday consumption of rubber on the Southeast Asian plantations where it was grown, in Europe, and particularly in the United States, where most rubber was consumed; and to examine how rubber companies tried to increase demand for their goods, especially through advertisements. In advertising to increase consumption, notions of race, gender, and class were critical in encouraging buyers to see purchases as expressions of identity. In that way, advertising reflects both the depth and the breadth of cultural assumptions about race, gender, and social class in the early twentieth century.

Everyday Consumption on Southeast Asian Plantations

Relatively few manufactured rubber goods made their way back to the rubber plantations. Most that did ended up in the hands of Europeans. Dunlop led advances in both tennis and golf balls, which were of course present on plantations on tennis courts and golf courses. On the Ladang Geddes estates, Dunlop had as many as five 9-hole golf courses. Sources refer occasionally to bicycles on plantations, which were useful for getting around the huge estates, but laborers could not afford to purchase their own, even if they did use those owned by the plantations.[3] There are references to latex gloves in plantation clinics, worn to prevent the spread of germs as staff treated laborers. Clerks used erasers along with pencils in keeping track of rubber production and laborers' wages and debts. By the early twentieth century, the small plantation factories that prepared rubber for shipment had rubber conveyor belts. Nevertheless, rubber goods were still comparatively expensive, so even rubber raincoats and rubber boots were hard to come by.

Instead, most rubber goods on the plantations were in the hands (or on the feet) of European and American staff. Rubber boots and tennis shoes were for Europeans and Americans.[4] Rubber ducks, balloons, and toys were for the children of the managers and assistants. Given the paucity of schools for laborers' children, even most erasers ended up in European hands. Europeans also rode bicycles (and, unlike Asian laborers in the Dutch East Indies, did not have to dismount and walk past any Europeans they met along the path). As the 1920s wore on, automobiles replaced buggies and, like elsewhere in the world, the making of tires for automobiles became the largest demand for rubber.

Individual managers and assistants bought automobiles in order to allow leisurely escape from plantations. Europeans in Southeast Asia sought relief from the heat at hill stations, mountain resorts with the cool, less humid air presumed necessary for the maintenance of European health "in the tropics." Automobiles made these kinds of quick day trips possible. The British were well known for their hill stations, where one could eat familiar (rather than tropical) fresh fruits, drink fresh milk, eat fresh butter, and breathe the cool, fresh air. Dutch planters from the Deli region of Sumatra savored the strawberries and cold water at Berastagi, British ones in Malaya went to the Cameron Highlands, while French ones from Indochina praised the strawberries and "Alpine" architecture in the highlands at Dalat.[5]

On a daily basis, automobiles took planters to the nearby town, where they gathered in the restaurant bar of a hotel or other sort of "club." Whereas in the early 1920s managers in Deli had cars and most assistants buggies, as wages and bonuses climbed in sync with rubber prices in the mid-1920s even assistants bought cars, very often simple Model T Fords, in order to get to town. As would be the case in Europe and North America, where automobile purchases reflected social status, managers then went more upscale, buying more expensive General Motors products that offered a choice of colors, and sometimes even

Pierce Arrows and Hudsons. Yet in Southeast Asia, even Ford owners regularly had drivers. Since club life consisted above all of heavy drinking, plantation assistants could party hard and then rely on their Asian driver to get them home safely. Roads were not particularly good, so cars rapidly went through set after set of tires. Thus, much of the rubber consumed in Southeast Asia was on the very automobiles that enabled leisure for European and American plantation employees. On plantations, laborers produced much of the rubber while consuming very little of it, as planters consumed much while overseeing production. On the one hand, plantation staffs were merely keeping up with the Joneses back in the United States and Europe. On the other, they proclaimed the need to consume heavily to survive "the tropics," and they could afford to do so. Due to very low wage rates for laborers, planters and their assistants could surround themselves with servants, thus leading lives in the colonies reserved for the very wealthy back home in Europe or the United States.

Class and Consumption in North America and Europe

Rubber consumption expanded in the nineteenth century. Rubber boots and soles, raincoats, balloons and other rubber toys, cervical caps, and condoms were increasingly available to Americans and Europeans. Rubber companies were often small. Several in the United States had Goodyear in the title, as they used the Goodyear patent in vulcanizing rubber (just as the later multinational would be named in honor of Charles Goodyear; founder F. A. Seiberling had no other connection to Charles Goodyear). As in society at large, advertising was minimal, consisting of catalogs for drug stores, handbills with appeals to particular trades (such as Goodrich ads, in German, for the German-speaking beer brewers who dominated that trade in the United States and used rubber hoses in their breweries), and world's fair exhibits. Rubber producers, like other manufacturers of the day, also widely disseminated trade cards, sort of combined business and post cards, which inevitably tied production to consumption, in order to advertise their goods. Often featuring an image of the factory owner, a picture of the factory in the background belching smoke, and the product in question, trade cards assumed a link between consumption and production.

The rubber industry changed dramatically with the advent of the bicycle and especially the automobile. Not only did automobile tires require large amounts of rubber, they also depended on people buying a large-ticket item that no one absolutely needed (somehow people had survived without the automobile up until that point in world history). Moreover, as expensive as automobiles were, tires were the most expensive component. For example, in 1898, Alexander Winton's 1-cylinder Phaeton cost $1,000 and was equipped with Goodrich pneumatic tires (with a useful life of 1,000 miles or so) costing $400 a set.[6] As a result, tire companies, like automobile manufacturers, spent heavily on advertising in order to create demand for automobiles and to encourage owners to drive them more. Advertisements coaxed the likely clientele for automobile tires to imagine how they might distinguish themselves— as well-off, as men, and as whites—from those assumed to be inferior, both at home and abroad. In the process, the dynamics of production became less visible. Consumption could bestow identities and dreamed-of lifestyles; ads hardly needed to remind buyers of the realities of the production process.

Before the first decade of the twentieth century, France was the world's largest market for automobiles and their tires. Not coincidentally, Michelin, which dominated that market, set a global standard, not only by exporting its products throughout the world and establishing a plant in New Jersey in 1908, but also by finding ways to create more demand for tires. Tapping into the rich tradition of poster art, identified with the beautiful works by Henri de Toulouse-Lautrec, Michelin posters portrayed its likely customer: a wealthy, even aristocratic, white man—the Michelin Man. Although today the Michelin Man is a largely gender-neutral, white, and puffy equivalent of the Pillsbury dough boy—albeit one made up of concentric rings suggestive of tires—the Michelin Man first appeared as a cigar-smoking, pince-nez- and ring-wearing, champagne-drinking man-about-town, one who appealed to fellow well-off European men. He appeared alternatively as a knight and as a rich man with a cane and top hat, offering advice to fellow automobile owners. Since the automobile was, in essence, an expensive toy for rich men, he appealed to them as one of their own—and appealed to upper-middle-class men who aspired to wealth. Since early automobiles were leisure craft for touring, Michelin found myriad ways to develop tourism by automobile in early twentieth-century France.

As early as 1900, Michelin began to publish a guidebook to hotels and garages, which became known as the red guide. Later the Michelin guide became famous for rating restaurants for the very well-heeled. The Continental tire company, Michelin's German competitor, soon followed suit, issuing its own guide to France that actually plagiarized large sections from Michelin's. Dunlop, the British firm, did its own work, and soon published extensive tourist guides to the British Isles, including Ireland. The American firm Goodrich, which established a manufacturing plant outside Paris in 1910, followed suit, retracing Michelin's footsteps and publishing a guidebook to World War I battle-fields in both English and French. It was Michelin that pioneered road maps for drivers of automobiles. Indeed, Michelin maps became the standard road atlas in Europe much as the one put out annually by Rand McNally eventually did in North America. Goodrich followed Michelin's lead, distributing more than a million state road maps in 1919. Well before national governments took charge of roadways, Michelin installed road signs, so that well-off tourists would not have to be dependent on locals for directions. In 1910, Goodrich followed Michelin and installed road signs in the United States; by 1917 Goodrich had marked more than 110,000 miles of road with 10-foot-high signs easily seen by motorists. Michelin even established a tourist office in Paris, which helped tourists by sending out individualized itineraries for trips, denoting distances and turn-offs. And the pattern repeated, as Dunlop did the same in London and Goodrich did likewise in Akron, its corporate headquarters handling some seven hundred requests per day in the summer of 1917. Goodrich also issued some thirty-seven different route books, tracing the precise directions for itin-eraries across the United States.[7]

Meanwhile, whenever possible, companies attempted to enhance their appeal to elite buyers by bragging about the royals and aristocrats who bought their tires. For example, in 1897, Dunlop let buyers know that those riding on Dunlops included the Prince of Wales, the Duke of Connaught, the German Emperor, and the King of Saxony, as well as well-known British politicians Joseph Chamberlain and A. J. Balfour.[8] Michelin, in turn, claimed that "the Michelin tire is not only the king of tires, it is the tire of kings." The German Emperor, the Russian Czar, the kings of Britain, Belgium, and Italy, and the Marquis de Dion and the Russian prince Wladimir Orloff all owned sets of Michelins.[9] By implication, buying the same tires as emperors, kings, and noblemen conferred status.

In the 1910s, automobile sales grew exponentially in the United States, as even farmers and workers could now afford a Ford Model T. Throughout the interwar years, the United States led demand for auto-mobiles; in 1929 Americans possessed 78 percent of cars in the world.[10] Tire companies no longer needed to create demand among the wealthy. Tires risked becoming a simple commodity, so now manufacturers needed to distinguish their products from those of the competition. Ads assisted in that process, which became known as branding. Tire companies competed fiercely with each other, hiring the major American advertising agencies, including J. Walter Thompson, Arthur Kudner, and Erwin, Wasey & Co., to design elaborate advertising campaigns. Nevertheless, ads continued to be upscale, if not for the wealthy few than for the American middle class. The strategy was two-fold: on the one hand, middle-class buyers could afford to pay more for tires, and usually drove more. On the other, for farmers and workers, the ads could still have an appeal in that ads then, as now, tend to be aspirational; anyone aspiring to have the life portrayed in ads, however far from their own, could sometimes find them appealing. Advertisements themselves departed from the simple trade cards of the past in order to tell stories, the narratives now being less about a description of the product and more about how it would transform the buyer's life.

Notions of social class remained critical in advertising, particularly as tire companies attempted to associate their tires with quality. Goodrich had the patent for the early production of Cord tires (tires that literally had cotton cords under the rubber, a feature that made them stronger and more durable). The process had been invented in Silvertown, in London's East End, but to American ears the silver of the name implied wealth and thus quality. Goodrich used the name Silvertown for its better tires, even naming one version "The Patrician." In 1929, J. Walter Thompson oversaw a national ad campaign that illustrated the quality of the tires by running a fleet of silver-colored cars, all equipped with Silvertown tires, more than 30,000 miles east and west, north and south, back and forth across the United States through forty-five of the forty-eight states. Some fifteen "pilots" and their "commander" met fourteen governors and hundreds of mayors. From Smith College in Massachusetts to Stanford University in California, the Silver Fleet appeared on college campuses. Entire faculties and student bodies turned out to have a look at them; at Southern Methodist University in Dallas and the University of California in Berkeley classes were canceled so that all could see the Silver Fleet. The lead (flagship) automobiles included large silver convertible Studebakers, Lincolns, and Buicks (tellingly *not* Fords or Chevies), brands that denoted a certain social status in the United States in 1929.[11]

Goodyear, by far the largest tire producer in the United States and the world (a fact that dominated its own advertising) in the 1920s, similarly used notions of social class to market their products. Goodyear's own version of the cord tire was dubbed by Arthur Kudner's firm "the masterpiece" in 1917 and appeared in ads as if a framed piece of art. In a wide array of magazines destined for the American middle class, Goodyear went one step farther in tying its higher-quality "Double Eagle" tire (the name itself a patriotic nod to the toughness of the iconic American eagle) to some of most famous works of European and

American art. As Goodyear put it in an ad that compared its tire to Frans Hals' *The Laughing Cavalier*:

> The Goodyear Double Eagle Tire may with propriety claim this kinship with every masterpiece of art: it is the very finest thing of its kind. It is more than an excellent tire—it is literally a much better tire than any normal need requires. It was built in the beginning without regard to cost; it has been scrupulously improved since as the art of tire-making has advanced.

Similar ads compared the tire to Boucher's *La Marquise de Pompadour*, Thomas Gainsborough's *Blue Boy*, Hans Holbein's *George Gisze*, Titian's *Portrait of a Man*, Valasquez's (sic.) *Portrait of a Lady*, Vermeer's *Young Woman in a Yellow Jacket*, and Whistler's *Portrait of Thomas Carlyle*, not to mention images of "the Winged Victory" of Samothrace and the Roman "Arch of Titus." The Taj Mahal was a notable outlier in coming from outside the tradition of "Western art," but it too was comparable to the Goodyear Double Eagle.[12]

Firestone employed a similar approach in advertisements that it placed in *American Magazine* and the *Saturday Evening Post*. In those ads, Firestone compared the production of its "Gum-Dipped Cord Tire" to great achievements in the past, including swords in Damascus, medieval tapestry, as well as the contributions of Gutenberg, Stradivarius, Christopher Wren, Richard Arkwright, Josiah Wedgwood, George Stephenson, Robert Fulton, and Robert Owen, among others. In an ongoing battle to compete with the Sears & Roebuck Company's inexpensive Allstate tire, Firestone redoubled its efforts to associate Firestone with culture, class, and quality. The Voice of Firestone made its radio debut on NBC in 1928. Featuring thirty minutes of classical music with an orchestra and vocalists, the Voice of Firestone was supposed to remind listeners of the inherent quality of Firestone products for more than thirty years (complemented by a television show of the same name from 1949 to 1959), making it the only radio program from the 1920s still to be on the air in 1959.[13]

Clearly, in the mass market for automobiles in the United States, as in the more limited European markets, tire companies—which gobbled up most of the world's rubber supply—used notions of social class to encourage buyers to imagine themselves as well-off men.

Race and Consumption in Europe and North America

In the United States, rates of automobile ownership, and thus rubber usage, were considerably lower in African-American, Hispanic, and Native American communities. Few people of color owned cars before

World War I, and rates of ownership remained low in the interwar years. While many could afford other rubber products, the "rubber sundries" available in drug stores, their business was taken for granted; advertising agencies aimed their campaigns at white, mostly middle-class America. People of color did not appear in ads, even tire ads, except as stereotypes: in this way, American ads differed little from European ones.

In both Europe and North America, the advertisements constituted what scholars call commodity racism. Unlike scientific racism, commodity racism was cultural and accompanied the simple products of everyday life. The infamous Pears Soap ads, in which black skin could be washed white with a bit of Pears Soap, are perhaps the best known. In the heyday of European empires, it was not at all unusual for advertisements—in Europe or the United States—to feature an array of stereotypical Africans or "Indians," with the latter term meaning everyone from inhabitants of the Indian subcontinent, to the indigenous peoples of the Dutch East Indies, to all the indigenous peoples of North, Central, and South America.

Clearly, advertisements were aimed at whites in Europe and the United States, encouraging them to see themselves as fundamentally different, and better, than non-whites. For example, two Africans appear riding bicycles on a prewar Michelin postcard drawn by Gaugé. An extremely skinny black man with huge lips and oversized hands, wearing a top hat and a ring in his nose, describes why he has Michelin tires and his wife does not. She, a fat woman with big pants to cover her huge hips, sits passively on tires called "Peach Pit" (indicating that they are as hard as rocks). The man announces: "Her, well-padded, mount Peach Pit. / Me, not well-padded, mount good Michelin tire."[14] Like so many American images of "mammy," as in the original Aunt Jemima ads in the United States, the African woman is assumed to be fat, while her slender and more delicate husband needs the comfort offered by Michelin tires. Moreover, the African man's ridiculous appearance is reminiscent of minstrel shows.

Michelin buyers could even make fun of Africans collecting rubber in the Congo, making light of the abuses so well publicized before World War I. In one poster, O'Galop portrayed the birth of the Michelin man. He descended from the clouds, hungry. His appetite was so ravenous that "all of the negroes spread out in the virgin forests and set about to gather and coagulate the precious rubber. The white brothers snatched up, for a king's ransom, these large masses and hurried to carry them into numerous factories."[15] The very suggestion that Africans were well paid for the rubber collected there is of course inaccurate, but what makes the poster interesting is that at least O'Galop thought it was funny. Only in a world where African lives were assumed to be less valuable than European ones could anyone find the reference even remotely funny, this just five years after the Belgian government took over King Leopold's Congo.

B. F. Goodrich featured Native Americans, casually mixing "red" Indians from North and South America with the "brown" Indians of Asia, in describing its inner tube (even automobile tires had inner tubes until after World War II), the "Goodrich Indian Tube." In one advertisement destined for Goodrich tire dealers, an American Indian holds the "Goodrich Indian Tube," while the text proclaims all of the excellent qualities of Indians:

> We give it this name because it is made of the cream of the finest rubber gathered by the native Indians in the richest rubber country.
> It is hardy, enduring, full of vitality—like an Indian.
> It is built for speed—like an Indian.
> It is brown—like an Indian.
> It is the "best in the long run"—like an Indian.
> You'll always know it by its color—copper-brown, Indian-brown.[16]

Obviously, here "the" Indian was essentially good, rather than the scalping, gambling, and drinking Indian of American Westerns at the time, even if "he" was essentialized in much the same way. African Americans fared less well; the following year, as minstrel shows took place in Akron, Goodrich made fun of a terrified African American named "Sambo" in a supposedly funny story entitled "Wherein One Darkey Gets Mighty Scared."[17] Clearly, the desired audience was not a black one.

Firestone and World's Fair authorities similarly denigrated Africans in appealing to white Americans. At the 1939–40 World's Fair in New York, Firestone mounted a huge diorama portraying the collection of rubber on one of its plantations in Liberia. In 1939 alone, some 5 million visitors saw the exhibit. A company survey revealed that visitors were exactly those targeted by Firestone, middle-class white Americans with "income and education" that "was above average." At the exhibit they heard African music and African voices, thereby having an "African" experience while viewing the diorama. As the Fair's press release described the Firestone scene:

> The rhythmic throb of African tom-toms, combined with native mumbojumbo, adds realism to one of the many features of the Firestone Tire & Rubber Company's exhibit at the New York World's Fair. Unintelligible mumblings and the thump-thump of taut goat skins come from the underbrush in a big diorama which depicts scenes on one of the big Firestone rubber plantations in Liberia, West Africa.[18]

Unlike the European classical music on the Voice of Firestone, African music was a "rhythmic throb" with a "thump-thump." Unlike the beautifully written English (a real language) ad copy for Goodyear Double Eagles, Goodrich Silvertowns, and Firestone Gum-Dripped Cords, here middle-class whites could hear "native mumbo jumbo" and "unintelligible mumblings" of Africa. Such racist advertising encouraged white visitors and potential tire buyers to feel superior to the "primitive" blacks at home and abroad.

Gender and Consumption in Europe and North America

In Europe and North America, the widespread notion of separate spheres for men and women made an inevitable distinction between production and consumption. Advertising did not create societal assumptions about women's and men's "natures," but it did reinforce them, making them stronger, through constant repetition. In principle, men left the home to work. Women took care of the home. Men produced. Women consumed. Men conquered. Women nurtured. Nevertheless, the actual purchasing of the automobile along with its tires, by far the most expensive household purchase after the house or apartment itself, fell to men. While today patterns of urban development seem to have made automobiles nearly indispensable, at least in North America, in the early twentieth century they were initially playthings for wealthy men. As the market became mass by the 1920s, automobiles remained status symbols for men in particular. Advertisements for automobile tires appealed to men and offered up strongly male identities to those who purchased a given manufacturer's tires. In the meantime, advertisements for rubber household goods targeted women, encouraging them to fulfill idealized roles of housewife and mother.

In nearly all of these ads, the right tires made the man, whether that be a worldly playboy or a good husband and father. In 1907, Michelin bragged about the "conquests of the Michelin Man." Returning from two wins at the automobile race course in Brescia, near Milan, the Michelin Man has to pass through French customs in the town of Modane. When the customs official asks the Michelin Man if he has anything to declare, he replies, "oh yes, two delightful women from Milan that I picked up on the race track at Brescia." With a blond on one side and a brunette on the other, the placement of his hands and the women's gorgeous appearance are unambiguous. The Michelin Man has made two "conquests" at the same time.[19] The message could not be any clearer to the man thinking of buying Michelin tires.

Michelin ads also equated cars with women. Having one is like having (with the ownership that verb implies) the other. Below an illustration of a man changing a tire and looking at a beautiful woman's raised heel at the same time, the Michelin Man quibbles with a pastor in Detroit who had compared the automobile to a man. Rather, declares the Michelin Man, the car and its needy tires resemble a woman:

> Woman, says the Arab proverb, shares our pains, doubles our joys, and triples our expenses. One can say the same thing about the automobile... The automobile, like woman, makes us see the country... To steer her one needs softness, a certain touch, and one recognizes this experience among those who have gotten around. You will tell me that the automobile has the superiority of silence. Would you be quiet! A pretty woman and a car, what could be better for expanding one's circle of acquaintances? The owner of a pretty car and the husband of a charming woman never risk having too few friends... And which costs the most, whether you are talking about a woman or a car? Maintenance [of cars and of women], I can't pursue that comparison; it could go on into infinity.[20]

Clearly, when it came to cars and tires, women were objects of men's attention. B. F. Goodrich was less direct but similarly associated tires with women. In the early twentieth century, the company's advertising included a well-known series of portraits of some gorgeous young women known as the "Goodrich girls." Their images appeared in magazine advertisements, calendars, handbills, and catalogs.

As automobile usage became increasingly widespread in interwar America, tire ads encouraged men to ensure the safety of their wives and children. The responsible man bought good tires to protect them. Some of the most heavy-handed of messages along these lines came from Arthur Kudner's efforts to sell Goodyear tires in 1937. The Goodyear "lifeguard" double-layered inner tube would "take the terror out of blowouts," as there always remained some air in the innermost chamber of the tube. Yet, the appeal was less technical than emotional. In one ad, a small child is in a wheelchair being pushed along by a woman, presumably his mother. He sighs, "Gee, I wish I could play again!" To be sure the reader did not miss the point, the text was unequivocal: "crippled for life in a blowout smash up! A pitiful accident that could never have happened if the car had been equipped with Lifeguard Tubes."[21] In another, a man in a suit looks out a window to the yard, where a nurse is helping a girl on crutches. The caption reads: "What a blithering idiot I was." Once again, lest the point is somehow lost on the viewer, the text explains: "Look at this sad picture, and ask yourself, 'Am I gambling the whole future of my loved ones on the

Figure 3.1 Goodrich girl. "Goodrich Automobile Tires, Adele," Goodrich Collection. Photo reprinted with permission of Archival Services, University Libraries, University of Akron.

Like automakers, tire makers associated products purchased by men with women desired by men. "Adele" was one of fifteen "Goodrich girls" whose appeal was supposed to help sell tires. The "Goodrich girls" are tame compared to many later images of nude or nearly nude women on automotive calendars destined for mechanics' workbenches. What does the image suggest that a man gets when he buys Goodrich tires?

possibility that a blowout can't happen to me.'"[22] In yet another, a woman sits crying, a picture of a man to her right. A young son asks, "Mummy, isn't daddy ever coming home?"[23]

The right tires could also allow men to disregard the presumably constant protests by women that they were driving too fast. According

Figure 3.2 "What a Blithering Idiot I Was." Goodyear ad, page proof, August 1937, Goodyear Collection. Photo reprinted with permission of Archival Services, University Libraries, University of Akron.

This image appeared in the well-illustrated magazines of the interwar years. How does it reinforce a notion of men's responsibility? What happens when a man makes a bad decision in not buying Goodyear tires? What is the construction of masculinity here?

to B. F. Goodrich, when she says, "Please don't drive so fast, we might have a blow out," he tells her, "Don't worry! Our tires have the new Goodrich golden ply."[24] Without Goodrich tires, the outcome would be different. She says, "Ted, you've been driving pretty fast. Aren't you afraid of a blow out?" as she sits in the front and the kids and grandma sit in the back seat. He says, "Why, these tires are only 4 months old. They won't blow out." Then there is a blow out, and the car goes over a cliff.[25] The subtext is clear. With the right (Goodrich) tires, a man can drive as fast as he likes. There is no danger—and no need to listen to his wife's annoying pleas to "slow down!" Without them, he is being irresponsible. Tellingly, Goodrich never suggests that men simply drive more slowly so that any sort of tire failure would be far less dangerous.

In the United States, to a far greater extent than in Europe, women took the wheel. That does not mean, however, that automobiles or their tires became the domain of women. Men remained the responsible parties. They needed to protect their families, particularly if presumably less-experienced "women drivers" were at the wheel. As Goodrich made clear: "when 'She' drives, your first consideration is safety for her and the youngsters. Specify for your new car, or equip your present car, with Goodrich Safety Tread Tires."[26] The company noted that "when your wife drives, when your family rides, you want SAFE tires on your family car— the best tires that money can buy. That means Goodyear Tires."[27]

By contrast, advertising for rubber household goods consistently pandered to women, even as they asserted that women's place was in the home. Many rubber items, including water bottles, balloons, and children's toys, were widely available in Europe and the United States in the late nineteenth century. In the early twentieth century, shipment of concentrated liquid latex became technologically possible, so that rubber did not have to be shipped as blocks of crepe sheets or smoked balls, then masticated and reconstituted in the production process. US Rubber began shipping latex as a liquid in 1913. By the early 1920s, tank cars moved latex from plantations to ports, where it could be shipped via tankers to the United States. There, latex could be used to create stronger, thin rubber gloves, which increasingly became a household item, having been developed for antiseptic surgery at the turn of the century. Latex helped make varied elastics possible, which transformed the manufacture of items such as bathing caps and swimwear. Lightweight rubber hot water bottles and syringes appeared on the market. Latex became a base for household paints. Whipped latex, called Airfoam by Goodyear and Dunlopillo by Dunlop, became foam rubber for use in pillows, mattresses, and upholstered furniture of various sorts. Eventually, many of these products became omnipresent in American and European homes. Initially, however, they were more expensive, and advertising attempted to convince women not only that the products would be useful, but that they would be fulfilling their duties to keep their families and homes scrupulously clean and well organized.

In the interwar years, B. F. Goodrich's Waldo Semon developed the first plasticized PVC (polyvinyl chloride), a rubber-related material that was a predecessor of many of today's plastics. Koroseal became the registered trademark. Goodrich's admen put the Koroseal name into advertising for a wide array of products, notably footwear and flooring, tablecloths, aprons, raincoats, shower caps, diapers, capes to be worn as women applied make-up, shower curtains, and ironing-board covers. Images reminded one and all that smart women who understood the importance of "modern hygiene" would be the buyers of these products. Said buyers were also assumed to be white, as in one ad featuring a thin, elegant white woman placing a Koroseal pad on the ironing board while a large, happy, black woman, obviously the maid and family "mammy," waits to iron the clothes.[28]

The idea that household products could replace maids—while still reminding buyers of them—was critical to the marketing success of Rubbermaid. In 1933, James Caldwell founded the company and began selling molded rubber dustpans door to door. (Absorbed by a balloon manufacturer, the Wooster Rubber Company of Wooster, Ohio in 1934, Rubbermaid remained the name on household products.) By the late 1930s, company employees were dipping wire dish drainers into latex tanks used for latex gloves and balloons, making a dish drainer that did not chip fine china. Bathtub mats, sink mats, spatulas, and drain-board trays to go under (rubber-covered) wire dish drainers followed. They all carried the name Rubbermaid, and the logo included a maid wearing a maid's cap. Buyers of these products could imagine that they were hiring a maid, the ultimate symbol of bourgeois prosperity in the nineteenth and early twentieth centuries, or replacing one they could never have afforded in the first place.[29]

Women buyers were also deemed to be the primary market for the thriving trade in water bottles, large rubber syringes/bulbs, and various combinations of the two. In colder climates, hot water bottles were often placed in cold beds before bedtime. Rubber syringes were sold as "hygienic" items. As with other rubber products, the US Commerce Department carefully assisted US rubber manufacturers of rubber bottles and syringes, undertaking detailed reports about the consumption of the products worldwide. The reports make clear that demand for such products was, in Jamaica, "restricted by the lower purchasing power of the colored people" and that "the colored women have little knowledge of the use of syringes, never having been given any idea of modern sanitation and hygiene."[30] Like ads for rubber syringes in the United States, the report was not exactly explicit. Rubber syringes were sometimes used for enemas. More often they were used for "feminine hygiene," meaning douching. Douching with water and, in the early 1920s, with Lysol and other products was the most widely used, although not effective, female contraceptive in the United States.[31] In retrospect, there is no little irony in the advertisers' efforts to convince women to keep cleaner and thus healthier home environments in order to meet presumed social expectations about their roles as good wives and mothers. Vaginal douching can be dangerous, even more so with a strong antiseptic such as Lysol.

Gendering Reproduction

Since the mid-nineteenth century, rubber has implied contraception and thus sex. As indicated by Northern American slang, "rubber" has long meant condom (it is a longstanding joke among Brits who entered American stores asking to buy a "rubber," when they wanted an eraser). Condoms existed long before they were made of rubber. Sheep intestines were the material of choice before the 1850s, when the first rubber condoms debuted. The latter soon dominated sales. And, despite the advent of rubber diaphragms and cervical caps of various sorts, condoms remained the manufactured contraceptive (as opposed to abstinence, douching, the rhythm method, or withdrawal) of choice in many countries well into the twentieth century.

Condom consumption was heavily gendered in several ways. Most obviously, unlike douching, condoms require male assent and participation. This was even more the case before the advent of latex condoms in the interwar years. In the late nineteenth century, condom production began with a mold more or less in the shape of a penis, to which workers affixed strips of rubber, before it was then cured with heat. The resulting product was thick and had a usable shelf life (actually, reusable) of about three months, as histories of condoms regularly point out. Some had seams. More significant was the issue of size. Rubber condoms came in various sizes, more or less matching different penis sizes, and men needed not only to don the condom but to choose the appropriate size. In some cases, doctors helped with the measuring, especially for models designed to fit primarily the glans.

After World War I, Fred Killian of Akron patented a method of dipping the mold into latex, which revolutionized condom manufacture. The resulting disposable latex condoms had a shelf life of about five years. The fact that they were thin, blocking sensation less than had earlier condoms, led to their widespread adoption in the United States, to such an extent that the US Food and Drug Administration tested them and the Consumers' Union (later publisher of *Consumer Reports*) recommended certain more reliable brands. A comparable method also simplified the production of diaphragms.

National norms determined contraceptive use. In the United States, the Comstock Laws limited the dissemination of information about condoms and other contraceptives. During World War I—much to the frustration of their French counterparts, let alone French civilians—the American military leadership did not distribute condoms to the American Expeditionary Force in France, an established practice in the British, French, and German armies. The American doughboys quickly became important vectors in the spread of venereal disease, pushing the US Army to reconsider its policy. In World War II, in an effort to avert the disaster of the previous war, condoms were standard issue for American troops in Europe and Asia, along with cigarettes, Wrigley's chewing gum, and Hershey chocolate bars.

In France, where prostitution was legal in the early twentieth century, sex was not the problem. Rather, after the losses of World War I and the preoccupation with French "depopulation," it was contraception itself that presented a problem. In 1920, the French National Assembly made the dissemination even of information about birth control, and thus birth control itself, illegal. Until the 1960s, diaphragms and cervical caps were essentially illegal, as the pill would be. Yet condoms, the form of contraception most dependent on men's participation (a fact not missed by feminists), remained legal, as they were deemed necessary for the prevention of venereal disease. Interestingly, despite the legislation, the French birthrate did not rebound enough to recover from the primary cause of French "depopulation": world war. In the 1930s, during several years there were more deaths than births. Economic uncertainty did not encourage couples to have large families; condoms were the artificial contraceptive of choice in France, and they saw wide use.

Outside Europe, evidence of the use of condoms, such as on Southeast Asian plantations, is indirect. European assistants could, and probably did, use condoms (or in British and Dutch colonies, diaphragms and cervical caps as well as condoms) with their wives, given that many assistants and their wives often had no, one, or two children. We have no idea, of course, of actual usage among plantations assistants who had sex with their "housekeepers." Obviously these unions created numerous mixed-race babies, who were recognized (or not) as bastards but not taken back to Britain, France, or Holland when the assistant returned to the metropole, any more frequently than their mothers. Given the social shame that such women faced in communities where they almost always remained, it seems doubtful that they had access to, or control of, effective contraception. More tellingly, venereal disease was rampant among female plantation laborers at the turn of the century, so it seems likely that condoms were not in widespread use: "A Deli doctor reported that more than half the women in one estate district had venereal disease. And from one estate district... a manager complained to his head office that thirty-five of his female workers were hospitalized with syphilis."[32]

In the case of condom consumption, as in so many other instances, notions of gender combined with those of race to produce results that tell us much about how societies construct both categories. In 1923, the Firestone Tire and Rubber Company began producing condoms (this situation was rare and temporary; condoms seemed illicit in a sometimes puritanical United States, and tire manufacturers did not generally want their brand names tied to condoms). Black with raised letters that read "nonskid," the condoms were a sort of advertisement for Firestone tires. Its trademarked "non-skid" tires were black, like other tires after the introduction of carbon black in the manufacturing process (early tires had been a shade of gray, much like latex itself). The Firestone "nonskid" condom was sold through garages and gas stations, male haunts at the time. Even if it seemed "natural" that a rubber company would produce "rubbers," Firestone's production of condoms was short-lived, as race, gender, and sex were a threatening combination when they took the form of a black condom in the United States.

"We were forced into it," claimed Firestone executives at the time. "We called ourselves a rubber company, so the guys at the club were always kidding around and asking for free samples. We didn't have much choice really." Its unusual design drew mixed reactions from the public. While women were enthusiastic about the texture: "like hundreds of little auto tires urging me to let go," the coloration was another matter. Firestone withdrew from the market after an intense campaign by the Ku Klux Klan, who feared that it would cause white women to develop a taste for black genitalia.[33]

Of course, the issue for the KKK would not have been interracial sex per se, as white men "picking" black women for sex as well as household help was no more unacceptable than white plantation managers "picking" Asian women for sex and housekeeping. The issue all along had been the presumed danger of men of color "possessing" white women who "belonged" to white men. Condoms, like other everyday consumer products, thus reveal much about the broader social context in which they were used.

READING

The Romance and Drama of the Rubber Industry,
Harvey S. Firestone, Jr.

In 1931–32, as part of the "Voice of Firestone" music program, Harvey Firestone, Jr. (son of founder Harvey S. Firestone, Sr.) narrated the history of rubber from its "discovery," to its various places of production, to its consumption in the United States. The series title was "Romance and

Drama of the Rubber Industry." The following is an excerpt from the August 28, 1931 program, entitled "The Discovery of Rubber."

- How does Harvey Firestone encourage the consumption of rubber?
- With what are raw rubber and manufactured rubber products associated (note key words such as crude, primitive, civilization, Indian, white man, and "modern")?
- What are his assumptions about race?
- How would he define civilization?
- In expressions such as "white man" and "white men," are women assumed or excluded (or both)?

We who enjoy the benefits of rubber in its many forms so vitally linked with modern life, may find it very interesting to go back to the crude beginnings to see how this remarkable material, from the laboratory of Nature, first came to the attention of the white man.

Spanish explorers found it in Mexico about the year 1521. They saw it used by the native Indians in various ways. The thing which startled and fascinated those Spanish explorers was the fact that the native Indians made bouncing balls of the material. White men had never before seen a solid substance that would bound away from another solid material when thrown against it. They saw the Indians playing games with those bouncing balls.

The native Indians found other and more practical uses of the milky substance from the rubber tree. How long they had used rubber no one knows, but in the activities of their crude and primitive life they had found a material that was destined to be a basic necessity in the development of our modern civilization.

Today rubber enters into almost every phase and activity of life. Without it, no factory could run, no modern building could operate, no fast railroad train could travel across the country, and no steamship could sail the high seas. No home could be conducted in the modern sense without the articles and implements of rubber that are made for our daily use. From the first cry of the new-born babe until the last slow march to the grave, things made of rubber are indispensable to our modern life.

One of the greatest of these things of basic importance is the automobile tire that serves the commerce of the world, speeds the business of every civilized nation, and adds convenience and happiness to millions upon millions of our people.[34]

Notes

1 "Le lundi de Michelin," *Le journal* (13 January 1913), p. 5.
2 Daniel R. Headrick, *The Tools of Empire: Technology and European Imperialism in the Nineteenth Century* (New York: Oxford University Press, 1981).

3 According to Leong Yee Fong, in the late 1930s Chinese laborers on plantations had bicycles: *Labour and Trade Unionism in Colonial Malaya: A Study of the Socio-Economic and Political Bases of the Malayan Labour Movement, 1930–1957* (Pulau Pinang: Penerbit Universitii Sains Malaysia, 1999), p. 42.

4 When the US Commerce Department grew concerned about Japanese exports of rubber boots and canvas shoes with rubber soles to Southeast Asia in the late 1920s and early 1930s (a presumed threat to US industry), at issue was not footwear for laborers, but boots and tennis shoes for Europeans and Americans: P. W. Barker, Acting Chief of Rubber Division, to F. G. Patterson, of United States Rubber Export Co., 5 May 1930, in National Archives II, RG 151 Records of the Bureau of Foreign and Domestic Commerce, General Records, 1914–1958, 254.20 Rubber Goods, Footwear, Japan.

5 Dane Kennedy, *The Magic Mountains: Hill Stations and the British Raj* (Berkeley, CA: University of California Press, 1996); Eric Jennings, *Imperial Heights: Dalat and the Making and Undoing of French Indochina* (Berkeley, CA: University of California Press, 2011).

6 The car belongs to the Smithsonian and was on display in December 2004 at the Western Reserve Historical Society.

7 Harp, *Marketing Michelin*, chapter 2; *Rules of the Road and Saving Hints to the "Man Behind the Wheel"* (Akron: B. F. Goodrich, 1917), p. 33 in the Warshaw Collection, Box 2, National Museum of American History Library, Smithsonian Institution; *Goodrich* (February 1919): 7 in BFG K-2 in University of Akron Archives (UAA).

8 *The Dunlop News* 8 (May 1897): 2.

9 "Le lundi de Michelin," *L'Auto* (9 October 1905): 8; Michelin, "Le pneumatique et l'automobile, 1894–1914: Influence du perfectionnement du pneumatique sur le développement de l'industrie automobile" (Clermont-Ferrand: Michelin, 1904), p. 27; "Le lundi de Michelin," *Le Journal* (25 November 1912): 5.

10 Richard P. Tucker, *Insatiable Appetite: The United States and the Economic Degradation of the Tropical World* (Berkeley, CA: University of California Press, 2000), pp. 226–282.

11 E. R. Schaeffer to P. J. Kelly, Advertising Manager at B. F. Goodrich, November 12, 1929, in J. Walter Thompson files, "Goodrich Silvertown Fleet, 1929," in the Hartman Center, Duke University Libraries.

12 Versions of Arthur Kudner's "The Masterpiece" appeared in the *Saturday Evening Post* in 1917 and again in *Atlantic Monthly* in 1936, and the other ads, by Erwin, Wasey & Co., appeared in *Country Life, Highway Traveler, Life, New Yorker, Saturday Evening Post, Sportsman, Spur, Town and Country, Vanity Fair,* 1931–33; these are all also in uncatalogued Goodyear advertising files, UAA.

13 John Wendell Spalding, "An Historical and Descriptive Analysis of the *Voice of Firestone* Radio and Television Program, 1928–1959" (PhD thesis, University of Michigan, 1961), pp. 1, 35.

14 Gaugé, postcard collection, Michelin Conservatoire.

15 O'Galop, "La bicyclette à travers les ages," poster, Michelin Conservatoire.

16 *The Goodrich* (January 1914): 17, in the UAA.

17 *The Goodrich* (May 1915): 5, in the UAA.

18 C. D. Smith of Firestone to Walter M. Langsdorf, Associate Director of Exhibits, 29 November 1939; and Press Release 792, issued by the New York World's Fair, 1939, in Firestone Tire & Rubber Co., Automotive Participation, 1939, Box 124, in the World's Fair Records of the New York Public Library.

19 Ad in *L'auto* (23 September 1907): 8.

20 "Le lundi de Michelin," *Le journal* (6 April 1914): 5.

21 Proof from uncatalogued Goodyear advertising files at the UAA; it ran in *Life*, 2 August 1937.

22 Proof from uncatalogued Goodyear advertising files at the UAA; it ran in the *Atlantic Monthly*, August 1937.

23 Proof from uncatalogued Goodyear advertising files at the UAA; it ran in *Forbes*, *Newsweek*, *U.S. News*, and *The Wall Street Journal*, in late August and September 1937.

24 Goodrich ad, Goodrich Box B-A-4, UAA; the ad ran in the *Saturday Evening Post*, 24 June 1933.

25 Goodrich ad, Goodrich Box B-A-4, UAA; the ad ran in the *American Magazine*, August 1934.

26 Goodrich ad, Goodrich Box B-A-2, UAA; the ad ran in *Munsey's Magazine*, June 1914.

27 Goodyear ad, by Erwin, Wasey & Co, in the uncatalogued Goodyear advertising files, UAA; it ran in *Time*, 9 May 1932.

28 Goodrich advertising, File "Development Series, 1940–41," in BA-7, in the UAA.

29 Donald E. Noble, *Like Only Yesterday: The Memoirs of Donald E. Noble* (Wooster, OH: Wooster Book Company, 1996), pp. 56–63.

30 E. G. Holt, Assistant Chief, Rubber Division, "Export Trade Notes on Rubber Specialties Markets for Water Bottles and Syringes," 18 March 1924, National Archives II RG 15, Box 1186, 254.24–254.26 File "Rubber Goods—Water bottles—1924–1928," Records of the Bureau of Foreign and Domestic Commerce, General Records.

31 Andrea Tone, *Devices and Desires: A History of Contraceptives in America* (New York: Hill and Wang, 2001), p. 158.

32 Stoler, *Capitalism*, p. 32.

33 Jim Wilson, "Hall of Erotic Technology," *Forum International* 15, no. 5 (December 1985): 1–9, in Kinsey Institute Archives, Indiana University: J 520 F74 v. 15 n.3, photo of a Firestone "nonskid" condom, p. 9.

34 Text of the broadcast later appeared in Harvey S. Firestone, Jr., *The Romance and Drama of the Rubber Industry* (Akron, OH: Firestone, 1936 [1932]), pp. 18–19.

4

World Wars, Nationalism, and Imperialism

Suggested film clip: FDR's Newsreel address regarding scrap rubber
https://archive.org/details/1942-06-15_Scrap_Rubber_Needed

Take away from us the motor vehicle, and I do not know what would happen. The damage would be more serious and lasting than if our land were laid waste by an invader. We could recover from the blowing up of New York City and all the big cities on the Atlantic seaboard more quickly than we could recover from the loss of our rubber.[1]

Thus proclaimed Harvey S. Firestone in 1926, as he compared possible apocalypses for the American public. Firestone, who like other tire and auto manufacturers did so much to make the United States more dependent on rubber, now wanted to mobilize US citizens to be concerned about the possible loss of "our rubber." By 1926, his perspective was news to no one, as a line about the need for the United States to have "our" rubber had appeared for years on nearly all Firestone advertisements. Meanwhile, US Secretary of Commerce Herbert Hoover sought publicity for his own efforts to secure cheap rubber for US industry; his advocacy for American business abroad would soon help propel him to the presidency. And Firestone and Hoover were just the two most prominent advocates of American rubber. At a time when US firms controlled no more than 3 percent of supply but the United States consumed about 70 percent of the world's rubber, Firestone's formulation, however widespread, is nevertheless fascinating. In referring to

A World History of Rubber: Empire, Industry, and the Everyday, First Edition.
Stephen L. Harp.
© 2016 John Wiley & Sons, Inc. Published 2016 by John Wiley & Sons, Inc.

"our" rubber, he implied that most of the world's rubber somehow *belonged* to the United States, wherever in the world it was produced. Rubber had become an important commodity by World War I and it only grew in importance thereafter. Entire national economies, and particularly that of the United States, became overwhelmingly dependent on rubber during the interwar years. Not surprisingly during this era of intense, even virulent nationalism, when government officials and corporate leaders described rubber, they spoke in a language of nationalism. The rubber from the Malay Peninsula and Ceylon (today Sri Lanka) was "British" rubber, that from Sumatra "Dutch," that from Cochinchina and Cambodia "French," *belonging* to the metropoles—and not the colonies themselves. Since the Americans used most of the rubber the world produced, they in turn claimed pretty much all of it as "theirs." In this chapter, we trace the ways in which rubber became an object of nationalism in Europe and the United States. In the next, we will see how it also became a symbol of both imperialism and nationalism for the peoples of Southeast Asia.

World War I

Although rubber was a colonial product well before the onset of World War I, it was not generally viewed through a nationalist lens. European empire had always been partly about international competition, between the Portuguese and Spanish, Spanish and British, Dutch and British, British and French, and so on. Nevertheless, the late nineteenth- and early twentieth-century plantation economies complicated national identities. In Southeast Asia, although surrounded by Asians, plantation managers and assistants saw other Europeans—and even white Americans—as being more like them than different. To some extent, *European* identities were forged in the colonies as "white" identities of colonizers in the face of "brown" and "black" colonized. British estates had staff members from other European countries, but especially whites from Britain and the British Dominions of Australia, Canada, and New Zealand. In Sumatra, where the Dutch encouraged international investment, British and American plantation staff worked (often in English) alongside the Dutch and some Germans who did not find the linguistic leap from German to rudimentary Dutch very difficult. In French Indochina, French-speaking Belgians sometimes served on plantation staffs. By the early twentieth century, all whites on plantations called themselves Europeans. They were distinct from the locals, those inhabiting the presumably timeless and unchanging "East" or "Orient."

World wars altered the dynamic. Although little publicized among the American people, during World War I Britain threatened to suspend rubber shipments to the United States permanently until the latter (still neutral at the time) agreed not to supply the German war machine. Had Britain done so, the US economy would have ground to a halt, as most rubber was grown in British colonies and passed through the hands of British traders in Singapore and London (aside from Goodyear and US Rubber plantations in Southeast Asia, US companies had virtually no plantations as compared to US consumption). Moreover, in the cataclysm that was the Great War, rubber proved its mettle. In September 1914, French forces halted the German onslaught, saving Paris from invasion. Trucks and government-requisitioned Renault taxicabs from Paris hauled men and materiel to the front in the famous French victory at the Battle of the Marne. In 1916, Verdun was the site of a long, brutal battle that came to symbolize the entire French war effort (about 80 percent of French troops served for a time at Verdun, 300,000 of whom died). There the "sacred way" (*voie sacrée*) received much credit for victory. On that narrow road, trucks ran round the clock, bumper to bumper, in an endless convoy to and from the front, carrying men and supplies. After the battle of Verdun, the future seemed clear. Tire-clad trucks would be critical in future wars. The generals could have gotten around without their cars (and drivers), reverting to horses, but trucks on rubber tires seemed indispensable. Meanwhile the Germans, cut off by the British blockade from rubber supplies, faced a severe shortage of the precious commodity, prompting German chemists to begin experimentation in the production of synthetic rubber, with very mixed results. The lack of rubber did not cause German defeat even if abundant rubber assisted in French and British victory. Still, the lesson had not been lost on the leaders of the major combatant powers. Future wars would be fought largely on rubber.

For its part Michelin, the dominant tire manufacturer in Europe, did not miss the opportunity to educate the postwar public about the importance of rubber tires in the recent victory as it promoted battlefield tourism. In some twenty-nine guidebooks to World War I battlefields, nineteen of which appeared in English as well as French, Michelin not only encouraged tourists to visit the battlefields by car, but also carefully pointed out the importance of tires in victory. In its guidebook to Verdun, the company included a detailed map of the "sacred way," the guide noting that because the Germans had fourteen different railways supplying their forces while all but one French rail link had been destroyed, only the "sacred way" remained as a supply route. In Michelin's words, "the motor service along the 'sacred way' was organised to such a pitch that it was able to ensure the transport of the troops, the evacuation of the wounded, and the revictualing of 250,000 combatants."[2] The US firm B. F. Goodrich, which had a factory in France, similarly produced a guidebook to World War I battlefields, in both French and English editions. In its rendition Goodrich did not hesitate to point out that many of the trucks along the "sacred way" had been equipped with Goodrich tires (since Michelin made only pneumatic tires, they were not used on the trucks, which ran on solid rubber ones):

> among the diverse types of pneumatic and solid rubber tires used, they [Goodrichs] distinguished themselves in their resistance and their adaptability to different kinds of terrain. There was more than one tire failure among the roads of Verdun, but never on vehicles equipped with Goodrichs.[3]

The message was clear: rubber tires had helped the French and the Americans win World War I.

"See America First" on "Good Roads"

Initially, the effects of World War I indirectly affected the United States, which remained neutral in the conflict during the first three years. The United States did not declare war until April 1917, instead producing for, and profiting from, the British and the French combatants. Only in 1918 did American troops arrive in significant numbers on the western front. Meanwhile, American rubber manufacturers thrived throughout the war. They too produced for the British and French war machines. As significantly, since the American economy thrived from supplying the British and French, then American, war efforts, the rubber industry still raced to keep up with demand from American consumers who bought cars and tires like never before.

A "good roads" movement had existed (in many of the states of) the United States well before the outbreak of war in Europe in 1914. Prewar commentators admired French roads made of paving stones (*pavés*) and lamented the unpaved rutted trails, many of them no more than dirt roads (impassible mud holes in the rain), of the United States. Citing the French as if they were competitors in having roads, American pro-moters of "good roads" used patriotic appeals to get individuals and state governments, and the federal government, to spend money to upgrade and pave roads. Before the war, a patriotic "See America First" campaign, supported by railway companies, attempted to persuade Americans to see the wonders of the United States, including the national parks, before embarking on "foreign trip" to Europe. Once war broke out in Europe, tire companies jumped on the bandwagon. B. F. Goodrich used advertisements to tell elite Americans repeatedly to "See America First" in their cars now that Europe was closed for tourism. As the company put it:

> See America First on Goodrich tires. America will look mighty good to you this year—better than it's ever looked before. You are going to take that motor trip this season, through the most wonderful land under the sun—a land with every variety of climate and scenery, and with marvels that you cannot match in any country the world over. Your golden opportunity has arrived—you can now "discover America." Where is the equal of the Grand Canyon, the Garden of the Gods, the Petrified Forest of Arizona? It's a land of a score of "Switzerlands"—of inland lakes that elsewhere would be called seas. Your car brings it all to you—and, greatest help of all, Goodrich points the way.... Ride into Dixie Land, speed across golden California or through Colorado's Wonder Lands.[4]

In 1917, Goodyear began supplying tires for the truck and bus fleet at Yellowstone National Park—thus associating the brand with American national identity as embodied by the treasured park—and put that fact in its advertising into the 1930s. In 1927, it compared the famous geyser to the Goodyear tire, in ads entitled "Ten Years of Old Faithful." Goodyear could thus associate itself with a national icon and also suggest that its tires were every bit as reliable as Old Faithful.

Before the war, advocates of US automobile tourism had already seized on the patriotic idea of a transcontinental road, an idea that harkened back to the building of the transcontinental railroad in the nineteenth century. The most important, publicity laden of those efforts were the actions of the Lincoln Highway Association (LHA), formed in 1913. Some fifty years after the Civil War, Abraham Lincoln still embodied American unity for the northern industrialists who formed the association (a north–south initiative was by contrast named the "Dixie Highway"). Their objective was the establishment of a paved highway running all the way from New York City to San Francisco, uniting the country from east to west. F. A. Seiberling, the founder of Goodyear, was a key contributor to the effort and served as the association's president. Although contributors to the association included President Woodrow Wilson, most supporters were connected to the automobile and tire industries. Even Harvey Firestone, Seiberling's chief rival, contributed. The association was essentially a lobbying arm of tire and automobile industries. Its lobbying paid off: in 1917, Seiberling bragged that for every $1 raised (and spent lobbying) for the Lincoln Highway, $100, mostly from taxpayers, was spent to pave the road.[5]

As intended, the Lincoln Highway Association was a success, resulting in an improved highway from coast to coast that is today largely US Route 30, from New York to San Francisco, as the federal government replaced highway names with numbers in the 1920s.

Rubber companies understood fully what they had to gain from transcontinental automotive tourism and, in their dreams, the new (and future) roads would see a high volume of truck transport, actually competing with railroads. World War I brought home just how important truck traffic might be. In 1917, just after the US declaration of war, Goodyear launched a publicity convoy of Goodyear trucks from Akron to Boston in order to illustrate both the potential of trucks for long-distance hauling as well as the biggest obstacle: poor-quality roadways. It took 28 days for the trucks to make the round-trip journey of some 1300 miles. Later that same year, to ease the crunch faced by railways moving goods and men across country, the US quartermaster ordered that all trucks sent to Europe to be used in the war effort be driven to Atlantic ports, where they were loaded onto ships. The loaded vehicles literally destroyed the barely paved surfaces in eastern states during the winter of 1917–18.[6]

Supply and mobilization for World War I thus illustrated that rubber-tire-clad trucks would be necessary in any future war, but only if roads could handle the traffic. In 1919, Lieutenant Colonel Dwight D. Eisenhower took part in an 81-vehicle Army convoy from Washington, DC to San Francisco, charged with determining necessary road improvements for potential use by the US Army. Covering some 3,251 miles in 62 days, Eisenhower saw the limits of US roads at first hand. State and federal funding, made possible by a tax on gasoline, increased steadily. Later, in the 1950s, during the Cold War, none other than President Eisenhower signed the Interstate Highway Act establishing today's limited-access interstates across the United States. As after World War I, after World War II the presumed needs of national defense justified extensive road building. And in the 1950s, as in the 1910s and 1920s, rubber companies stood happily at the forefront of such efforts, patriotically proclaiming the "need" for highways—which did much to increase tire usage among the US public as well as to reduce (in this case greatly) usage of passenger rail in the United States.

Flying for the Nation

In the early twentieth century, rubber companies also associated themselves with the national cause through support for aviation. In this case, they could link their products both with patriotism and with modernity, as nothing suggested the future quite like air travel. Among rubber manufacturers, Michelin was the first to use advocacy of flight to tie its name to the future of the nation. Among scores of initiatives, the company sponsored a Michelin Cup for flying prowess, won by the Wright brothers in 1908. During World War I, Michelin built airplanes for the French military and conducted tests for bombing. In arguing for French aviation, it could seem disinterested as the company stopped producing planes after World War I. Yet, the contributions were not anonymous, and its advocacy of French aviation served as excellent publicity, connecting the Michelin name with both France and the future.[7]

In the United States, Goodyear, the largest of the world's tire companies, followed suit. Early in World War I, it built hot air balloons to be used in reconnaissance by the British military. When the United States entered the war, Goodyear produced lighter-than-air ships (sometimes called "airplanes" into the 1920s and now regularly called "blimps") for the US Navy. Among other uses, the blimps were assigned to ships, charged with looking for German submarines and alerting the mother ship. These wartime contributions were useful to the rubber companies throughout the interwar years in tire advertisements. Inevitably, Goodyear reminded the public of its service to the nation—without bothering to mention how profitable wartime production had been for the company.

After World War I, Goodyear continued both to promote aviation and to build airships. The Navy ordered two huge Goodyear airships, the USS *Akron* and the USS *Macon*. Goodyear took out national ads for the commissioning of the *Akron* and marked the occasion on its NBC radio program with John Philip Sousa and his band performing patriotic music. Filled with helium rather than hydrogen and smaller than the later German *Hindenburg*, the *Akron* and the *Macon* were nevertheless large enough to carry fighter jets. Both airships were lost in crashes in the 1930s, and it became clear that airplanes—not airships—were the future of aviation. In fact, the crash of the *Akron* resulted in more fatalities than the much better-known *Hindenburg* explosion (seventy-three vs. thirty-six).

After the failure of its large airships, Goodyear focused on the blimp, which was essentially a 200-foot-long oblong balloon with a small motorized gondola.[8] Very much subject to the wind, the blimp increasingly lost its association with national interests, coming instead simply to be a fixture at major outdoor events. To pay the bills for an expensive project during the Depression, Goodyear ran advertising in banners behind the blimp and on the neon display under it. Goodyear dealers could invite a blimp to town. At the Chicago World's Fair in 1933–34, the company offered rides for $3 per person, adult or child, for a short trip at the edge of Lake Michigan (this at a time when an agricultural laborer in the Midwest might earn about 10 cents per hour).[9] Goodyear took the blimp to the New York World's Fair in 1939–40, again offering paying customers blimp rides. After World War II, blimps remained a fixture at major outdoor sporting events. In an age of space exploration, the blimp lost any association with the future, much as it mostly lost the link to American nationalism. Like Michelin's "Man," the Goodyear blimp is now simply a company icon.

Restricting Rubber in the Wake of War

After World War I, the supply of rubber remained the object of nationalist arguments, particularly between Britain and the United States. The war had spiked demand for various raw materials, including rubber. During the course of the war, planters in Southeast Asia planted ever more hevea trees. After the end of the conflict the tables turned and, with demand unable to keep up with an increasing supply, rubber prices plummeted. In 1922, rubber fell below 12.5 cents per pound, less than the cost of production (having been priced during the war at over $1 per pound, and as high as $3 in 1909). Rather suddenly, many planters faced bankruptcy. In 1920s, British-controlled Malaysia and Ceylon produced over 70 percent of the world's rubber supply, while the United States consumed more than 70 percent.[10] For the British Rubber Growers' Association, a powerful planters' lobby, the solution seemed simple. Britain, the self-proclaimed prewar champion of free trade, needed to protect British planters by increasing the price of rubber at the expense of manufacturers (there had been many exceptions in the past, from the Corn Laws of early nineteenth-century Britain to the restrictions on importation of textile machines to colonial India). Secretary of State for the Colonies Winston Churchill agreed and established a committee headed by Sir James Stevenson, a Churchill crony who had made his name and much of his fortune as managing director of the Johnnie Walker whisky company. Rubber growers dominated the Stevenson Committee, but no rubber manufacturer served on it.

The Stevenson Committee considered various means for raising the price of rubber and proposed legislation establishing rubber production quotas. Parliamentary passage was swift, as nationalist sentiment was strong. Britain had borrowed heavily from the United States to fight World War I and British members of parliament thought it only fair that

"British rubber" (from British-controlled colonies) fetch a decent price. Churchill specifically cited British war debts in defending the plan. Restriction could have the "double object of saving the rubber planters, and, by making the Americans pay, [it would] contribute materially to stabilizing the dollar exchange [with the British pound]. [It was] the principal means of paying" its "debt to the United States."[11] As the result of the legislation, all rubber plantations in British colonies, even those owned by foreign companies, received precise quotas for rubber production. Producers in Dutch and other colonies were invited to join.

Within the British empire, participation in the Stevenson plan was obligatory. In Malaysia, Chinese and Malay smallholders who had recently planted rubber groves were forbidden to tap or expand production, a ban that led to both resistance and smuggling. Planters in the Dutch East Indies and French Indochina opted not to participate, although British-owned plantations in the Dutch East Indies were supposed to take part. As rubber prices rose as a result of the Stevenson scheme, planters in both of those colonies expanded their acreage. In French Indochina, Michelin and investment companies leased and planted vast new tracts of land. In the Dutch East Indies, indigenous smallholders significantly extended the size of their rubber groves, tapped them, and profited handsomely. In the short term, however, the policy worked for British growers. In 1925, rubber was selling at $1.23 per pound.[12]

American Assertions: Herbert Hoover and US Trade

Although British nationalism, as stoked by planters, was critical in passing the Stevenson restrictions, the US responses were more fiercely nationalistic. Herbert Hoover led the charge. After his successful work in European war relief during World War I, Hoover served as the secretary of commerce from 1921 to 1928 under Presidents Harding and Coolidge, until he resigned to run for president himself. Hoover was arguably the most visible Cabinet member at the time. He had been trained as an engineer and became a technocrat. The Commerce Department generated huge amounts of information in support of US industry as part of the public–private partnership that Hoover believed would ensure US prosperity. Under his leadership, US Commerce forcefully asserted itself in the protection of US business interests abroad. That began with ensuring the supply of raw materials for industry. At Hoover's direction, in 1921 Commerce created an entire division devoted exclusively to rubber. Throughout the 1920s, American consuls throughout the world made voluminous reports to Commerce about both rubber supplies and the market for rubber goods. In turn, Commerce assisted American rubber manufacturers by providing them with detailed knowledge of conditions abroad, and arguing on their behalf both within the US government and with foreign governments.

Secretary Hoover personally took a major role, meeting frequently with the American Rubber Manufacturers' Association (founded in 1915 and dominated by major US tire firms) and individual company leaders, particularly Harvey Firestone. A darling of the press for his work in war relief, Hoover brilliantly courted journalists as secretary of commerce. His slogans included "Help Hoover against the English Rubber Trust" and "1776–1925." Hoover's efforts, peppered with direct quotations, regularly appeared in the major newspapers, including those influential ones of record, the *New York Times* and the *Washington Post*. Like Firestone, Hoover referred frequently to "our rubber" and argued that "America needs its own rubber." He thus cast himself as a champion of "free enterprise" in attacking "foreign monopolies," while protecting the American public as well as American business, a strong Republican constituency.

Hoover attacked the Stevenson plan on several fronts. Much as Americans had been exhorted to "Hooverize," or conserve, during World War I, now they were to exercise their patriotism by turning in old rubber products or parts for reprocessing (called "reclaiming" rather than "recycling" at the time). Moreover, after meeting with Harvey Firestone, Hoover strongly supported the latter's plan for a Congressional Appropriation of $500,000 largely to undertake a series of "rubber surveys" in different parts of the world. These studies focused on the Philippines, Central and South America, Africa, and Southeast Asia, laying out the various conditions that would help or hinder the establishment of American-owned plantations in each place. Initially, attention focused most sharply on the Philippines. Rubber grew "wild" there, as did the related gutta percha (the rubber its latex rendered used to protect transcontinental cable and telephone lines), and the climate seemed ideal for the planting of hevea trees. Since the Philippines were an American colony, investments there would have the protection of the US government. The biggest obstacle was that Philippine land law forbad the establishment of estates of more than 2,500 acres, parcels much smaller than those sought by US rubber interests. Despite extensive lobbying, the Philippine assembly refused to change the law, out of fear that large estates owned by US business would become an obstacle to eventual independence. Moreover, the cost of labor in the Philippines was higher than in British and Dutch colonies employing contract laborers, to the extent that some American businessmen suggested that cheaper Chinese "coolies" would have to be imported to the Philippines should the plantations get the green light. Naturally, such (quite) public plans did nothing to allay widespread Filipino fears that large rubber estates would ultimately serve as an obstacle to national independence for the Philippines. The US government, concerned about political stability in the Philippines, did not force the issue.

Other regions presented different obstacles. While the hevea tree was native to the Amazon basin, it grew there as an isolated tree, typically only a couple per acre. The establishment of hevea plantations would mean chemically conquering a fungal disease to which the trees were subject if living too near to one another, known as leaf blight. The alternative was the cultivation of other latex-producing plants, most notably guayule, but these plants did not have the latex yield of the hevea. Central America seemed a better option than did most of South America. In short, the powers behind the Planning Commission figured that US business and government would have an easier time dominating the politics of Central American nations. *Castilloa elastica* was already being grown in Central America and it seemed to have some potential; only later would it be clear that hevea was much superior and thus cheaper. Still, neither Central nor South America had the incredibly cheap labor available in Southeast Asia. American policymakers and businessmen may have wanted "America's own rubber," but it needed to be at least competitive in price with imports from British colonies, not more expensive.

Although rubber grew naturally in parts of Africa, and there were some small plantations there, notably in prewar German East Africa (today the country of Tanzania), Africa presented another challenge. In the early 1920s, save for Ethiopia and Liberia, the entire African continent consisted of European colonies. Ethiopia did not have the proper climate, but Liberia did. Founded by freed and resettled slaves from the United States, Liberia had been a virtual American colony since the nineteenth century. Here the climate was appropriate, labor was cheap, and the US government would be able to protect investments. As a result, the Department of Commerce encouraged rubber companies to invest in Liberia. Few did besides Harvey Firestone, who famously acquired a lease there for one million acres.

Had American companies chosen to invest in British colonies within Southeast and South Asia, they would have been subject to the Stevenson plan, just like British companies; this left investment in the Dutch East Indies (Indonesia today). Here Hoover's intervention was critical. Meeting with the Dutch envoy early in 1923, Hoover pressed him to guarantee that the Dutch would not join the Stevenson scheme.

Anxious to increase investment and thus "development" of the colony, the Dutch government assured Commerce that it would continue to welcome US investment and would in no way restrict the unbridled production of rubber.[13] It was no coincidence that US Rubber and Goodyear holdings soon expanded into the area. Smaller firms also invested there. After peaking at well over $1, the price of rubber hovered at 50 cents a pound in 1926. Hoover publicly declared victory, taking credit for the decline. As rubber prices continued to fall, a fact mostly attributable to increased production on the part of indigenous smallholders in the Dutch East Indies (a 900 percent increase between 1920 and 1930), the British government realized the limits of the Stevenson plan and repealed it in 1928. Having wrapped himself in the American flag and presumably won, Hoover was well positioned. His protection of US business abroad had given him national name recognition and an important base of donors. In the successful presidential campaign of 1928, the Republican Party promised prosperity in the form of "a chicken in every pot and a car in every backyard." Rubber tires would of course be on every such car. Undoubtedly, patriotic calls for the cheap supply of rubber helped elect Herbert Hoover president. Prosperity was supposed to ensue.

Firestone and Friends

Like Hoover, Harvey Firestone repeatedly appealed to American patriotism in his public campaign against the Stevenson plan. As early as 1922, before it was even implemented, Firestone was adamant in his opposition. The American Rubber Manufacturers' Association was lukewarm but not violently opposed, because other rubber companies had less to lose than Firestone. US Rubber already had huge holdings in Sumatra and thus had a distinct advantage over its American competitors. The largest global tire company, Goodyear, was in limbo. Goodyear's holdings included some in Sumatra, so it had limited protection. More significant was the fact that Seiberling had bought rubber futures before the price plummeted and now could not sell tires at a high enough price to break even. The predicament caused him to lose control of Goodyear to his bankers in 1921 (pushed out entirely, he subsequently founded another firm, Seiberling Rubber Company, that was never able to rival Goodyear or the other major producers). For his part, Firestone bought rubber on the open market and was fully exposed to any spike in rubber prices. Thus, Firestone's subsequent attacks on the British producer "monopolists" were privately self-serving as well as publicly patriotic.

The broader context for Firestone's campaign was simple: by this time the rubber industry was not especially profitable. Companies had prospered by steadily increasing demand, even as they made less money per unit sold. Technical improvements could only temporarily increase profits; that is, until competitors learned of upgrades. Competition was fierce, as company executives and engineers never tired of trying to snatch market share and trade secrets from each other. When Paul Litchfield of Goodyear visited Michelin's hometown of Clermont-Ferrand, he was not only denied entry into the Michelin works, he was also tailed by a private detective.[14] Harvey Firestone was so suspicious of competitors and afraid that his executives would spill trade secrets at Akron's Portage Path Country Club that he built the famous Firestone Country Club to keep them miles away as they drank and golfed (the club was long the host of the World Series of Golf and is now the host of the WGC Bridgestone Invitational).

Tire producers were thus not passive, merely meeting presumably inevitable demand in a global commodity chain. They created demand not only through advertising but by keeping prices low. Lower costs encouraged demand by increasing the size of the market; workers and farmers in the United States could afford Model Ts, and cheap tires kept them buying replacements more often. Manufacturers made a profit by buying rubber at what was, in essence, a non-negotiable global price (although they played the market by contracting for future shipments at a given price, in essence trading in "futures") and producing rubber goods for a lower price than the competition. Naturally, then, tire companies rose and fell with the global price of rubber. If the British could keep the price of rubber high, the market for tires would not continue to grow. Moreover, if Firestone was at a cost disadvantage compared to other American producers, his firm would be the most threatened.

Not one to back down from a fight, Firestone very effectively worked the media. In addition to operating behind the scenes with Secretary Hoover and other officials at Commerce, Firestone testified in congressional hearings regarding the rubber supply that were duly reported in the newspapers. He made frequent grand pronouncements to the press. In the late 1920s and 1930s, his son Harvey Firestone, Jr. gave radio talks on rubber during the Voice of Firestone programs. In the late 1910s and early 1920s, Harvey Sr. gained fame as a participant in the famous camping trips with his friends Henry Ford, Thomas Edison, and the naturalist John Burroughs. Calling themselves "the vagabonds," they were anything but. While in principle roughing it, the men were in fact followed by a retinue of journalists and photographers who recorded their every move. These were well-organized, made-for-media events, with a sitting president, Warren Harding, joining the four in 1921.

A few years later the men paid visit during their trip to President Coolidge at his summer home in Vermont. They had elaborate tents, a mobile kitchen truck, a dining table, and plentiful help, including drivers, staff members, and cooks. Horses came along in trailers. Their wives and other family members also accompanied them. Here Firestone was in very good company, as Ford and Edison were already stars of the American media, well known across the country, and he gained much publicity in their presence.

Firestone also had Ford's and Edison's ears, and the three men talked extensively about the rubber crisis that the United States supposedly faced due to the Stevenson plan. Personally taking the charge to "grow America's own rubber," Edison devoted the last years of his life to botanical expeditions and experiments in an effort to find an adequate latex-yielding plant well suited to growing conditions in the United States. In 1927, Firestone, Ford, and Edison each contributed $25,000 to establish the Edison Botanic Research Corporation, a botanical garden and rubber laboratory at Edison's winter home in Ft. Myers, Florida. Edison and his staff ultimately chose goldenrod over the slower-growing guayule as the best alternative source, but neither plant ever proved commercially competitive on a scale that could rival the hevea tree.

For his part, Ford bought just less than 2.5 million acres in the Tapajós valley in Brazil and set up a plantation modestly named after himself, "Fordlandia," and a second named Belterra. Creating a veritable American town within the rainforest, Ford attempted to grow hevea trees to supply rubber for his factories. The result was a complete fiasco. Leaf blight and pests ruined the trees. Ford's treatment of Brazilian laborers, including a classically paternalistic Fordian ban on alcohol and tobacco use even in laborers' dwellings, led to significant conflict. In 1945, Henry Ford II "turned Fordlandia and Belterra, valued at nearly $8 million, with $20 million invested in them, over to the Brazilian government for $244,200."[15] In retrospect, Fordlandia was Ford's folly, but his motivation was the same as Firestone's: the production of rubber cheap enough to undermine British efforts to maintain high rubber prices. In the meantime, Ford's efforts drew attention to and legitimized Firestone's vocal arguments for "our rubber."

Firestone in Liberia

Harvey Firestone regularly announced to the press his intention to "grow American rubber." At the same time that the US government was undertaking the aforementioned rubber surveys, Firestone sent his own men to the Philippines, Mexico, and Liberia to investigate possibilities and begin negotiations with local authorities. He ended up choosing Liberia. Firestone succinctly described the resulting deal in a letter to his brother:

> I have had a Mr. Barclay—a man of deep color—who is Secretary of State of the Liberian government here [in Akron] for about two months. He just returned last Saturday. I closed a concession with him for a million acres of land in Liberia for which I pay six cents an acre, and I also arranged for a banker's loan in New York for the Liberian government of $5 million. This was made through our State Department, which gives us full control over Liberia, that is, all their finances, as the financial advisor is appointed by the President of the United States and all his assistants by the Secretary of State and they also appoint four senior army officers to control their army. So you can see we are well protected from a Government standpoint on going into Liberia.... I put Harvey [Jr., his son] in charge of this and we are now increasing our organization in Liberia and will send out about 50 [white] men as overseers [sic—in the US this term of course connoted those who had overseen slaves' work].[16]

A few days later, Firestone followed up with formal thanks to President Calvin Coolidge and US Secretary of State Frank Kellogg for their help in setting up the deal.[17]

Although Firestone publicly presented his Liberian adventure as patriotism, his justification to the company's board of directors was solely about profitability:

> The indigenous labor supply of Liberia effects a large savings [sic]. It costs $48.00 to recruit and bring a Javanese coolie to Sumatra.... Using an average of $50.00 per head and converting this into terms of our present labor force of 6,000, our saving to date is $300,000 without taking into account the addition to this figure which [labor] turnover would require. In Liberia our land costs practically nothing, while land in [Southeast Asia] ranges from $10 to $50 per acre. This is only one of the many concessions which we have been able to secure from the government of Liberia.

Aside from the savings in not having to recruit at $50 a head, Firestone could pay less in wages. Its laborers in Liberia earned 24 cents per day, compared with 25 cents in Sumatra and 50–70 cents in the Philippines. Moreover, Liberia had no import duty on necessary machinery, no income tax on profits, and no land tax, whereas in the Dutch East Indies, "every company is subjected to the well-known policy of the Dutch government of taxing to the full extent of reasonable limits."

The biggest problem was supposedly conditioning "primitive" Liberians to stay put:

> our labor turnover to date has been high due, we believe, principally to the fact that we have no permanent quarters established. However, we believe a great deal of education is necessary to train labor to remain permanently on our property even after permanent quarters have been supplied. Basically, the problem is to convert a primitive people to industrious and organized community life.[18]

Interestingly, Firestone did not seem to think that labor turnover resulted from working conditions, low wages, or living conditions. Tapping into the same language that European planters used in Southeast Asia to describe indigenous peoples who saw little reason to work themselves hard for European profits, for Firestone the problem was that "primitive" people had to learn to be "industrious."

Even leading newspapers fawned, praising Firestone's patriotic actions as well as his effort to bring "civilization" to the "primitive." The *New York Times* entitled an article "American Rubber Empire Rises in Africa: Colossal Enterprise to Conquer and Cultivate 1,000,000 acres." Here readers learned that Harvey S. Firestone was "the directing genius of this enterprise," who "supplied the imagination and... the capital [so] that American motorists might ride upon American-owned rubber." The expression had the ring of patriotic philanthropy. According to the *Times*, once up and running the Firestone holdings were to produce "more than one-half of the present American consumption." Firestone even got credit for undertaking the white man's burden in Africa, by "introducing a new phase of life to this primitive part of sun-baked Africa." The article went on to say that "the hand of civilization has at last touched Liberia... an utterly primitive country." The *Chicago Tribune* admiringly reported that the "American rubber empire in Liberia" would enable Harvey Firestone to "figure possibly as an American Cecil Rhodes" in "the latest romance of American big business."[19] Here was a tangible expression of patriotic pride in the notion that Firestone was becoming an imperial as well as an industrial magnate, and that his expansion reflected well on the United States. Today's prevalent image of Rhodes—the lying, ruthless, and manipulative British diamond king of Southern Africa—was clearly not shared by the *Chicago Tribune* in 1926.

From the late 1920s and into the 1950s, when Liberia was finally able to pay back the loan, Firestone essentially controlled Liberia. The $5 million loan of 1926 had, as mentioned, been issued at

Firestone's insistence. The loaned money largely went to pay off earlier multinational, largely British, loans, in the process essentially refinancing them at 7 percent (they had been at 5 percent). In pressing for the loan, Firestone was concerned about the threat of both French and British influence in Liberia, which the new loan and its American financial enforcers eliminated. The various US advisers would be paid by the Liberians. Beginning in 1933, however, the Roosevelt administration was less accommodating than that of Coolidge. When the Liberians could not keep up with loan payments, Roosevelt refused Firestone's request that the US government force payment with "gunboat diplomacy"; that is, sending a warship to Liberia to force payment. After nearly mothballing the operation early in the depths of the Depression, Firestone came to an agreement with the Liberians and expanded the size of his operations there. In the late 1930s, Firestone was Liberia's largest employer, with at least 10,000 workers, a number that more than doubled during World War II. In cooperation with the Liberian government, many of those workers were recruited by force, hence the low cost, with community chiefs receiving payment for men from their villages. Into the twenty-first century, to many international critics eyeing such payments, recruitment for Firestone plantations seemed remarkably like a modern-day form of the slave trade.[20]

Germany: Colonies and Chemicals

While Americans were busy demanding their right to "our" rubber, meaning either that others needed to supply it at a low price or that Americans would embark on their own imperial ventures, German nationalists were learning a different lesson in the first years of World War I. Before the start of the conflict, most rubber that found its way into the German economy came from British and Dutch plantations. Indigenous tappers did collect varieties of latex in German New Guinea. And German firms established plantations in German East Africa (Tanzania), but all of these concerns together could hardly supply Europe's largest economy, especially in wartime. During the war the British naval blockade effectively halted rubber from anywhere making its way into Germany, even that from the neutral Dutch East Indies. The wartime German rubber shortage was acute, despite two famously daring trips of the submarine *Deutschland* through the blockade to the United States (still neutral before April 1917, its ports in Baltimore, Maryland and New London, Connecticut welcomed the sub), where

Figure 4.1 Firestone brochure for the Century of Progress International Exposition in Chicago, 1934. Century of Progress records, series 16, box 18, folder 267, Special Collections, University of Illinois at Chicago Library.

Just as Briton Rudyard Kipling's poem "The White Man's Burden" was directed at American men to get them to realize their duty to "civilize" the "natives" of the Philippines, this image reveals American participation in global, imperial practices. Do you think most rubber gatherers were this large or well fed? If the Firestone factory represents American progress and modernity, what do barely dressed Liberian rubber gatherers symbolize? Like other Chicago World's Fair exhibits and paraphernalia, this brochure initially ended up in the Chicago Museum of Science and Industry; can you make out the Library's ink stamps on the image? What do they say about the importance of archives and libraries in preserving traces of our collective past?

dyestuffs and pharmaceuticals such as Novocaine were delivered in return for rubber. Rubber sold for the equivalent of $20 per pound in Germany, compared to about $1 per pound in the United States. German military hospitals soon ran out of rubber gloves, tubes, and syringes, and there was a severe shortage of truck tires.

In the early twentieth century, Germany was the world's chemical powerhouse, providing most of the textile dyes, artificial fertilizer, and pharmaceuticals (such as Bayer aspirin) consumed in the United States and elsewhere. German chemists worked to come up with substitute ("ersatz") rubber, just as they had developed ersatz versions of other products. They only managed to develop a form of synthetic rubber that was essentially useless, too hard even for use as truck tires. Still, research continued in the 1920s at IG Farben, the huge chemical conglomerate that brought together Bayer and so many other firms in 1925. In the late 1920s, IG Farben chemists worked with butadiene, combining it with styrene to create Buna, a more pliant synthetic rubber.

When Hitler came to power in 1933, he immediately began to plan for war. To avoid a repetition of World War I, in which Germany had faced an especially bitter defeat, he demanded autarky (economic self-sufficiency), especially in metals and rubber. He turned to IG Farben, the largest company in Europe (in the world only GM, US Steel, and Standard Oil of New Jersey were bigger), to refine and develop Buna for military use. Germans used two raw materials that they had in abundance, coal and limestone, to create the acetylene base for Buna (the Soviets and Americans would use grain alcohol and petroleum instead; the Germans would later employ natural gas as well). Chemists at IG Farben shortened the production time and found that although still less elastic than natural rubber, synthetic rubber was actually better at resisting the deleterious effects of sunlight and petroleum products including gasoline, a decided advantage on the battlefield. The problem was cost. German economists estimated that a tire made of Buna would cost 90 marks to produce, compared to 18 marks for one made of natural rubber.[21] Clearly, a fivefold price difference was not justifiable, unless the purpose of developing Buna was for war. Hitler personally authorized a significant subsidy to bring Buna tires to market. With government support, the product became a success story, even winning a gold medal at the Paris World's Fair in 1937. In the process, IG Farben became a critical pillar in the war economy of the Third Reich, purging Nobel Prize–winning Jewish chemists from its ranks, receiving huge subsidies from the Reich, and profiting handsomely.

Buna literally made World War II possible, from beginning to end. Of necessity, over the course of the war, IG Farben continued to refine synthetic rubber and mostly replaced Germany's use of natural rubber. The USSR continued to ship natural rubber to Nazi Germany before the German invasion in 1941, but after that date the Nazi war machine had virtually no natural rubber beyond scrap rubber. German occupying forces seized natural rubber stockpiles in France for the German war machine, but these stores were limited. By February 1943, German tires contained only about 8 percent natural rubber. IG Farben produced 70,000 tons of Buna in 1939 and 140,000 tons in 1944.[22]

World War II and the US Scramble for Rubber

The United States had not developed and marketed synthetic rubber for the same reason that Germany had not done so before the Nazi seizure of power: it was not any more economically competitive than the natural rubber alternatives to latex that Edison studied. Hevea rubber was extremely plentiful and cheap in the 1930s. Later, during World War II, earlier US policy seemed shortsighted, yet no one could deny that it had been economically sound in the 1930s.

In the last years of that decade the United States began to stockpile rubber, as it seemed critical for a war effort that was starting to seem inevitable. Stockpiling intensified in 1940 and 1941, as the Japanese threat became clear. Yet, it was still surprising to many contemporaries that Japan took Southeast Asia so quickly and easily. In early 1942, just after the attack on Pearl Harbor, the Japanese invaded and occupied British and Dutch colonies. Vichy France formally controlled French Indochina, so the Japanese saw little reason to invade it until late in the war. Japan's primary interest in Southeast Asia was not rubber, but oil for its own war effort. At the same time, however, the Japanese invasion simultaneously cut the United States off from about 98 percent of its prewar supply of rubber.

The United States had stockpiled proportionately less rubber than had Britain, and the result was panic. Nationalist talk about the need for "our rubber" in the 1920s had done a good job of priming Americans for what was, this time, a genuine national crisis. Without rubber, the United States simply could not fight this war it had entered:

> Each Sherman tank—and the United States eventually produced 50,000 of them—required about a half a ton of rubber. Each of the nation's heavy bombers needed about a ton. Each battleship contained more than 20,000 rubber parts, totaling about 160,000 pounds on each ship. Americans produced 1.4 million rubber airplane tires in 1944 alone. American soldiers wore 45 million pairs of rubber boots, 77 million pairs of shoes with rubber soles, and 104 million pairs of shoes with rubber heels. Every industrial facility contained rubber conveyor belts and wheels.[23]

This was without mentioning the rubber gaskets within the machines themselves, let alone the tires for farmers and truckers on the home front.

The American public was fully aware of the "rubber crisis" in 1942, as one anguished article after another appeared in the press. President Roosevelt did a filmed Universal newsreel speech (shown before movies in those days) asking citizens to gather their scrap rubber and turn it into their local gas stations for a penny a pound. Roosevelt also imposed a national speed limit of 35 miles per hour—not to conserve gasoline, but to conserve tires. Not only did a low speed limit discourage long trips, and thus rubber usage, but tires wore more slowly at low speeds. Moreover, since consumers could not buy new replacement tires during the war years, they kept bald ones that would have been even less safe at higher speeds. Conservation was the first and obvious step, although it was wholly inadequate. As the Rubber Survey Committee, created by Roosevelt to address the rubber crisis, succinctly put it:

> Of all the critical and strategic materials, rubber is the one which presents the greatest threat to the safety of our Nation and the success of the Allied cause… if we fail to secure quickly a large new rubber supply, our war effort and our domestic economy will collapse.[24]

Alternative supplies of natural rubber were one solution. By this time Ceylon was the largest source of natural rubber, producing about 98,000 tons in 1943. India produced some 17,000 tons. Firestone managed to double production in Liberia, so that the entire country produced about 15,000 tons in 1943. Natural rubber collection became economically viable again elsewhere in Africa, even Madagascar, but notably in British-held Nigeria, the Belgian Congo, and French Equatorial Africa. Although never on the scale of the days of Leopold II,

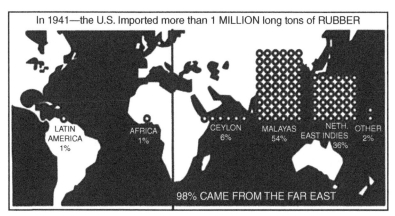

Figure 4.2 Prewar US Rubber Supply. May 1942. Farm Security Administration/Office of War Information. Image courtesy of the Library of Congress Prints & Photographs Division Washington, DC 20540, US. LC-USE613-D-002953-a.

How is an image such as this one worth a proverbial thousand words? How does the map itself (bereft of any commentary) make an argument about the war, the importance of rubber conservation, or the need to defeat the Japanese?

Classification

D-6400 President Roosevelt is welcomed to the Firestone rubber plantation during his inspection trip of the Republic of Liberia. (JAN. 1943) PLEASE CREDIT: OFFICIAL NAVY PHOTO FROM ONI.

OFFICE OF WAR INFORMATION

Figure 4.3 Roosevelt in Liberia. Office of War Information. Photo courtesy of the Library of Congress Prints & Photographs Division Washington, DC 20540, US. LC-DIG-ds-00622.

After the Casablanca meeting with British Prime Minister Winston Churchill in January 1943, President Roosevelt visited the Firestone plantation in Liberia. What does his visit say about the importance of natural rubber in fighting World War II? Are you surprised that a black employee was meeting the President, shaking his hand and wearing a colonial pith helmet? How might an image like this have been used in African-American communities during the war?

abuses occurred in the Congo as those profiting from the rubber trade forced others to gather rubber. In Nigeria as many as 100,000 Africans were conscripted to collect rubber for the Allied war effort. In French Equatorial Africa, some Africans resisted rubber collection despite pressure, until they earned payment and found goods imported from the United States; some former gatherers in French Equatorial Africa later remember World War II as a time of prosperity, when they could afford to buy goods, participating in the global economy.[25] South and Central American production also increased. In Brazil, *seringueiros* (tappers) were again pressed into service, often by force, as if it were the equivalent of military conscription. Yet, the global supply of natural rubber remained woefully inadequate given growing wartime demand.

The other solution was, of course, synthetic rubber. Both German and Soviet vehicles rolled into battle on tires that were mostly synthetic (some natural rubber remained necessary in tire construction, including those for large trucks). Ironically, because of a corporate partnership between IG Farben and Standard Oil of New Jersey, Buna technology should have been available in the United States. However, while Standard offered up its own interwar discoveries to IG Farben, even on the eve of war the latter did not share its knowledge of the production of Buna. Since Standard legally held the patent to Buna in the United States, Goodrich, Goodyear, and Dow Chemical held back from the development of synthetic rubber in the late 1930s. Bizarrely, IG Farben clearly assisted in the war preparedness of the Nazi regime, while Standard's actions actually set back US development of synthetic rubber. Congressional hearings followed, but during wartime mobilization the US government avoided what would have been a distraction from the war effort. Standard's executives were essentially off the hook since the United States was busy playing catch-up.

Suspending the enforcement of anti-trust law, the federal government worked with rubber companies and invested heavily in the development and production of synthetic rubber. One estimate had the total governmental investment at some $750 million.[26] Initially, grain alcohol served as the base for American synthetic rubber, because this made the process simpler and the Midwest had a grain surplus. By the end of the war, petroleum served as the base for synthetic rubber, as it would in the postwar years. The manufacturing process for using petroleum was more complex, but on average, petroleum was also cheaper. Progress was rapid. B. F. Goodrich had done early work in synthetics, and became the largest producer of synthetic rubber during the war, as patriotically announced to the US public in ads for its trademarked "Ameripol" (as in "American" and "polymer," the latter referring to the molecule that would also serve as the basis for plastics). Ultimately, US firms built fifty-one synthetic rubber factories between 1942 and 1945. During the same period, production climbed from 24,640 tons of synthetic rubber in 1942 to more than 784,000 tons in 1945.

Nazi Racism and Buna at Auschwitz

Given the state of synthetic rubber development in the United States before the war, its wartime advance was astonishing, making it one of the great success stories of World War II. In retrospect, the gap between the United States and Germany, where Buna production merely doubled between 1941 and 1944, is remarkable. Why the difference? When the head of IG Farben, Carl Bosch, told Hitler in 1932 that the dismissal of Jewish scientists from IG Farben "could set back German science by a century, Hitler replied, 'Then we'll work a hundred years without physics and chemistry.'"[27] All Jewish scientists had been forced out of IG Farben by 1937. Scientific research depended on talent, and many of the most talented engineers, scientists, and academics were forced to leave Germany in the 1930s. It is no coincidence that the leading physicist at the time, Albert Einstein, figured among the émigrés from the Third Reich.

When we move from research to production of synthetic rubber, the gap between US and German experiences becomes even clearer. Historians have long noted that the diversion of trains to haul people to extermination camps hampered the movement of German troops and war materiel. Wartime production also suffered from the regime's imperial racial ambitions. In 1941, IG Farben began construction of a huge Buna plant, projected to supply all of Germany's needs. Near Auschwitz, in occupied Poland, the company found the necessary coal and limestone. The site was at the time outside the range of Allied bombers (although that would change as the front ultimately advanced). There was abundant water for processing. There was also abundant cheap labor, as IG Farben contracted with the SS (the Nazi party's paramilitary unit) for slave labor. Near the town of Monowitz, this new Auschwitz camp, about five miles from the gas chambers, was often referred to simply as "Buna." As many as 20,000 inmates were at work at Monowitz at any given time, and as many as 300,000 worked there during the war. The horrific conditions at Monowitz have been immortalized by Primo Levi, who described his experiences there in his well-known *Survival in Auschwitz*. At Buna laborers were quite literally worked to death at the construction site. Prisoners of war were a second source of labor, along with some German civilians.

Yet, in the words of Primo Levi, "the Buna factory, on which the Germans were busy for four years and for which countless of us suffered and died, never produced a pound of synthetic rubber."[28] Significantly, while decently paid American workers rapidly built synthetic rubber facilities, at Buna most workers were slave laborers. Quite literally starved to death (average weight loss was 6.5–9 pounds each week), they were not particularly productive. In 1941, as building began, IG Farben carefully calculated that concentration camp inmates would only be about 75 percent as productive as a well-fed worker, although in reality 33 percent seems to have been more accurate.[29] Some survivors reported efforts to sabotage the building site. By 1944, Allied bombers also took a toll, so it is impossible to judge just how much either an abused, underfed workforce or sabotage undermined Buna. Still, the contrast with the US experience remains marked.

In a sense, the Nazis implemented, with violent and "efficient" twentieth-century means, a nineteenth-century imperial agenda. Using the same nineteenth-century notions of empire, white superiority, and racial hierarchy, Nazi imperial expansion was directed eastward. Hitler greatly admired US "manifest destiny" and "Indian removal," seeing America's westward expansion against "inferior" Indians as a model for his eastward expansion against Slavs for German *Lebensraum*. Among German and other European anti-Semites, Jews were referred to as "Asiatics," even as "Mongols." Clearly, the assumptions about a modern, "civilized" West as superior to a barbaric East found yet another permutation in Nazi ideology. It is always tempting to see the Third Reich as an aberration in European history, but such an approach ignores the ideological continuities between nineteenth-century empires and the Third Reich.[30]

Imperialism and Nationalism in the Wake of World War II

The world wars revealed some of the horrible effects of the intense nationalism, militarism, and racism that composed the edifice of imperialism. European nationalisms were critical in setting the stage for both world wars, and well-entrenched European (and by extension US) ideas of global "races" were omnipresent before and during the wars. However, to the extent that the Nazis took notions of racial superiority to the "final solution" of exterminating the presumably inferior "races," they also laid those notions bare in ways that were hard for the world to ignore after the war. Not coincidentally, the thriving early twentieth-century eugenics movements of Britain and the United States mostly disappeared in the face of revelations of Nazi euthanasia and the concentration camps. "Race science" no longer seemed legitimate. When Americans and Europeans founded the United Nations in the wake of World War II, they made specific reference to universal human rights, although they and others would struggle to implement that idea at home and abroad. On the level of ideas, after World War II it became increasingly harder to justify racism (and the denial of human rights), even if some people and countries continued, and still continue, to do so.

READING

Life, Work, and Death at Buna Monowitz

The following are two accounts of life and work in the construction of Buna. The first is that of Kai Feinberg, a Norwegian Jew. The second is from a British prisoner of war, Denis Avey.

- How might conditions at Buna have reduced workers' productivity?
- How might conditions have encouraged sabotage?
- Does brutality make human beings submissive, or does it cause us to resist?

After three weeks, on December 23, 1942, my father, his two brothers, and I were quartered in the special concentration camp of Monowitz. Conditions were unbearable. It was almost impossible to breathe. We had to get up at 4:30 a.m. It took three quarters of an hour to march to our place to work. On the first day—the day before Christmas, 24 December 1942—we had to work through until 3:00 a.m., 25 December, without food. We unloaded boxcars, iron poles and bags containing cement.... On January 5, 1943, my father was already so weakened that when we had to drag a 50-kilogram bag at doubled pace he collapsed before my very eyes. He was carried to the camp by his comrades. He had been beaten constantly by the guards, and this most severely on the last day.... He died in my presence on 7 January 1943. One brother of my father injured his right arm during work, and he was gassed. One brother of my father had become so weak that he died while at work, about one or two weeks after my father in Buna. I myself was able to stand the work until 15 January 1943; then I contracted pneumonia and resumed work from 15 February until the end of February. Then I was declared unfit for work because I was no longer able to walk and it was decided that I should be gassed. It so happened that on that day no truck came to the Buna works and I was returned instead to the concentration camp at Auschwitz.[31]

We weren't allowed to rivet at first but after a while they let us do it so long as we were supervised; but they couldn't always watch us that closely, you see, because there were too many of us. So when they weren't looking we used to weaken the rivets, so that after a couple of months they would pop and they'd have to do it all over.... Other times we'd take grease off the engines, mix it with sand, and then put it back so that when they started them up it would wreck the gears. Or we'd bend the blades of cooling fans, things like that. Anything we could get away with, basically. You had to be careful, though, because the Germans were always on the lookout for sabotage and would test everything. They'd shoot you if you got caught. But I had a stooge on the inside of the chief

108

engineer's office and we'd know when certain things were going to be used and so we'd only go after the stuff that was going to be lying idle for a few weeks. That way, when it didn't work, they didn't know who had worked on it. It caused them no end of problems.[32]

Notes

1 Harvey S. Firestone, *Men and Rubber: The Story of Business* (Garden City, NY: Doubleday, Page, 1926), p. 254.

2 Michelin, *The Battle of Verdun (1914–1918)* (Clermont-Ferrand: Michelin, 1919), pp. 9, 12.

3 Goodrich, *L'automobiliste en voyage* (n.p.: Goodrich, n.d.), p. 73; in the former Touring Club de France library in the City of Paris library branch of the 16e arrondissement.

4 Goodrich advertisement in Goodrich file BA 2-3, University of Akron Archives (UAA).

5 F. A. Seiberling to A. F. Bement, 19 March 1918, and the accompanying form letter from Seiberling to potential contributors, Seiberling papers, Mss 347, Box 40, Ohio Historical Society.

6 Peter J. Hugill, "Good Roads and the Automobile in the United States, 1880–1929," *The Geographical Review* 72, no. 3 (July 1982): 340–341.

7 Harp, *Marketing Michelin*, pp. 155–186.

8 The noteworthy exception was Goodyear Aeronautics' production of Corsair airplanes during World War II.

9 Hugh Allen, "Winter Airship Plans," in Goodyear Advertising 1932, file 10372, UAA; Blair Williams of Goodyear to L. Sellmer of the Century of Progress Information Bureau, 31 May 1934, in Chicago World's Fair files 1-6460, in the Special Collections section of the University of Illinois—Chicago Library.

10 Memorandum Submitted by the Rubber Manufacturers'Association of America to the Department of Commerce, 16 July 1925, in Commerce Papers: Rubber, Box 531, Herbert Hoover Presidential Library; E. G. Holt, Chief Rubber Division, Department of Commerce, "Five Years of Restriction," *India Rubber World* 77, no. 5 (1 February 1928): 55–57.

11 James Cooper Lawrence, *The World's Struggle with Rubber, 1905–1931* (New York: Harper & Bros, 1931), p. 37.

12 E. G. Holt, Chief Rubber Division, Department of Commerce, "Five Years of Restriction," *India Rubber World* 77, no. 5 (1 February 1928): 55–57.

13 Joseph Brandes, *Herbert Hoover and Economic Diplomacy: Department of Commerce Policy, 1921–1928* (Pittsburgh, PA: University of Pittsburgh Press, 1962), p. 114. The Dutch were also concerned with increasing political instability had smallholders been forced to take part: Anne L. Foster, *Projections of Power: The United States and Europe in Colonial Southeast Asia, 1919–1941* (Durham, NC: Duke University Press, 2010), p. 54.

14 Paul W. Litchfield, *Industrial Voyage: My Life as an Industrial Lieutenant* (Garden City, NY: Doubleday, 1954), p. 133.

15 Greg Grandin, *Fordlandia: The Rise and Fall of Henry Ford's Forgotten Jungle City* (New York: Metropolitan Books/Henry Holt, 2009), p. 350.
16 Harvey S. Firestone to his brother Elmer S. Firestone, 1 October 1925, in Overman files on Liberia, Folder 2, Holsoe Collection, Archives of Traditional Music, Indiana University.
17 Harvey S. Firestone to Coolidge and Kellogg, 2 October 1925, in Overman files on Liberia, Folder 2, Holsoe Collection, Archives of Traditional Music, Indiana University.
18 The original report was from Harvey Firestone, Jr., C.A. Myers, and D.A. Ross (a planter from Southeast Asia who became the director of the Firestone plantation), 8 April 1927, and became part of Harvey Firestone, Sr.'s report to the Firestone Board of Directors, 24 May 1927, Folder 2 in the Holsoe Collection, the Archives of Traditional Music, Indiana University.
19 James C. Young, "American Rubber Empire Rises in Africa: Colossal Enterprise to Conquer and Cultivate 1,000,000 acres," *New York Times* (19 December 1926); in 1934, the author of the article published a book of veritable Firestone propaganda: James C. Young, *Liberia Rediscovered* (Garden City, NY: Doubleday, Doran, 1934). David Darrah, "U.S. in Liberia," *The Chicago Tribune* (19 December 1926), clippings among many others from 1920s in "Rubber," Box 532, Commerce Papers, Herbert Hoover Presidential Library.
20 Ibrahim Sundiata, *Brothers and Strangers: Black Zion, Black Slavery, 1914–1940* (Durham, NC: Duke University Press, 2003).
21 Diarmuid Jeffreys, *Hell's Cartel: IG Farben and the Making of Hitler's War Machine* (New York: Metropolitan Books/Henry Holt, 2008), p. 203.
22 John Tully, *Devil's Milk: A Social History of Rubber* (New York: Monthly Review Press, 2011), pp. 293–295.
23 Mark R. Finlay, *Growing American Rubber: Strategic Plants and the Politics of National Security* (New Brunswick, NJ: Rutgers University Press, 2009), p. 171.
24 Frank Robert Chalk, "The United States and the International Struggle for Rubber, 1914–1941" (PhD thesis, University of Wisconsin, 1970), p. 237.
25 Eric Jennings, *Free French Africa in World War II: The African Resistance* (Cambridge: Cambridge University Press, 2015), pp. 179–204; Tamara Giles-Vernick, *Cutting the Vines of the Past: Environmental Histories of the Central African Rain Forest* (Charlottesville, VA: University of Virginia Press, 2002), p. 163.
26 "Synthetic Rubber, 1946," in Goodrich files, JBL-35 in UAA.
27 Joseph Borkin, *The Crime and Punishment of IG Farben* (New York: Free Press, 1978), p. 57.
28 Primo Levi, *Survival in Auschwitz: The Nazi Assault on Humanity*, trans. Stuart Woolf (New York: Simon and Schuster, 1996 [1958]), p. 73.
29 Borkin, *Crime and Punishment*, pp. 117–127.
30 Shelley Baranowski, *Nazi Empire: German Colonialism and Imperialism from Bismarck to Hitler* (Cambridge: Cambridge University Press, 2011).
31 Testimony at the Nuremberg trial of IG Farben executives, quoted in Josiah E. DuBois, *The Devil's Chemists* (Boston, MA: Beacon Press, 1952), p. 223.
32 Jeffreys, *Hell's Cartel*, p. 340, from an interview in January 2005.

5

Resistance and Independence

Suggested film: newsreel, "Malaya's Jungle Fight in 1952"
http://www.youtube.com/watch?v=oAO9xqXZ6BQ

In spite of the absolute absence of the suggestion of labor unions, do not think for one minute that the native coolie is without his weapon, and be assured that it is the most powerful of any. It is known as "passive submission" [today we would use the term "passive resistance"]. In other words—he submits one day and the next is back doing the job in his own way. Again he is corrected, and, by some, beaten mildly or fined a small share of his microscopic wages.... They seem to think it is impolite to say "no" to a white man. The result is that they may say "yes" and then go ahead according to their own ideas. To the phlegmatic Dutch in the Netherlands, to the firm-as-a-rock Britisher in Malaysia or Ceylon, this method is exasperating beyond anything and to the quick nervous American it takes away whatever pleasure there may be in living in the Tropics.[1]

Because so many of the sources for the history of imperialism are from above, at the level of colonial governments and thus reflect officials' prejudices, it is easy to assume that there was not much indigenous resistance to European empires until the post–World War II years, when suddenly nationalists and communists rose up and seized control, quickly creating independent countries. Yet, as this chapter will illustrate, laborers employed various forms of resistance to imperial policies, even on strictly controlled rubber plantations. Contrary to common belief,

A World History of Rubber: Empire, Industry, and the Everyday, First Edition.
Stephen L. Harp.
© 2016 John Wiley & Sons, Inc. Published 2016 by John Wiley & Sons, Inc.

resistance began as soon as empire began. Over time, it took different forms on plantations, on rubber smallholdings, and in rubber factories.

The quotation that opens this chapter, from a Goodyear company newsletter, tells us more about the dynamics of laborers' resistance, both on rubber plantations and in rubber factories, than its author probably intended. It begins with reference to labor unions. Not coincidentally, Goodyear and other rubber companies fought hard against efforts to unionize their workforces in North America and Europe in the interwar years. Unionization would eventually succeed, largely because white workers in Europe and the United States could win in the court of public opinion during the 1930s, when governments increasingly helped to protect those workers' rights. Yet, contrary to what Goodyear said, there was not an "absolute absence of the suggestion of labor unions" for workers in the colonies. Rather, labor unions remained illegal in those places in the interwar years, as the colonized did not yet receive the rights afforded their white counterparts, despite what was in essence a global struggle on the part of workers for fair treatment in the workplace.

The quotation also echoes the persistent American myth of the "happy slave." In spite of all evidence to the contrary, there also existed a widespread imperial myth of the "happy coolie," who was simple, more or less satisfied, and hardworking enough—if kept on task by overseers and European managers. "He" might drag his feet a bit, prove stubborn or suspicious, but was ultimately controllable. Beneath it all, there existed a notion that "coolies" (like the word describing them; European workers were never called coolies) were fundamentally different, human to some extent, but less "civilized," more "primitive," with fewer needs and lower expectations. To use Goodyear's language, firm-as-a-rock Britishers, phlegmatic Dutchmen, and quick, nervous Americans may have differed from each other, as clearly national stereotypes are operative here, but there was presumed to be a much bigger gap between white and non-white "races." It was not assumed that "coolies" were in any way equals, persons who had simply signed contracts to avoid destitution at home, or even that they had a sense of justice—and as a result resisted when plantations seemed to violate contracts through intimidation, humiliation, abuse, or unilateral changes in the terms of agreements.

Plantations and Resistance

The myth of the content, "submissive coolie" did not materialize out of thin air. Rather, it was repeated, as by Goodyear above, to European and American audiences over and over again. As in other advertising, at the ever important world's fairs across Europe and North America, visitors received assurances that all was well on rubber plantations, that the "coolies" were content with their conditions. For example, in a printed text for the Paris Colonial Exposition of 1931, French labor inspector E. Delamarre informed fairgoers that "during the period from 30 June 1929 to 30 June 1930, on all of the plantations of Cochinchina [southern Vietnam] there were only four collective refusals to work; only one, at Phú Riêng, February 4–8, necessitated police intervention, whose presence sufficed to maintain order."[2] His brief reference encouraged fairgoers to admire the employment of overwhelmingly satisfied indigenous laborers.

We need to go deeper, beyond the comforting words of Delamarre, to consider the documentary evidence of laborers' resistance. As we follow the paper trail, it becomes clear that Delamarre and fellow officials withheld a great deal of information from the public. In fact, like so many planters and colonial officials, Delamarre misrepresented both the reality of life on the plantations as well as the extent of workers' acceptance of what they considered gross injustices. In fact, as we know, he had inspected plantations and written critical confidential reports to his superiors, squarely blaming plantation owners for conditions that led laborers to stop work, to strike, and even to attack their overseers. In their sense of fairness and justice, plantation laborers in Southeast Asia did not differ fundamentally from factory workers in Europe and North America. However, Americans and Europeans often assumed otherwise, casting them as passive or active, docile, or irrationally violent.

Over and over again, working conditions spurred responses among plantation workers in French Indochina, British Malaya, and the Dutch East Indies. Combinations of reform and repression, as well as police intervention, temporarily ended incidents of resistance. And then they broke out again. Plantation workers responded to what they understood as exploitation. In the end, their expectations of fairness were remarkably like those of European and American factory workers during the same period, even if that message did not normally reach the American or European publics.

Selective resistance to plantation labor began long before the plantations produced anything at all. When plantation companies first gained leases to lands, they attempted to hire local populations to clear the rainforest and work on the plantations. Planters found few takers on the Malay Peninsula, on Sumatra, or in Vietnam and Cambodia. Local populations generally lived well enough without needing to accept dangerous work and cruel treatment on plantations. Their reluctance to do so became part of colonizers' lore. Malays in British Malaya were consistently presumed "lazy," as were the native Sumatrans in the

Dutch East Indies. In French Indochina, the director of one plantation explained that "the natives from the region [of Cochinchina] have the weakness of being unstable.... They have a tendency toward sabotage... because of [their] indolence."[3]

Compared to locals, migrant laborers were desperate, as they generally signed the labor contracts in order to escape destitution. Once they arrived on plantations, the gap between promised and actual working conditions could be stark. Legally, they had few options, as most had signed contracts that bound them to the work. Among planters, there was frequent mention of work slowdowns and sabotage. When conditions were particularly bad, another response was desertion. Between June 1927 and March 1928, on the Michelin plantation at Phú Riêng, 161 of 990 total laborers deserted.[4] Escapees were rounded up by plantation guards, police, and the local mountain people, who were paid bounties. Since the escapees came from northern Vietnam, they did not know the terrain. If they escaped capture, they still did not always survive in the jungle. Officials as well as planters kept careful track of desertion rates and presented their decline as "progress," although they did not note whether workers were better treated or just more effectively controlled. Other workers committed suicide. In the British-controlled Federated Malay States, forty-three Tamil laborers killed themselves in 1928, and forty-five in 1929, making "suicide the foremost working hazard for coolies in both years."[5]

Such passive resistance was not the only option. In fact, laborers were far less accepting of their plight than the Goodyear quotation that opens this chapter implies. Physical retaliation for abusive treatment occurred with astounding frequency. In the plantation region of Sumatra, in the 1920s there was an attack on a European assistant about each month, a situation deemed bad enough that Europeans often carried a revolver. In fact, "[i]n 1924 it was calculated that an assistant in fifteen years of service had a 3% chance of being killed by a worker and at least a 50% probability of being physically assaulted."[6] Laborers clearing the rainforest for new plantations had access to saws, machetes, and knives. Domestic help of course used knives on a daily basis. Even rubber tappers regularly carried a small (farrier's) knife used to skin the bark of hevea trees in order to let the latex flow. Europeans on plantations feared what they called "coolie attacks," which they consistently attributed to the "primitive" nature of non-Europeans and their supposed lack of appreciation for human life.

Generally, our records of revolts come only from government officials and planters. Yet, for a few of the uprisings in French Indochina, historians are fortunate to have detailed accounts from two separate perspectives: that of government officials, including labor inspectors whose reports were sometimes also leaked to the press; and that of the plantation laborer Tran Tu Binh, who ultimately rose to a position of importance in the Communist Party in North Vietnam. Taken together, they offer remarkable detail about the dynamics of laborers' active resistance. In workers' eyes, mistreatment justified peaceful protests and, when those proved ineffective, violent action. In his autobiography, Tran Tu Binh refers repeatedly to "justice." Government officials, in describing the same events that Tran Tu Binh does, sometimes conceded that planters' treatment of laborers was a factor in revolts. At other times, officials agreed with planters, using the word "mutiny" to describe incidents of laborers' active resistance, much as many British discredited the Indian uprising of 1857 with the term "mutiny" while many Indians have used the expressions "First War of Independence" and "Great Rebellion."

To gauge the difference between the official version and that of a laborer, consider two separate descriptions of the events of September 1927 on the Michelin plantation of Phú Riêng. Here a government report laid out what happened:

> In September 1927, a group of Tonkinois [from northern Vietnam] laborers, having recently arrived on the plantation of Phú-Riêng, mutinied after morning reveille. Those revolting attacked their overseer, Monsieur Monteil, and killed him. Then they invaded the plantation, and undertook hostile acts against the director and his European assistants, who, to save their lives, had to use their arms.... On 7 and 8 February, the lower criminal court of Saigon pronounced judgment on the murder of M. Monteil and issued the following sentences: one to death, two to forced labor for life.[7]

By contrast, Tran Tu Binh offered a good deal more background on the attack as well as more detail. He wrote that

> the chief overseers under Triai's [the European assistant under Monteil, whose actual name was Triaire, but Tran Tu Binh would never have seen it spelled out] authority followed his example, and were no less cruel. For example, there was Valentin, a huge [former] soldier. He beat very harshly, always punching and kicking the worker to the point of real danger. Another one was Monte [how Monteil sounded to him], famous as the most cruel of the overseers at Phú Riêng. He would beat from morning to night, until he had worn out whole sheaves of rods [rattan canes, widely used on plantations for beating].... The overseers commonly beat workers who had just arrived in order to intimidate them.... One youth with an upset stomach did not get into a straight line soon enough and Trial sprang toward him, drew back his leg and kicked the

Resistance and Independence

youth, rupturing his spleen. The incapacitated youth lay writhing at his feet. Straight-faced as if nothing had happened, [Trial] gave a sign to his subordinates. Valentin and Monte then came over and struck out with their rods, at once striking us and counting out the number of workers in a loud voice. When they reached me, I raised both arms to protect my head and spoke up quickly: "The contract forbids beatings. Why are you beating us?"... Triai stared at me angrily. Suddenly, he struck me hard on the head with his rod and shouted: "Let him feel the club!" At once French and Vietnamese overseers alike began caning me from left and right and kicking me with their hobnailed boots... I was beaten by Triai and Monte themselves. After they beat me to the ground, I drew myself up into a ball, using my legs to protect my stomach and chest. The two of them kept raining down blows.

Overseers then threw the bloodied Tran Tu Binh in a dark hut and shackled him for three days without food. He continued his tale:

Triai had driven my fellow workers out to the work area. After the first round of beatings to intimidate them, Triai urged the overseers to beat the workers unceasingly.... Monte and Valentin and their crew gave even fiercer beatings. Those who were beaten in that first round resigned themselves to retreating, trying to bear it, and waiting to see how things would work out.

One morning [at reveille]... Monte came. The roll call began. As usual, Monte struck everyone on the head with his cane, counting out loud in French. The workers pretended to take no special notice of it and just raised their hands to protect their heads. As Monte went deeper into the ranks, he came near Tu, who suddenly shouted, "brothers! Kill him!" The freshly sharpened crescent-shaped axe in Tu's hand flashed up, then slashed down. Monte ducked just in time. The axe sliced into the flesh of the overseer's shoulder. He spun around and fled to his bungalow, so scared of the smell of blood that he ran powerfully despite his wound. Tu brandished his axe and gave chase, shouting "After him! After him!" A number of the others raised their picks and pruning knives and chased off the panic-stricken foremen. Monte could not get back to his quarters to get his gun. He had just reached the wooden stairs outside his bungalow when the blades of nine axes descended on him. The final blow split off half his face....

All of the workers ran off into the forest. When Triai arrived he called out more soldiers, surrounded the workers on all four sides and chased them down. He caught forty or fifty people and brought them back. Those who came in range of his own gun he shot dead. The bodies of the dead were buried right out in the forest, and even those still writhing in pain were buried alive.

Those who were picked up in the forest were taken to Bien Hoa and turned over to the Secret Police. They were savagely tortured in an

116

attempt to learn who the instigator was. Finally, they found out it was brother Tu. The Bien Hoa court sentenced him to death and handed down life sentences to two other workers involved in the plot with Tu.[8]

Tran Tu Binh's account can easily cause us to wonder just how much detail was left out of other governmental reports that have survived. From his perspective, workers' actions were entirely justified, as their own violent actions seem a rational response to the brutality of overseers and the plantation manager. It is noteworthy that key facts, such as the court's sentences, are the same in both Tran Tu Binh's and the governor general's account.

In early 1930, at the start of Tet, the Vietnamese festival of the new lunar year, Phú Riêng was again the site of collective action on the part of contract laborers. Carrying a traditional festival dragon, more than 1,300 plantation laborers arrived at the plantation manager's villa, began a strike, seized the weapons of plantation guards, assaulted the plantation guards, sang the Communist anthem Internationale, and proceeded to make a series of demands, notably one for an eighthour workday (workdays had lasted for at least ten hours, and including time spent walking to and from living quarters to work areas were up to twelve hours). The protest ended when 800 heavily armed troops took over the plantation and arrested the strike's organizers, including Tran Tu Binh, who received a sentence of five years on the notorious Côn Sơn Island. In some ways, the actions of 1930 serve as a preview for developments both later in the 1930s and after 1945. First, the uprising of 1930 was not a spontaneous reaction so much as a planned strike with carefully defined goals. Second, at least some participants, including Tran Tu Binh, considered themselves communists, organized themselves in clandestine cells, and claimed to follow communist ideology. The appeal of international communism to the workers was obvious. The Soviet-sponsored Third International, founded after World War I, condemned colonialism. As plantation laborers saw it, there was no better example of how capitalism exploited workers than a rubber plantation. Admittedly, plantation workers were agricultural laborers, not the industrial ones that Karl Marx assumed, but their work was more tightly controlled and as carefully regulated as that of the industrial laborers in Michelin's tire plants in France. Like the better-known Yên Bái revolt of that same year, another defining event in Vietnamese history, the incidents at Phú-Riêng in 1930 were a hint of the ideological mix of nationalism, anti-imperialism, and communism that would characterize North Vietnamese efforts to achieve a particular form of Vietnamese independence after World War II.

Global Economic Crisis and Plantation Labor

In the early 1930s, the global economic depression had a profound effect on rubber plantations. Rubber prices had already begun to decline in the late 1920s as supply increased. Economic contraction after the Wall Street crash of 1929 brought shrinking demand, which reached a low point three years later. As car sales fell, tire companies in North America and Europe sold many fewer original equipment sets. As the unemployed and underemployed drove less often, sales of replacement tires plummeted. While other rubber goods continued to sell in varying amounts, most of those required so little rubber that their sale had little impact on global rubber prices.

For their part, in response to the Great Depression rubber plantations shed workers and slashed wages. For example, on East Sumatran plantations generally, in 1930 the workforce totaled 336,000; in 1934 only 160,000 remained.[9] From Sumatra, workers were shipped back to Java, from Malaya back to India. European assistants saw pay cuts, lost bonuses, increased workload,[10] and those who were laid off were sent back to Europe, for fear that the sight of poverty-stricken Europeans on the plantations would hurt "white prestige" in the colonies. In the deflationary environment of the Depression, laborers' wages became the next target. In the Dutch East Indies, when laborers' contracts expired they were replaced with "free workers" (*vrije arbeiders*), meaning former contract laborers now rehired at 25 percent of the former wage. The government also now allowed planters to offer only half pay for half-days of work and frequent unpaid "holidays." Plantations were thus released from their obligations to pay and feed laborers for the duration of contracts.

Plantation laborers, facing destitution if they returned home during the crisis, usually put up with the straitened circumstances. Laborers accepted lower wages—unless they felt they were not being treated fairly or legally, in which case they took action. By acting both unfairly and illegally, managers of a Michelin plantation once again found themselves at the center of labor conflict. In 1932, the Union of Rubber Planters in Indochina got an agreement from the governor general of Indochina that, when it was time to renew contracts, male contract laborers would see their wages reduced from 40 cents (of a Singapore dollar) to 30 cents, while female laborers who had been paid 30 cents would receive only 23 cents (thus did the government help planters avoid competing wage rates). The government agreed that contract renewals and new contracts would be for lower wages than existing contracts, which would allow French plantations to produce at the same cost as those in Malaya and the Dutch East Indies, as the governor general of French Indochina was concerned about maintaining the economic competitiveness of the colony. The new contracts were overwhelmingly accepted by those laborers whose old contracts, with more generous terms, had expired. Yet, in December 1932, Michelin reduced wages on existing contracts and cut rice rations, which made up most of workers' diets, from 800 to 700 grams per day for men, and from 700 to 600 grams per day for women. On Michelin's Dâu Tiêng plantation approximately one thousand laborers took their grievance to the local administrator at Thù Dâu Môt. Along the way, a scared guard shot at the crowd, killing four persons. When word got out, the French Communist party newspaper *Humanité* had a field day, and the topic was the source of debate in the French Parliament (*Assemblée Nationale*), but there is little evidence that the revolt was inspired or organized by the communists who had been so thoroughly repressed in Indochina after the uprisings of 1930. In reports not released to the public, government officials were clear that the laborers were not communist, not armed, and not aggressive; Michelin was entirely at fault.[11] The colonial government required Michelin to follow the law. The protests ended.

When rubber prices rebounded in the slow economic recovery of the late 1930s, wage rates increased. As would be the case in Europe and North America, colonial employers could increase profits when wages remained low. However, when wage rates began to rise, plantation laborers worried about the disparity of wage rates among the different plantations. In May 1937, again on the Dâu Tiêng plantation, some 1,500 workers gathered in front of the manager's office to demand that wages rise to 40 cents. Although they disbanded when the police force arrived, 1,200 assembled the next day and began walking toward Thù Dâu Môt, "announcing their intention to go to Saigon to explain their grievance to the governor. A reinforcement of one hundred policemen was sent." The governor met the group some 12 kilometers from Dâu Tiêng The assembly was dispersed but thirty leaders were arrested and taken to Thù Dâu Môt for interrogation. Calm was restored.[12] In the end, the workers only got an increase to 32 cents, but while the government helped to suppress their action, the governor general of Indochina noted that the workers' demands were reasonable: higher pay for experienced workers, a return of the rice ration to 800 grams, sufficient drinking water, a more equitable division of daily tasks on the plantations, and more gentle and humane treatment by overseers.[13] Behind the scenes, officials thus admitted that workers' protests were justified.

In 1937 in Selangor, on the Malay Peninsula, Chinese workers instigated a series of strikes on rubber estates. As in French Indochina, communist ideology seemed to have had little actual influence on the demands of strikers, which included not the overthrow of capitalism or even British rule so much as pay increases commensurate with the rising global price of rubber. Here too, the police fired on strikers and arrested two, which caused 1,200 others to march in protest. Waves of strikes and police repression followed, as workers demanded increased pay, "childcare for children under the age of five, schools for the coolies' children, and 'no dismissals without cause.'"[14] Police repressed the uprising, arresting leaders and forcing the others to return to work. During a wave of strikes between 1939 and 1941, on the eve of Japanese occupation, it became clear to officials in British Malaya that resistance was not limited to the supposedly troublesome Chinese, influenced by the strength of Chinese communists and nationalists on the mainland. In fact, the supposedly "mild Hindoo" Tamil laborers were every bit as "unruly" in demanding their rights. Tamil demands included, among others:

> pay parity between Indian and Chinese [laborers], removal of "brutal" [overseers], proper education for children, an end to the molestation of laborers' womenfolk by Europeans..., proper medical facilities,... freedom of speech and assembly, free access to estates for family and friends, laborers to remain mounted on bicycles in front of European and Asian staff, abolition of 10–12 hour days, and permission to form associations to represent their interests.

At least 20,000 workers from almost 100 estates participated. However, there was to be no compromise, as the legitimacy of planters' control and European rule generally seemed to rely on not compromising with striking workers. The government sent in the military. Five strikers were killed, sixty wounded, and the others compelled to return to work.[15] Protests were not always effective, but workers obviously resisted when they believed working or living conditions to be inadequate.

Success of the Smallholders

Resistance to European plantations, and the imperial power that supported them, also took the form of growing and tapping rubber outside the plantation system. Indigenous inhabitants of Malaya and Sumatra who steadfastly refused to work on European rubber plantations did not refuse to gather or grow rubber on their own terms. Before the establishment of plantations, indigenous peoples in Southeast Asia gathered a variety of latexes from the forest, including gutta percha, and sold them to Chinese and Dutch traders. Trees were found and tapped during the dry season, when labor was freed up from agriculture.

Beginning with the introduction of the hevea tree on plantations in Southeast Asia in the late nineteenth century, indigenous smallholders planted it in rubber groves, taking seeds and seedlings from nearby plantations. In comparison with the huge European plantations and the middle-sized Chinese ones (more than 100 acres, but generally not the thousands of acres of European ones), "smallholders" were quite literally those who farmed a small agricultural holding in the forest (in Malaya, the official definition of a "smallholding" was 100 acres or less, with what was called a "true smallholding" consisting of no more than 25 acres, much of which may not have been in cultivation; in the Dutch East Indies, there was no official definition). Colonial authorities paid relatively little attention to them as compared to European planters. Smallholders continued to live on lands not surveyed, registered, or leased out by the colonial government. In contrast with European planters, they received no state support.

Planters and colonial states first really noticed smallholders in the 1920s. In Malaya, British authorities strongly discouraged smallholder rubber planting, particularly during the Stevenson scheme years (1922–28). The fear was both that smallholders might undercut plantations, rendering the plan ineffective, and that indigenous people should grow rice, which could then be sold to the plantations. Some Malay rubber smallholders resisted the Stevenson plan by protesting, or as British authorities put it during repression, "rioting."[16] Most Malay smallholders traded with Chinese smugglers, undetected by colonial authorities. As rubber prices climbed, the smallholders increased production, flouting colonial government.

In the Dutch East Indies, colonial authorities simply left smallholders alone. The government did not know much about them or how much they had planted. That fact changed during the Stevenson years, when smallholders maximized tapping of their groves as the price of rubber soared. To many European and American observers, smallholders seemed to have come out of nowhere. Their rapid increase in production was the most important factor in undermining the Stevenson plan (due to smallholders' production, the British only controlled 53 percent of rubber production by 1928). Between 1920 and 1930, smallholder production in the Dutch East Indies grew ninefold, from 11,000 tons to almost 100,000. It grew to more than 290,000 tons by 1940, a year in which smallholders produced fully one half of total rubber output in the Dutch East Indies.[17]

The phenomenal increase in smallholders' rubber production shocked European planters and colonial authorities. In part, that was because smallholders were assumed to be backward, in technique and in efficiency, so barely worth notice. In fact, hevea cultivation fit neatly into the traditional swidden agriculture (often known pejoratively as "slash and burn"), in which farmers burned a portion of the forest, farmed there until the light soils were depleted, and then moved on, repeating the process. Smallholders worked out their own systems of planting heveas. They planted trees up to six times more densely than did plantations. Then they left the plot completely alone, moving on to another area of the jungle and starting anew. They planted rice in the marshy areas and hevea trees on higher ground, even on soil too poor for rice, but near rivers and streams so that the rubber could be moved to market. Smallholders developed a pattern, whereby they worked in rubber groves during the dry season and in rice fields during the rainy season. In fact, hevea trees did not produce as well in rainy conditions, and the cups for gathering latex filled with water anyway. Smallholders realized that latex flowed best in the morning, so during particularly busy times they tapped trees in the morning, worked in the rice paddy, then gathered the latex in the late afternoon. Although rubber trees could bear within about six years on plantations, as they fought undergrowth on the smallholder plots they required about ten years to mature enough to do so. Then smallholders would hack their way to the trees, still leaving much of the undergrowth, and tap them.

Smallholders adapted some techniques from local plantations while rejecting others. They used the same curved ("farrier's") knife for tapping. They cut the bark in the same herring bone pattern developed by H. N. Ridley. Smallholders did not, however, always regularly tap the trees; theirs could be left alone for months or even years. Smallholders planted more trees per acre, so their yields could be less per tree, yet still higher per acre. They even allowed the trees to reseed themselves over time. Most significantly, smallholders did not bother to "clean weed," eliminating all undergrowth and keeping the understory "clean" of any weeds, as most plantations did.

Particularly in the 1930s, planters resented the competition from smallholders. Smallholders' rubber was supposedly less pure, and therefore labeled "jungle rubber." Smallholders stood accused of "slaughter harvesting," meaning that they damaged trees during tapping so that their high yields could not be maintained over time. However, as smallholders' production exploded and then remained high, it became obvious that they were not in fact destroying their trees. Above all, planters believed that smallholders' "laziness" in not clean weeding allowed for the dreaded root disease to take hold, then to spread to European plantations.

Ironically, planters realized in the 1930s that leaving undergrowth undisturbed allowed for warmer temperatures, higher humidity, and better recovery of the bark after tapping. Moreover, undergrowth seemed actually to retard the spread of root disease. Now "clean weeding" appeared to be the culprit in the spread of root disease. Tellingly, planters attributed their abandonment of "clean weeding" not to the example of smallholders, but to some European planters' experiments with leaving undergrowth. In the context of the empire, where knowledge and science were supposed to be the preserve of Europeans, it would have seemed well-nigh impossible to attribute the change to the example of smallholders. Well after World War II, even after Dutch plantations were nationalized by the Indonesian government in the late 1950s, it was assumed that knowledge flowed downward from plantations to smallholders, never in the opposite direction. The myth was that plantations were always, by definition, more efficient. In retrospect, it is clear that smallholders could, quite simply, be more efficient producers. They had virtually no overhead. There were no managers or assistants from Europe, no salaried employees at all, no leave for European employees, and no estate buildings or bungalows to build and maintain. Experts estimated that smallholders could establish their rubber holdings for less than a tenth of what plantations spent.[18] Longstanding deeply held assumptions about indigenous sloth and European order were not borne out by reality on the ground.

Over time, smallholders proved incredibly resilient. They remained subsistence rice farmers, tapping trees when they had reason to do so. The most obvious reason was need, in times of scarcity; as the Kantu' people of Borneo put it, "If you have rice you do not tap rubber." High rubber prices were another reason, as high prices made tapping quite profitable. Yet, the opposite could also be true. Low prices could be a reason as well: if families had a need for a specific amount of money, such as school supplies, they simply tapped more trees to get the money.[19] Much as colonial authorities wanted to categorize small-holders in the money economy or the subsistence one, straddling proved an excellent tactic, insulating them from recessions as well as bad harvests. They could survive a failure of the rice crop since they also grew rubber for the market. And as subsistence farmers they survived the Depression, even when the price of rubber fell to 4.6 cents per pound, while plantations were in full-blown crisis.

As a result of the trouble in the plantation sector, the major rubber producers banded together to create a new restriction scheme designed to shore up rubber prices. In 1934, British, Dutch, and French authorities spearheaded the creation of the International Rubber Regulation Committee (IRRC). The agreement limited production through taxation, sales quotas, prohibition of new planting, and the felling of trees. In theory, it applied to both plantations and smallholders, although, like the Stevenson scheme in Malaya, it imposed particularly low quotas on smallholders. In addition, the new rules favored the replacement of older trees with new bud-grafted ones, dramatically increasing yields; US Rubber had pioneered that innovation, and while plantations were well placed to increase production with that process, smallholders were not. Under the IRRC, rubber was also taxed according to water content, an approach prejudicial to smallholders. Because plantations processed their own rubber, concentrating the latex by removing much of the water content, they were taxed less. Smallholders sold rubber with a higher water content, which would later be removed in processing, so faced higher taxes. Still, here too smallholders adjusted. Even in extremely remote areas on the island of Borneo, they purchased cast-iron rubber mangles, hand-powered machines with rollers that could wring out the water out of sheets of rubber. The machines became a fixture in smallholders' settlements.[20]

Smallholders resisted the power of plantations and colonial authorities in yet another way. Colonial land laws treated the forest as unoccupied and thus available land. Planters received concessions on unexploited lands. Often such land had in fact been used in swidden agriculture for generations, but once the forest grew back there was no evidence of settlement and the land could be seized. Had smallholders planted rubber trees native to Southeast Asia, the land could still be doled out to Europeans as concessions. However, hevea trees came from Brazil and could easily live for thirty years while reseeding themselves to create a permanent rubber grove. Their very presence in the forest gave smallholders legal proof that they previously had farmed an area and would be returning to it. At least part of the widespread though dispersed rubber groves in Indonesia today (which produce more than 90 percent of the country's total production), areas larger in surface than rubber plantations, result from smallholders' efforts to keep their land from being taken.[21]

Plantations under the Japanese

In early 1942, just weeks after the attack on Pearl Harbor, Japan quickly occupied much of Southeast Asia, incorporating it into its Greater East Asia Co-Prosperity Sphere. In Malaya and the Dutch East Indies, those European planters and their families who had not fled found themselves imprisoned. Like young plantation laborers (up to half of male Tamils in Malaya), European men were put to work on Japanese military projects, including the infamous Burma–Thailand Railway. Japanese officers now responsible for the plantations relied on the Asian clerks already in place to run operations. Officially, French Indochina remained under the control of Vichy, the collaborationist government of defeated France. Just as France was drained by Germany, Indochina was drained by Japan, for which it produced rice. Overall, Japan did not need much rubber for civilian use, and existing rubber stocks largely sufficed for the Japanese military. It was oil that the Japanese really needed. With little demand for the rubber, production ceased on most plantations in Southeast Asia.

Plantations had long imported food, notably rice, to feed laborers. Neighboring smallholders did not produce enough rice and other food-stuffs to feed plantation inhabitants, even before the war. During the conflict famine threatened, as plantations were not generating income to buy food and supply lines were disrupted. Although practices varied widely depending on region, in most cases both plantation laborers and nearby populations simply planted subsistence crops on plantation land, a practice returning Europeans would later call "squatting." Japanese authorities supported the effort, even granting leases to do so in some areas, particularly to plantation laborers. Since plantations had little land that had been cleared but not planted, squatting resulted in the destruction of existing rubber trees. Knowledgeable about the life cycle of trees (which were productive for about thirty years), squatters usually uprooted the older, least productive trees. Many of these were the older, seed-grown varieties with much lower yields than younger, bud-grafted trees that had been slowly replacing them on plantations before the war. Laborers had often had small garden plots on plantations so that they could grow vegetables to supplement rice. In a sense, they now expanded their plots, transforming themselves from paid laborers into subsistence farmers.

As elsewhere in the Greater East Asia Co-Prosperity Sphere, many plantation workers were brutalized by Japanese occupiers, with some drafted as veritable slave laborers. And while a notion of Asian racial kinship replaced the European/Asian racial divide of the European colonies, Japanese assertions of superiority among Asians replaced European racism with a Japanese version. Resistance followed; varied communist and nationalist movements fought the Japanese. Among the Chinese in Southeast Asia, Chinese nationalist and especially communist opposition to the Japanese on the main-land served as a model. Malayan and Indonesian nationalisms and ostensibly international communism attempted to pull together diverse ethnicities. The varieties of nationalism and communism in Southeast Asia would remain a volatile mix, but the Japanese occupation created a certain unity of different ethnic groups com-mitted to removing Japanese troops.

World War II armed plantations as it did Southeast Asia more generally. Weapons flowed freely by the end of the war, including on rubber plantations. Rubber was traded in Singapore for arms by late 1945. Japanese firearms were readily available. In Indonesia, several rubber plantation factories were converted to the manufacture of small arms, some destined for nationalist and communist revolutionaries.[22]

Britain, France, and the Netherlands were severely weakened by the war. France and the Netherlands were both occupied, and economically drained, by Nazi Germany. Britain, while victorious, was economically devastated—to bring home the point, historians often point out that beef was rationed in Britain until 1954. Although governments in all three countries recognized the profitability of plantations for their own balance of payments, causing all three to attempt to regain control of their colonies, none could easily afford to wage protracted imperial warfare.

World War II had significant lasting effects on the balance of power between Southeast Asians, including plantation workers and colonial authorities. For European imperial governments, the issue was not about maintaining control, but instead re-establishing their colonies as quickly and cheaply as possible. On plantations, returning Europeans faced widespread squatting, armed opposition, and national and communist movements. Southeast Asian resistance, on plantations and elsewhere, would prove organized, armed, and ultimately quite effective.

Independence and Decolonization

Plantations were targets for revolutionaries working to achieve independence from European and American political and economic dominance. Plantations seemed to embody imperialism itself, from the collaboration of some traditional elites who had signed off on land leases, to the huge profits for foreign capitalists, to the exploitation of Asian workers. Financially, plantations enriched colonial governments, as well as European and American investors. By going after plantations, revolutionaries could choke off revenue for investors and colonizing powers, raising the cost of empire at a time when Europeans were both broke and weary of war. Because plantations were usually far from urban areas and therefore concentrations of police officers and troops, revolutionaries could easily attack both the roads to plantations and the vast acreages themselves. It became standard practice for partisans to attack a plantation factory, office, or dwelling, then slip back into the huge plantation, or as necessary into the nearby jungle or village.

Postwar happenings on plantations also made them increasingly dangerous places. With the support of colonial authorities, European planters reasserted control of plantations and recommenced production. Despite the advent of synthetic rubber, overall demand for rubber grew quickly after the war, even before the spike in demand due to the Korean War in 1950–53. Planters forcibly reclaimed land from squatters who, according to the planters, had illegally occupied it.

Squatters were a direct challenge to managers' authority. Workers and squatters were, often as not, the same people. The ability of workers to fall back on farming in the event of low wages or a strike gave them an independence and leverage that they had never possessed before.[23]

Laborers watched as planters drove tractors over their homesteads, preparing the soil for the re-establishment of rubber trees. Planters also fought laborers' demands for fair pay. There was considerable resistance, sometimes on the part of plantation workers, sometimes on the part of those planters deemed outsiders; in fact, the very distinction between the two groups, divided by ethnicity and experience, became less important after the war, in part as result of planters' efforts to re-establish prewar controls.

Isolated plantations resembled armed camps. Barbed wire and floodlights surrounded the production facilities on plantations. Plantations employed private armies to protect production facilities, trees, and the planters themselves. Planters carried automatic weapons, drove vehicles fitted with armor, placed sandbags along the walls of their bungalows, and often evacuated their families to safer urban areas. The risk of ambush was high in some areas, so helicopters became a preferred means of transport into and out of plantations. In 1949, 745 planters and miners had police rank in Malaysia. Plantations were, like other places, sites of warfare in the late 1940s, even if former colonial powers officially avoided the term "war" for fear of legitimizing the opposition.

In Indonesia—where revolutionaries led by Sukarno proclaimed independence as early as August 17, 1945, just two days after Japanese emperor Hirohito announced that Japan would surrender—Dutch military offensives to reclaim control in 1947 and 1948–49 were known as "*Politionele Acties*" or "police actions." International (including American) investors supported Dutch intervention so that plantations might be secured against revolutionaries. In December 1949 the Netherlands formally withdrew, recognizing the newly independent country of Indonesia.

Until the 1960s, President Sukarno oversaw a left-leaning nationalist government that simultaneously worked with plantation owners, an important source of revenue, and increasingly militant plantation laborers. Conditions on rubber plantations improved significantly in the early 1950s. Despite the existence of synthetic rubber, there was strong global demand for natural rubber. Workers won an increase in the minimum wage at a time of stable prices, as well as a forty-hour work-week. Barrack housing disappeared, as workers were granted material and time to build and maintain individual dwellings. The workers' union managed to remove abusive foremen and pressured those accused of harassing women workers.[24] The union could easily target foreign-owned firms, exerting pressure for change.

Because the Netherlands was the former colonial power, Dutch firms were particularly targeted. In the late 1950s, as the original leases to Dutch plantations expired, Indonesia nationalized Dutch plantation holdings, and Indonesian army officers served on the boards of the plantations to ensure the transfer of control to the Indonesian state. Ironically, labor actions became rare in the aftermath. Workers' resistance became impossible when Suharto seized control of Indonesia in the 1960s and violently stamped out left-leaning organizations, including labor unions. The US government supported Suharto's regime because he was virulently anti-communist. Goodyear and many other foreign firms maintained some of their plantations, profiting from the "stability" offered by the regime. Other plantations were sold off, however, as the risks of directly owning plantations now exceeded the rewards.

Britain similarly mobilized troops to maintain control of the Malaya peninsula, where rubber production offset the British empire's postwar trade deficit with the United States (in 1948, the dollar value of rubber production from Malaya exceeded the total value of *all* British domestic exports to the United States). In Malaya, Britain fought what has since become known as a "forgotten" and "dirty" protracted war with communist revolutionaries from 1948 to 1960. At the time, British officials referred to the ongoing military action as the "emergency," a term that allowed plantation owners to collect insurance payments for destruction (insurance policies did not provide protection during "time of war"). Opponents were dubbed communist "terrorists" or "bandits," labels that made insurgents' actions seem illegitimate and illegal:

As J. D. Higham, head of the Colonial Office's Eastern Department, noted in a letter in November 1948, "It has been decided that the criminal elements engaged in acts of violence in Malaya should be referred to as *bandits*. On no account should the term *insurgent*, which might suggest a genuine popular uprising, be used."[25]

Newsreels showed US and European publics how valiant British plantation managers struggled against "communist terrorists" and "bandits," the "unseen enemy" in Malaya.

Communist guerillas, sometimes supported by Chinese squatters on plantations, slashed rubber trees, attacked factories, and killed plantation staff. Dunlop alone estimated that 14,492 trees were slashed in 1950 and 16,715 in 1951; the company used as many as seventy armored vehicles by 1953.[26] By 1954, taking the rubber plantations as a whole, eighty-six planters had been killed, "of whom eighty-two were European, approximately seven percent of their number."[27] Britain deported some Chinese back to the mainland, even many who had lived on the Malay Peninsula for generations. That did not end the "emergency," however, as Tamils also resisted, and some joined communist and nationalist forces.

The "emergency" weakened Malayan communists, but ultimately strengthened the hand of Malayan nationalists as Britain prepared to hand over power. In 1957, an independent Federation of Malaya emerged and joined the British Commonwealth. In 1963, the states of Sabah and Sarawak on Borneo joined Malaya to create the Federation of Malaysia. In the early 1960s, most plantations remained in the hands of European staff, with profits going to investors. Over the next two decades, the number of British personnel slowly declined both in tin mines and on rubber plantations, as the Malaysian government took over many foreign, and especially British, firms in a process called "Malayanization." Much like Indonesia, Malaysia remains a major rubber producer, but plantations are largely in the hands of Malyasian nationals as the number of local smallholders continues to grow.

"Malaysian national" is itself a general term that hides the incredible ethnic diversity of the country, a diversity that results in large part from the vast plantations of the early twentieth century. In 1931, the population of British Malaya consisted of 1,934,900 "Malaysians" (which included Malay migrants from Java), 1,707,915 Chinese, and 623,224 Indians, so Chinese and Indians significantly outnumbered Malays.[28] While many Chinese small businesspeople already lived in Malaya before the arrival of the British, the recruitment of plantation laborers added huge populations of Chinese and Indian laborers, most of whom remained in the postwar years. The social and cultural divide between native Malays and the new immigrants remained vast, but Chinese and Tamil immigrant communities were equally distinct from each other. It is telling that nationalist movements in British Malaya included Chinese ones inspired by Chinese nationalists and communists, a Tamil one following the Indian National Congress and the creation of independent India, a Tamil one inspired by Tamil nationalists opposed to the Indian government, as well as a local Malayan one with nationalists fighting for an independent

Malaya dominated by Malays. After independence, Malaysia has of course struggled to integrate diverse populations that remained quite separate communities throughout the colonial era.

In French Indochina, Japanese forces had not invaded until early 1945 when the collaborationist Vichy government gradually collapsed. Advised by officials from the American Office of Strategic Services (the predecessor of the CIA) during World War II, the Vietnamese Independence League, the Viet Minh, fought the Japanese. When Japan surrendered, Viet Minh leader Ho Chi Minh issued a Vietnamese Declaration of Independence, directed against the French. Since the rubber plantations were in Cambodia and especially Cochinchina, or southern Vietnam, production recommenced after the war even while French forces fought the Viet Minh, largely in the north.

In Vietnam, rubber plantations actually fostered national unity. France had long divided French Indochina into Cambodia, Laos, Cochinchina, Annam, and Tonkin, an administrative stratagem that denied the legitimacy of Cambodian, Laotian, and Vietnamese nationalities and thus independent states. The movement of laborers from northern to southern Vietnam tended to reinforce the nationalist cause within the country, as people could recognize cultural and linguistic unity in opposition to the French. Rubber plantations became a symbol of French imperialism, and workers' resistance to planters and the French became a symbol of Vietnamese nationalism.

To an even greater extent than Indonesia or Malaysia, Vietnam got caught in the crosshairs of the Cold War. Concerned about Communist China as well as the Soviet Union, the United States bankrolled the French war effort. After a colossal French defeat at the Battle of Dien Bien Phu in 1954, the United States, increasingly worried that Vietnam would "fall" completely to communism, sponsored, advised, and then fought alongside the forces of South Vietnam, particularly after 1964. In South Vietnam, Vietnamese Communists sporadically attacked rubber plantations. Several plantations, including Michelin's, continued to produce rubber during the war in Vietnam. In the late 1960s, the Michelin plantation Dâu Tiêng was the site of battles between the VC and American troops. Today, the rubber plantation is a frequent stop, along with the Cu Chi Tunnels, on US veterans' tours of former battlefields. Of course, Michelin lost its plantations when North Vietnam won the war in 1975 and nationalized plantation holdings. The plantations are still in operation. Dâu Tiêng has developed into such an important icon of the struggle for Vietnamese national independence that it became, in 2011, the home of a small museum in the reconstructed laborers' barracks.

United Rubber Workers

Decolonization and independence occurred during the same post–World War II years in which European and American factory workers prospered because their labor unions succeeded after the 1930s. Consumer societies emerged in Europe as well as the United States, and many consumers bought cars and thus tires. Management met demand and cooperated with unions, largely avoiding conflict with pro-labor governments (of Democrats in the United States and of Social Democratic and Labor parties in Europe). In Europe, some labor unions in tire plants maintained ties to communist parties, thus to the parties that sided, at least in principle, with anti-colonial movements for independence. In the United States, the United Rubber Workers represented American workers; the "united" in the name referred to the unions that combined to form the URW, not any sort of global unity of international workers. Instead, as occurred across US industry, American rubber workers focused on their own wages and benefits, not international solidarity. During the Cold War, they could not and did not have any international or communist affiliation. Financially, US rubber workers did well, essentially joining the middle class, taking vacations, and often sending their children to college. However, the URW did not side with Vietnamese or other Southeast Asians fighting for independence. Instead, it focused on successful strikes and negotiations.

In the end, it was not decolonization or independence movements that disrupted US rubber workers' prosperity, but multinational tire manufacturers who sought non-union wages both in the US South and abroad. In the 1970s, US tire manufacturers foundered in meeting the challenge of Michelin, whose radial tires were a better product, getting better mileage and lasting longer; Michelin seemed the enemy to workers as well as managers. As the American war in Vietnam ended, there developed fascinating Akron myths about Michelin that circulate to this day. First, like some American soldiers, Akron workers claimed that Michelin made secret payments to the Viet Cong, an unproven charge that seems incredibly unlikely given the Michelin family's right-wing politics (payments instead went from the US government to Michelin as compensation for the rubber trees destroyed). Secondly, many Akron rubber workers believed that Michelin's success was due to its exploitation of the Vietnamese, as it was widely said that one "coolie" died for every rubber tree planted on a Michelin plantation—as if Goodyear and Firestone had not also established plantations with comparable working conditions. The charges are interesting. Just as much of the French public came to believe that the Americans were in the wrong in fighting in Vietnam, ignoring the French role there, some Americans criticized Michelin's role in imperialism as a way to undermine the company's image in the United States. In fact, American rubber workers cared a good deal more about threats to their middle-class lifestyles than about working conditions, anti-colonial resistance, or independence in Southeast Asia. Global connections do not necessarily lead to global solidarity.

READING

Describing Smallholders in the Dutch East Indies

Hugh Allen was the head of advertising at Goodyear. The following is his description of indigenous smallholders in the Dutch East Indies.

- How does he manage both to admit their achievements on one level and to belittle them on another?
- How does Allen manipulate longstanding stereotypes about "the native" to explain what would have been called "efficiency" were it practiced by an American or European?
- How might Allen reflect the views of European and American plantation owners, who needed to explain smallholder success without admitting that they produced rubber more efficiently, as efficiency was in their minds the preserve of plantations—and of Europeans?
- What does it mean that the smallholder "was not a businessman" but that his "challenge was that of numbers"?

It was the little brown man who in the end broke the British monopoly. He had no town sites to keep up, no payrolls to maintain, no managing directors. His overheads were zero, his tastes were simple, he had no tailor bills, no Scotch-and-soda chits, no sons to be educated in Europe, no daughters to be presented at court. Give him his holiday festivals and enough to eat and he was content. He was not a businessman, had no ambition to build an industrial empire. His challenge was that of numbers, of the vast areas of trees that he held.[29]

READING

Explaining Indigenous Resistance

Dutchwoman Madelon Lulofs lived in Sumatra in the 1920s and penned an autobiographical novel about life on a rubber plantation. Like fiction generally, for historians her book is less useful in its details than in the assumptions that she makes about people and their motives; that is, about the "mentalities" of Europeans as they viewed the "natives." Her report of an attack on a European assistant dehumanizes the attacker.

- Rather than explaining the laborer's action as a reaction to his own humiliation from a beating, how does Lulofs imply that there was something fundamentally primitive about him?

Her account begins with a discussion of the laborer's unwillingness to work and ends with the death of a European assistant; it is worth quoting at length because the complex context of the attack is in fact embedded in her narrative.

> As they walked, Jake [the European assistant] asked for particulars. Modestly, in accordance with custom, the mandur [overseer] walked two steps behind Jake while he told the story.
> "On the night of pay-day Tukimin gambled away all his money. He's a new coolie. Sir [*Tuan*, in Malay] knows him; he arrived with the last gang from Java. Yesterday he was quarreling all day. And last night the chief mandur beat him because he threatened [another] with a knife. And now he sits in front of his room and refuses to work."
> "Oh, does he?" said Jake. "He'll have to, though."…
> They walked into the compound….
> "Is your name Tukimin?"
> The coolie nodded with downcast eyes.
> "Answer!" said the mandur roughly.
> From beneath Tukimin's eyelids a sideways glance went out to Kassan [the mandur] and returned to the cover of the eyelids.
> "Is your name Tukimin?" repeated Jake.
> "Yes, Tuan."
> "Are you going to work or not?"
> The coolie remained silent.
> "Answer!" shouted the mandur, and again that same look appeared under the coolie's half-closed eyelids. It was a look full of hatred for the mandur. It darted back like the quick, pointed tongue of a serpent.
> "Will you work or not?" repeated Jake.
> "I will not work."
> "Why will you not work?"
> The coolie remained silent.
> "Answer!" shouted the mandur.
> Tukimin kept his eyelids down. He had allowed his sarong to drop a little, thus freeing one arm. He was drawing figures on the sand with his finger.
> "Why won't you work, Tukimin?"

Tukimin kept silent. The mandur, in whom a wild anger was beginning to seethe, stepped towards him. But Jake held him back with a gesture of the hand.

"You know you must work. You've signed the contract. All contractants are workmen. You have no right to refuse..... Will you work, Tukimin?" The coolie kept silent. Jake felt an impatience rise in him, but, controlling himself, he continued quietly: "Do not be foolish, Tukimin. Go to your work. Why will you not work?"

The coolie did not reply.

"Have you been gambling?"

The coolie did not reply.

"Come, get up and go to your work."

"I won't," said Tukimin darkly.

"Why won't you?"

The coolie kept silent. He had withdrawn his hand under his sarong.

"Stand up and go to your work."

Tukimin did not move.

"Did you hear what I said? Stand up and go to your work!... Tukimin," forcing himself to be calm, though he was trembling with nervous excitement, "Tukimin, listen to me. Go do your work."

The coolie did not move. Kassan could restrain himself no longer. A blind anger overpowered him. He approached the crouching form in one big step, bent down, took Tukimin's ear lobe between his thumb and finger, pinched and twisted it till it was almost white. Tukimin pulled himself free and half rose like an animal on the defensive. His eyes were mad with fury. He drew up his shoulders, dropped his sarong to the ground, and stood there challengingly, his body naked save for his short pants. The two men faced each other silently, and both felt a desire to kill. Jake moved Kassan aside.

"Go to your work at once. And now, by God, I've had enough of your nonsense. D'you understand me? Get on. To your work!"

Jake stepped threateningly towards the coolie. Tukimin stepped back. Jake took another step. Then, with a movement as quick as lightning, the coolie crouched down, drew his knife, and sprang at Jake. Kassan shouted, but it was too late. Without a word, Jake dropped down. A stream of blood gushed from his mouth. Kassan bent over him [and] lifted Jake's head from the ground. Another stream of blood washed over Kassan's hands. Then life left Jake's eyes and his head fell sideways....

Tukimin was crouching down again, indifferent, cool, almost unconscious. He had placed the bloody knife at his side. The primitive creature within him, which had been roused for a moment to sudden unreasonable and uncontrollable passion, had fallen asleep once more.

... Kassan picked up the knife.

"Get up and come with me to the office," he ordered Tukimin.

The coolie stood up without resistance, drew his sarong over his shoulders, and followed the mandur without a word, walking, in accordance with customary deference, two steps behind him. His instinct had had free run. His eye had been darkened and he had killed. That was all. It happened that this meant a clash between primitive ages and the twentieth century. He had taken the life of a fellow human-being, but it made no difference to him whether that human-being happened to be an assistant or a mandur. As for the fact that he was going to be hanged, he did not even think of it. He scarcely knew that there was a penalty. Vengeance he understood. Immediate punishment also. But imprisonment, a sentence in three or perhaps six months, by which time he would have forgotten what he had done, and especially why he had done it, that was altogether beyond his comprehension.[30]

Notes

1 Goodyear, *Wingfoot Clan*, 8, no. 19 (March 8, 1919): 8.
2 E. Delamarre, *L'émigration et l'immigration ouvrière en Indochine* (Exposition Coloniale Internationale, Paris 1931/Indochine Française/Section des Services d'Intérêt Social/Inspection Générale du Travail de l'Indochine) (Hanoi: Imprimerie d'Extrême Orient, 1931), p. 28.
3 H. Célarié, *Promenades en Indochine* (Paris: Editions Baudinière, 1937), p. 229.
4 Main d'oeuvre en Indochine, Procès-Verbal de la visite de la Plantation de Phú Riêng 2 mars 1928—première inspection, in FM 7 Affaires Economiques carton 25, Centre des Archives d'Outre Mer (CAOM).
5 Martin Thomas, *Violence and Colonial Order: Police, Workers and Protest in the European Colonial Empires, 1918–1940* (Cambridge: Cambridge University Press, 2012), p. 191.
6 W. Middendorp, *De Poenale Sanctie* (Haarlem: Tjeenk Willink, 1924), p. 4, cited in Stoler, *Capitalism*, p. 61.
7 Governor General of Indochina to the Minister of the Colonies in Paris, 5 June 1930, in CAOM FM INDO NF 2614.
8 Tran Tu Binh, *The Red Earth*, pp. 34–39. There also exists a petition from those laborers charged with killing Monteil that largely concurs with Tran Tu Binh's focus on abuses before the incident, reprinted in François Graveline, *Des hévéas et des hommes: L'aventure des plantations Michelin* (Paris: Editions Nicolas Chaudin, 2006), p. 48.
9 Stoler, *Capitalism*, pp. 87–88.
10 Report of the Incorporated Society of Planters of Malaya, 1934, in British National Archives CO/602/22.
11 Sûreté Générale, "Note au sujet des incidents qui sont produits les 16 et 17 décembre sur la plantation Michelin de Dâu Tiêng," 6 January 1933, in CAOM FM INDO NF 2616.
12 Governor General of Indochina to Minister of the Colonies in Paris, May 1937, CAOM FM INDO NF 2404.
13 Governor General of Indochina to Minister of the Colonies in Paris, 24 June 1937, in CAOM FM INDO NF 2404.

14 Tully, *Devil's Milk*, 270–272, citing "Labour Disputes in Malaya, Federal Council Minutes, Samson's report," in CO 273/632/9 Straits in the British National Archives.

15 Tully, *Devil's Milk*, pp. 276–277; Leong Yee Fong, *Labour and Trade Unionism in Colonial Malaya: A Study of the Socio-Economic and Political Bases of the Malayan Labour Movement, 1930–1957* (Pulau Pinang: Penerbit Universitii Sains Malaysia, 1999), pp. 86–90.

16 Tully, *Devil's Milk*, p. 191.

17 Michael R. Dove, *The Banana Tree at the Gate: A History of Marginal Peoples and Global Markets in Borneo* (New Haven, CT: Yale University Press, 2011), pp. 7, 135.

18 P. T. Bauer, *The Rubber Industry: A Study in Competition and Monopoly* (Cambridge, MA: Harvard University Press, 1948), p. 68; Colin Barlow "Changes in the Economic Position of Workers on Rubber Estates and Smallholders in Peninsular Malaysia, 1910–1985," in Peter J. Rimmer and Lisa M. Allen, eds. *The Underside of Malaysian History: Pullers, Prostitutes, Plantation Workers* (Singapore: Singapore University Press, 1990), p. 32.

19 Dove, *Banana Tree*, pp. 15, 163.

20 Dove, *Banana Tree*, p. 117 (picture on p. 118).

21 *The Evolution of the Rubber Industry in Malaysia: Navigating and Re-Inventing the Industry* (Kuala Lumpur: Malayan Rubber Board, 2005), p. 32; B. R. Mitchell, *International Historical Statistics: Africa, Asia, and Oceania* (New York: Palgrave-Macmillan, 2005), p. 279; Dove, *Banana Tree*, p. 90.

22 Stoler, *Capitalism*, pp. 105–106.

23 Christopher Bayly and Tim Harper, *Forgotten Wars: The End of Britain's Asian Empire* (London : Penguin, 2007), p. 421.

24 Stoler, *Capitalism*, pp. 147–148.

25 J. D. Higham. Assistant Secretary and Head of the Eastern Department, Colonial Office, to Mr. Blackburne, November 1948, BNA CO 537/4762, cited in Benjamin Grob-Fitzgibbon, *Imperial Endgame: Britain's Dirty Wars and the End of Empire* (New York: Palgrave Macmillan, 2011), pp. 116–117.

26 Dunlop, *The Plantation Courier: A Digest of Dunlop Activities* 53, no. 1 (1953): 9–13.

27 Letter from Rex Duncan, General Secretary and Treasurer of the Incorporated Society of Planters, Malaya to the editor of the *Straits Times* (19 July 1954), in BNA CO/1030/15.

28 Yee Fong, *Labour and Trade Unionism*, p. 318.

29 Typescript of the revised *House of Goodyear*, no page numbering, in Goodyear History, Box 2, University of Akron Archives.

30 Madelon H. Lulofs, *Rubber: A Romance of the Dutch East Indies*, trans. G. J. Renier and Irene Clephane (London: Cassell, 1933), pp. 193–198.

Conclusion: Forgetting and Remembering Rubber

In contrast with the first half of the twentieth century, the history of rubber is no longer well known. Rubber is now a commodity that is largely behind the scenes, in contexts where we take it for granted. As in the case of another former colonial commodity, cotton, few of us know who grows it, where, or how. Like sugar, rivaled by high-fructose corn syrup, natural rubber has stiff competition from a synthetically produced counterpart. Natural rubber is still present in industry, medicine, transportation, and the bedroom, in various forms. Conveyor belts, latex gloves, some tire sidewalls, and latex condoms continue to use natural rubber. Plantations still exist, although owners are rarely European or American rubber companies; international complaints about working conditions, political deals during civil unrest, and environmental degradation make Firestone's Liberia holdings a public relations disaster for the parent company Bridgestone-Firestone. Malaysian and Indonesian governments and individuals own most plantations in those countries. In Southeast Asia, Thai and Indonesian smallholders produce more rubber than do plantations. China produces more natural rubber all the time. Overall, rubber growers produce more natural rubber today, 12.2 million tons, than ever before (as compared to over 15.5 million tons of synthetic rubber produced each year).[1]

In an era of HIV/AIDS, it is especially ironic that natural rubber is little known today, as sales of natural rubber condoms have surged since the 1980s (arresting a slow decline, due to the advent of the contraceptive pill). Scientists now believe that HIV first made the jump from primates to humans in the early twentieth century in west central

A World History of Rubber: Empire, Industry, and the Everyday, First Edition.
Stephen L. Harp.
© 2016 John Wiley & Sons, Inc. Published 2016 by John Wiley & Sons, Inc.

Africa. The first well-documented case was in the Belgian Congo in the late 1950s, in an area of natural rubber exploitation since the late nineteenth century. Clinically identified in 1981 in the United States, HIV often spreads through sexual contact. Rubber condoms block transmission of the virus (the few condoms still made of sheep intestine, mostly for people with a latex allergy, have tiny pores through which the virus can pass). Increasingly, AIDS education campaigns publicly advocate condom use and make them easier to obtain. Nevertheless, many consumers still do not realize that condoms are almost always fabricated from natural, rather than synthetic, rubber. And few know where or how that rubber is grown.

Meanwhile, former "rubber cities" are known as such only by their inhabitants. Michelin produces comparatively few tires in Clermont-Ferrand. Once the largest and best-known "rubber city," Akron has virtually no tire production today. Multinational tire companies concentrated production where wages are lower and unions weak, nearly busting the once mighty United Rubber Workers. Akron is one of the many rust-belt cities, like Gary, Detroit, and Pittsburgh, long vulnerable to global competition. Old-timers talk nostalgically of glory days of abundant, well-paying factory jobs at Goodyear, Firestone, or Goodrich. Globalization usually takes the blame for the postindustrial landscape that remains, even though it had always been a global commodity chain that made so Akron prosperous in the first place. The city was never an island of good fortune disconnected from the rest of the world.

Why has the production of natural rubber, so well known to so many before and during World War II, been largely forgotten since? The wartime development of synthetic rubber is one reason. During and after the war, American rubber and petroleum companies trumpeted this triumph of modern chemistry. US success in producing synthetic rubber symbolized a widespread faith in American technological know-how. Chemicals were good, a symbol of American progress, at least until increased environmental consciousness by the 1970s (it is no coincidence that Chemlawn has now become TruGreen; as a word "chemical" had a mostly good reputation that has gone mostly bad in the popular consciousness). In practical terms, synthetic rubber diversified supplies, giving tire companies considerable leverage at the very time that the most important producers, Malaysia, Indonesia, and Vietnam, achieved independence. Natural rubber had to compete with synthetic in a global marketplace. Until the oil shocks of the 1970s petroleum was inexpensive, and synthetic rubber constituted up to three-quarters of global rubber production. In the recent run-up of oil prices in the twenty-first century, natural rubber has increased market share. Yet, in the popular imagination after World War II, especially in the United States, synthetic rubber replaced natural.

Knowledge of natural rubber also suffers from a broader colonial amnesia, particularly in Europe. Despite some remnant nostalgia for empire in Britain, France, and the Netherlands (as in the case of the film *Indochine* and the tales of Madame de la Souchère in Chapter 2), former imperial powers feature little public discussion of past empires. Decolonization in the 1950s and 1960s did not lead to a rethinking of global relations so much as a sort of collective amnesia about an uncomfortable history.[2] Tellingly, British, Dutch, and French school textbooks largely ignore the imperial pasts of each country, just as American schoolchildren learn little about both formal and informal American colonies, from the Philippines to Liberia. American participation in imperial exploitation, as was certainly the case with rubber, is also largely absent.

Moreover, advertising of rubber products does not encourage consumers to consider the impacts of production on laborers or the environment. Instead, consumers learn to associate their tires with speed as they watch automobile racing, or with safety as they watch television ads of babies riding around inside tires. In North American ads, the Michelin Man does not build tires so much as protect babies. In Europe, through the famous Michelin guidebooks, he serves as a helpful tour guide. Goodyear maintains blimps that have little to do with tires and nothing to do with the reality of the tire business. Goodyear has not really tried to defend itself publicly for paying manager Lily Ledbetter much less well than her male colleagues or attempting to rectify the inequality; by aggressively fighting her claim all the way to the US Supreme Court, the company helped to ensure Congressional passage of the Lily Ledbetter Fair Pay Act of 2009, facilitating lawsuits against unequal pay, however long ago the infraction occurred. Rather, Goodyear advertising focused on the performance and safety of its tires and kept its blimps hovering over racetracks and ball fields. For Goodyear and the others, company reputations float through the air untethered to the realities of production, namely the treatment of labor or the impacts of company operations on the environment. Goodyear's advertising is in no way unique. In advanced capitalism, mass media have had a way of making histories of labor and production disappear before our eyes. Products represent spectacular dream worlds. The commodity instead stands on its own, a veritable fetish, with its consumption disconnected from its production. In the end, it is no coincidence that the words "rubber" and "latex" today often suggest sex and sexual fetishes, just as the pick-up truck has become a fetish of perceived masculinity (strength, ruggedness) in the United States.

Realities of global production have a way of disappearing in the dreamscape of modern consumerism.

Finally, the history of rubber has also been actively obscured by company policies regarding their records. Government sources are widely accessible, as are those from agency houses, such as Harrisons & Crosfield's deposited at Guildhall Library in the City of London. However, the sources most lacking are company documents from the most important tire producers that also owned large plantations. Most Dunlop, Goodyear, and US Rubber records have not survived. While Firestone and Michelin, by contrast, have substantial archival holdings concerning their plantations, they continue to deny scholars access. No scholar receives permission to consult Firestone documents from Liberia, even though these are currently housed in the University of Akron Archives; like so many other students of history, I have awaited more than a decade and a half for a response to my requests to consult Firestone holdings. (For the discussion of Firestone in this book, I have used the Svend E. Holsoe Collection on Liberia at the Archives for Traditional Music at Indiana University Bloomington; an ethnomusicologist, Holsoe had access to Firestone documents before Bridgestone-Firestone limited scholarly access to its archives.) Publicity about Firestone's willingness to give strongman Charles Taylor run of its plantation during the Liberian civil war will likely make the company even more skittish about scholars.[3] Michelin is not much better, granting access only if projects will cast the company in a favorable light.[4] That is, of course, not something that serious historians can guarantee. Overall, unlike in the early twentieth century, when tire companies tried to mobilize the public to support government policies protecting their supply of rubber, today they would prefer that we forget the global commodity chain that spanned—and continues to span—from Southeast Asia and Africa to Europe and to North America.

That is too bad. The historical record does not always make anyone feel comfortable. Nevertheless, the study of history can challenge us to consider the complex legacies of the varieties of global exploitation and discrimination that have characterized our world. Ideally, confronting the realities of the past will make us wiser, better-informed global citizens in the future. I hope this book has helped to do just that.

Notes

1 2013 numbers from the International Rubber Study Group, at http://www.rubberstudy.com/documents/WebSiteData_3.0c.pdf, accessed July 28, 2014.

2 On the forgetting of the empire, see Ann Stoler, "Colonial Aphasia: Race and Disabled Histories in France," *Public Culture* 23, no. 1 (2011): 121–156; and Todd Shepard, *The Invention of Decolonization: The Algerian War and the Remaking of France* (Ithaca, NY: Cornell University Press, 2008).

3 T. Christian Miller and Jonathan Jones, "Firestone and the Warlord: The Untold Story of Firestone, Charles Taylor and the Tragedy of Liberia," November 18, 2014 on the Public Broadcasting System's *Frontline* program with an accompanying article on Propublica at https://www.propublica.org/article/firestone-and-the-warlord-intro, accessed December 6, 2014.

4 Even Eric Panthou, a trained historian and librarian in Michelin's hometown of Clermont-Ferrand, has been unable to gain access, instead piecing together some of the facts of Michelin's plantations from other sources: *Les plantations Michelin au Viêt-Nam: Le particularisme des plantations Michelin* (Clermont-Ferrand: Editions "La Galipote," 2013). Michelin did allow François Graveline (who is not a historian) some limited access for a nostalgic portrayal of Michelin plantations that resembles an early twentieth-century history of rubber, using terms like "adventure" to describe Europeans' experience there: *Des hévéas et des hommes: L'aventure des plantations Michelin* (Paris: Editions Nicolas Chaudin, 2006). Zambian historian Webby Silupya Kalikiti also received limited access, and his unpublished thesis argues unconvincingly that Michelin's plantations have been unfairly criticized both by contemporaries and by historians: "Plantation Labour: Rubber Planters and the Colonial State in French Indochina, 1890–1939," University of London School of Oriental and African Studies, 2000.

Suggested Readings

The following books and articles are a first step for further research, constituting a fraction of the relevant materials. Missing are printed primary sources, dissertations not yet in print, and many of the works not in English.

Adas, Michael. *Machines as the Measure of Men: Science, Technology, and Ideologies of Western Dominance*. Ithaca, NY: Cornell University Press, 1989.

Alatas, Syed Hussein. *The Myth of the Lazy Native: A Study of the Image of the Malays, Filipinos and Javanese from the 16th to the 20th Century and Its Function in the Ideology of Colonial Capitalism*. London: Frank Cass, 1977.

von Albertini, Rudolf, with Albert Wirz. *European Colonial Rule, 1880–1940: The Impact of the West on India, Southeast Asia, and Africa*. Westport, CT: Greenwood Press, 1982.

Allen, G.C., and Audrey G. Donnithorne. *Western Enterprise in Indonesia and Malaya: A Study in Economic Development*. New York: Augustus M. Kelley, 1968 [1954].

Allen, P.W. *Natural Rubber and the Synthetics*. New York: John Wiley & Sons, 1972.

Anstey, Roger. *King Leopold's Legacy: The Congo under Belgian Rule, 1908–1960*. London: Oxford, 1966.

Appadurai, Arjun, ed. *The Social Life of Things: Commodities in Cultural Perspective*. Cambridge: Cambridge University Press, 1986.

August, Thomas G. *The Selling of the Empire: British and French Imperialist Propaganda, 1890–1940*. Westport, CT: Greenwood Press, 1985.

Babcock, Glenn D. *A History of the United States Rubber Company: A Case Study in Corporation Management*. Bloomington, IN: Indiana University Graduate School of Business, 1966.

Barham, Bradford L., and Oliver T. Coomes, *Prosperity's Promise: The Amazon Rubber Boom and Distorted Economic Development*. Boulder, CO: Westview Press, 1996.

A World History of Rubber: Empire, Industry, and the Everyday, First Edition.
Stephen L. Harp.
© 2016 John Wiley & Sons, Inc. Published 2016 by John Wiley & Sons, Inc.

Barker, P.W. and E.G. Holt. *Rubber: History, Production, and Manufacture.* US Dept. of Commerce, Bureau of Foreign and Domestic Commerce. Washington, DC: United States Government Printing Office, 1940.

Barker, P.W. and E.G. Holt. *Rubber Industry of the United States, 1839–1939.* United States Department of Commerce, Bureau of Foreign and Domestic Commerce. Washington, DC: United States Government Printing Office, 1939.

Barlow, Colin. *The Natural Rubber Industry: Its Development, Technology, and Economy in Malaysia.* Kuala Lumpur: Oxford University Press, 1978.

Barlow, Colin, Sisira Jayasuriya, and C. Suan Tan. *The World Rubber Industry.* London: Routledge, 1994.

Bauer, P.T. *Report on a Visit to the Rubber Growing Smallholdings of Malaya, July–September 1946.* London: Colonial Office/His Majesty's Stationery Office, 1948.

Bauer, P.T. *The Rubber Industry: A Study in Competition and Monopoly.* Cambridge, MA: Harvard University Press, 1948.

Bayly, C.A. *The Birth of the Modern World, 1780–1914 : Global Connections and Comparisons.* London: Blackwell, 2004.

Bayly, Christopher, and Tim Harper. *Forgotten Wars: The End of Britain's Asian Empire.* Harmondsworth: Penguin, 2007.

Beckert, Sven. *Empire of Cotton: A Global History.* New York: Knopf, 2014.

Beisel, Nicola. *Imperiled Innocents: Anthony Comstock and Family Reproduction in Victorian America.* Princeton, NJ: Princeton University Press, 1997.

Binh, Tran Tu. *The Red Earth: A Vietnamese Memoir of Life on a Colonial Rubber Plantation.* Trans. by John Spragens. Edited by David G. Marr. Athens, OH: Ohio University Center of International Studies, 1985.

Black, Brian C. *Crude Reality: Petroleum in World History.* Lanham, MD: Rowman & Littlefield, 2012.

Blaszczyk, Regina Lee. *Imagining Consumers: Design and Innovation from Wedgwood to Corning.* Baltimore, MD: Johns Hopkins University Press, 2000.

Bloor, Janet, and John D. Sinclair. *Rubber: Fun, Fashion, Fetish.* London: Thames & Hudson, 2004.

Boisseau, Tracey Jean. *White Queen: May French-Sheldon and the Imperial Origins of American Feminist Identity.* Bloomington, IN: Indiana University Press, 2004.

Bonneuil, Christophe, and Mina Kleiche. *Du jardin d'essais colonial à la station expérimentale, 1880–1930: Éléments pour une histoire du CIRAD.* Paris: CIRAD, 1993.

Boomgaard, Peter, and Ian Brown, eds. *Weathering the Storm: The Economies of Southeast Asia in the 1930s Depression.* Leiden: KITLV Press/Singapore: Institute of Southeast Asian Studies, 2000.

Borkin, Daniel. *The Crime and Punishment of IG Farben.* New York: Free Press, 1978.

Boucheret, Marianne. "Le pouvoir colonial et la question de la main d'oeuvre en Indochine dans les années vingt." *Cahiers d'histoire: Revue d'histoire critique.* 85 (2001): 29–55.

Boucheret, Marianne. "Les organisations de planteurs de caoutchouc indochinois et l'état du début du XXe siècle à la veille de la Seconde Guerre Mondiale." In *L'esprit économique imperial (1830–1970): Groupes de pression et réseaux du patronat colonial en France et dans l'empire.* Edited by Hubert

Bonin, Catherine Hodeir, and Jean-François Klein. Publications de la Société française d'histoire d'outre-mer, 2008, pp. 715–733.

Boulle, Pierre. *Sacrilege in Malaya*. Trans. by Xan Fielding. Kuala Lumpur: Oxford University Press, 1983.

Bouvier, René. *Le caoutchouc: Brillante et dramatique histoire de l'hévéa*. Paris: Flammarion, 1947.

Bradley, Mark Philip. *Imagining Vietnam and America: The Making of Postcolonial Vietnam, 1919–1950*. Chapel Hill: UNC Press, 2000.

Brandes, Joseph. *Herbert Hoover and Economic Diplomacy: Department of Commerce Policy, 1921–1928*. Pittsburgh, PA: University of Pittsburgh Press, 1962.

Brauer, Norman. *There to Breathe the Beauty: The Camping Trips of Henry Ford, Thomas Edison, Harvey Firestone, John Burroughs*. Dalton, PA: Norman Brauer Publications, 1995.

Breman, Jan. *Taming the Coolie Beast: Plantation Society and the Colonial Order in Southeast Asia*. Delhi: Oxford University Press, 1989.

Brinkley, Douglas. *Wheels for the World: Henry Ford, His Company, and a Century of Progress, 1903–2003*. New York: Viking Penguin, 2003.

Brocheux, Pierre. "Le prolétariat des plantations d'hévéas au Vietnam méridional: Aspects sociaux et politiques (1927–1937)." *Movement social* 90 (January–March 1975): 54–86.

Brocheux, Pierre. *The Mekong Delta: Ecology, Economy, and Revolution, 1860–1960*. Madison, WI: University of Wisconsin Center for Southeast Asian Studies, 1995.

Brocheux, Pierre, and Daniel Hémery. *Indochine: La colonisation ambiguë (1858–1954)*. Paris: Editions La Découverte, 1995.

Brockway, Lucile H. *Science and Colonial Expansion: The Role of the British Royal Botanic Gardens*. New York: Academic Press, 1979.

Brodie, Janet Farrell. *Contraception and Abortion in Nineteenth-Century America*. Ithaca, NY: Cornell University Press, 1994.

Brown, Rajeswary Ampalavanar. *Capital and Entrepreneurship in South-East Asia*. New York: St. Martin's, 1994.

Bullough, Vern L. "A Brief Note on Rubber Technology and Contraception: The Diaphragm and the Condom." *Technology and Culture* 22 (1981): 104–111.

Burbank, Jane, and Frederick Cooper. *Empires in World History: Power and the Politics of Difference*. Princeton, NJ: Princeton University Press, 2010.

Burleigh, Michael. *Small Wars, Far Away Places: The Genesis of the Modern World, 1945–65*. London: Macmillan, 2013.

Butcher, John G. *The British in Malaya, 1880–1941: The Social History of a European Community in Colonial South-East Asia*. Kuala Lumpur: Oxford University Press, 1979.

Chakrabarty, Dipesh. *Provincializing Europe: Postcolonial Thought and Historical Difference*. Princeton, NJ: Princeton University Press, 2000.

Chandler, Alfred D. *The Visible Hand: The Managerial Revolution in American Business*. Cambridge, MA: Harvard University Press, 1977.

Clancy-Smith, Julia, and Frances Gouda, eds. *Domesticating the Empire: Race, Gender, and Family Life in French and Dutch Colonialism*. Charlottesville, VA: University Press of Virginia, 1998.

Clarence-Smith, William. "The Rivaud-Hallet Plantation Group in the Economic Crises of the Inter-War Years." In *Private Enterprises during Economic Crises: Tactics and Strategies*. Edited by Pierre Lanthier and Hubert Watelet. Ottawa: Legas, 1997, pp. 117–132.

Clarence-Smith, William. "La SOCFIN (Groupe Rivaud) entre l'Axe et les Alliés." In *Les Entreprises et l'outre-mer français pendant la Seconde Guerre Mondiale*. Edited by Hubert Bonin, Christophe Bouneau, and Hervé Joly. Pessac: Maison des Sciences de l'Homme d'Aquitaine, 2010, pp. 99–113.

Clarence-Smith, William. "The Portuguese Empire and the 'Battle for Rubber' in the Second World War." *Portuguese Studies Review*, 19, nos. 1–2 (2011): 177–196.

Clarence-Smith, William. "The Battle for Rubber in the Second World War: Cooperation and Resistance." In *Global Histories, Imperial Commodities, Local Interactions*. Edited by Jonathan Curry-Machado. Basingstoke: Palgrave Macmillan, 2013, pp. 204–223.

Clarence-Smith, William. "Rubber Cultivation in Indonesia and the Congo from the 1910s to the 1950s: Divergent Paths." In *Colonial Exploitation and Economic Development: The Belgian Congo and the Netherlands Indies Compared*. Edited by Ewout Frankema and Frans Buelens. London: Routledge, 2013, pp. 193–210.

Clements, Kendrick A. *Hoover, Conservation, and Consumerism: Engineering the Good Life*. Lawrence, KS: University Press of Kansas, 2000.

Cline, Catherine Ann. *E. D. Morel, 1873–1924: The Strategies of Protest*. Belfast: Blackstaff Press, 1980.

Coates, Austin. *The Commerce in Rubber: The First 250 Years* (Commissioned by the Singapore International Chamber of Commerce Rubber Association). Singapore: Oxford University Press, 1987.

Comber, Leon. *Malaya's Secret Police, 1945–60: The Role of the Special Branch in the Malayan Emergency*. Monash, Australia: Monash Asia Institute/Singapore: ISEAS, 2008.

Compagnon, P. *Le caoutchouc naturel: Biologie, culture, production*. Paris: Editions G.P. Maisonneuve et Larose, 1986.

Conklin, Alice L. *A Mission to Civilize: The Republican Idea of Empire in France and West Africa, 1895–1930*. Stanford, CA: Stanford University Press, 1997.

Constantine, Stephen. *Buy and Build: The Advertising Posters of the Empire Marketing Board*. London: Her Majesty's Stationery Office, 1986.

Cook, Hera. *The Long Sexual Revolution: English Women, Sex, and Contraception, 1800–1975*. New York: Oxford University Press, 2004.

Cooper, Frederick, and Ann Laura Stoler, eds. *Tensions of Empire: Colonial Cultures in a Bourgeois World*. Berkeley, CA: University of California Press, 1997.

Cooper, Nicola. *France in Indochina: Colonial Encounters*. Oxford: Berg, 2001.

Coquéry-Vidrovitch, Catherine. *Le Congo au temps des grandes compagnies concessionnaires, 1898–1930*. Paris: Mouton, 1972.

Costello, John. *Love, Sex, and War: Changing Values, 1939–45*. London: Collins, 1985.

Courtwright, David T. *Forces of Habit: Drugs and the Making of the Modern World*. Cambridge, MA: Harvard University Press, 2001.

Curry-Machado, Jonathan, ed. *Global Histories, Imperial Commodities, Local Interactions*. New York: Palgrave Macmillan, 2013.

Curtin, Philip D. *Cross-Cultural Trade in World History*. Cambridge: Cambridge University Press, 1984.

Curtin, Philip D. *The World and the West: The European Challenge and the Overseas Response in the Age of Empire*. Cambridge: Cambridge University Press, 2000.

Daughton, J.P. "Behind the Imperial Curtain: International Humanitarian Efforts and the Critique of French Colonialism in the Interwar Years." *French Historical Studies* 34, no. 3 (Summer 2011): 503–528.

Daunton, Martin, and Matthew Hilton, eds. *The Politics of Consumption: Material Culture and Citizenship in Europe and America*. Oxford: Berg, 2001.

Davis, Donald Finlay. *Conspicuous Production: Automobiles and Elites in Detroit, 1899–1933*. Philadelphia, PA: Temple University Press, 1988.

D'Emilio, John, and Estelle B. Freedman. *Intimate Matters: A History of Sexuality in America*. New York: Harper & Row, 1988.

Dean, Warren. *Brazil and the Struggle for Rubber: A Study in Environmental History*. Cambridge: Cambridge University Press, 1987.

Dorgelès, Roland. *Sur la route mandarine*. Paris: Albin Michel, 1925.

Douglas, Mary, and Baron Isherwood. *The World of Goods: Towards an Anthropology of Consumption*. London: Routledge, 1996 [1979].

Dove, Michael R. *Swidden Agriculture in Indonesia: The Subsistence Strategies of the Kalimantan Kantu'*. Berlin: Mouton, 1985.

Dove, Michael R. *The Banana Tree at the Gate: A History of Marginal Peoples and Global Markets in Borneo*. New Haven, CT: Yale University Press, 2011.

Drabble, J.H. *Rubber in Malaya, 1876–1922: The Genesis of the Industry*. Kuala Lumpur: Oxford University Press, 1973.

Drabble, John H. *Malayan Rubber: The Interwar Years*. London: Macmillan, 1991.

Duiker, William J. *The Rise of Nationalism in Vietnam, 1900–1941*. Ithaca, NY: Cornell University Press, 1976.

Edgar, A.T. *Manual of Rubber Planting (Malaya)*. Kuala Lumpur: Incorporated Society of Planters, 1958.

Erker, Paul. *Wachsen im Wettbewerb: Eine Zeitgeschichte der Continental Aktiengesellschaft (1971–1996)*. Düsseldorf: Econ, 1996.

Erker, Paul. *Vom nationalen zum globalen Wettbewerb: Die deutsche und die amerikanische Reifenindustrie im 19. und 20. Jahrhundert*. Paderborn: Ferdinand Schöningh, 2005.

Ewen, Stuart. *Captains of Consciousness: Advertising and the Social Roots of the Consumer Culture*. New York: McGraw-Hill, 1976.

Ewen, Stuart. *All Consuming Images: The Politics of Style in Contemporary Culture*. New York: Basic Books, 1988.

Fauconnier, Henri. *The Soul of Malaya*. Trans. by Eric Sutton. Singapore: Archipelago Press, 1983 [1931].

Fenichell, Stephen. *Plastic: The Making of a Synthetic Century*. New York: HarperCollins, 1996.

Ferro, Marc, ed. *Le livre noir du colonialisme: XVIe–XXIe siècle: de l'extermination à la repentance*. Paris: Robert Laffont, 2003.

Fieldhouse, D.K. *The West and the Third World: Trade, Colonialism, Dependence, and Development*. Oxford: Blackwell, 1999.

Figart, David M. *The Plantation Rubber Industry in the Middle East*. Department of Commerce, Trade Promotion Series no. 2, Crude Rubber Survey. Washington, DC: Government Printing Office, 1925.

Filene, Peter G. *Him/Her/Self: Sex Roles in Modern America*. Baltimore, MD: Johns Hopkins University Press, 1986 [1974].

Findlay, Eileen J. *Imposing Decency: The Politics of Sexuality and Race in Puerto Rico, 1870–1920*. Durham, NC: Duke University Press, 1999.

Finlay, Mark R. *Growing American Rubber: Strategic Plants and the Politics of National Security*. New Brunswick, NJ: Rutgers University Press, 2009.

Firchow, Peter Edgerly. *Envisioning Africa: Racism and Imperialism in Conrad's* Heart of Darkness. Lexington, KT: University Press of Kentucky, 2000.

Firestone. *Pioneer and Pacemaker: The Story of Firestone*. Akron, OH: Firestone Tire and Rubber Company, n.d.

Firestone Plantations Company. *Liberia and Firestone: The Development of a Rubber Industry, A Story of Friendship and Progress*. Harbel, Liberia and Akron, OH: Firestone Plantations Company, n.d. (but at least after 1952).

Firestone, Harvey S., Jr. *The Romance and Drama of the Rubber Industry*. Akron, OH: Firestone Tire and Rubber Company, 1932.

Firestone, Harvey S., Jr. *Man on the Move: The Story of Transportation*. New York: G.P. Putnam's Sons, 1967.

Flink, James J. *The Automobile Age*. Cambridge, MA: MIT Press, 1988.

Foster, Anne L. *Projectons of Power: The United States and Europe in Colonial Southeast Asia, 1919–1941*. Durham, NC : Duke University Press, 2010.

Fox, Richard Wightman, and T.J. Jackson Lears. *The Culture of Consumption: Critical Essays in American History, 1880–1980*. New York: Pantheon, 1983.

Fox, Stephen. *The Mirror Makers: A History of American Advertising and Its Creators*. New York: William Morrow, 1984.

Frank, Zephyr, and Aldo Musacchio. "Brazil in the International Rubber Trade." In *From Silver to Cocaine: Latin American Commodity Chains and the Building of the World Economy, 1500–2000*. Edited by Steven Topik, Carlos Marichal, and Zephyr Frank. Durham, NC: Duke University Press, 2006, pp. 271–299.

Franzke, Lothar. *Vom Kautschuk zum Buna*. Berlin: Wilhelm Limpert Verlag, 1939.

Frémeaux, Jacques. *Les empires coloniaux dans le processus de mondialisation*. Paris: Maisonneuve et Larose, 2002.

French, Michael. "Structure, Personality, and Business Strategy in the U.S. Tire Industry: The Seiberling Rubber Company, 1922–1964." *Business History Review* 67 (Summer 1993): 246–278.

Fridenson, Patrick. "French Automobile Marketing, 1890–1979." In *International Conference on Business History 7: Development of Mass Marketing: The Automobile and Retailing Industries*. Edited by Akio Okochi and Koichi Shimokawa. Tokyo: University of Tokyo Press, 1981, pp. 127–154.

Fridenson, Patrick. "Some Economic and Social Effects of Motor Vehicles in France since 1890." *The Economic and Social Effects of the Spread of Motor*

Vehicles: An International Centenary Tribute. Edited by Theo Barker. London: Macmillan, 1987, pp. 130–147.

Friedel, Robert. *Pioneer Plastic: The Making and Selling of Celluloid.* Madison, WI: University of Wisconsin Press, 1983.

Galambos, Louis. *The Public Image of Big Business in America, 1880–1940.* Baltimore, MD: Johns Hopkins University Press, 1975.

Galang, Francisco G. *The Rubber Industry in the Middle East.* Government of the Philippine Islands; Department of Agriculture and Natural Resources, Bureau of Agriculture, Manila. Manila: Bureau of Printing, 1925.

Galey, John. "Industrialist in the Wilderness: Henry Ford's Amazon Venture." In *Henry Ford: Critical Evaluations in Business and Management,* vol. 2. Edited by John C. Wood and Michael C. Wood. London: Routledge, 2003, pp. 357–365.

Gareffi, Gary, and Miguel Korzeniewicz, eds. *Commodity Chains and Global Capitalism.* Westport, CT: Greenwood Press, 1994.

Gide, André. *Travels in the Congo.* Trans. by Dorothy Bussy. Hopewell, NJ: Ecco Press, 1994 [1929].

Giles-Vernick, Tamara. *Cutting the Vines of the Past: Environmental Histories of the Central African Rain Forest.* Charlottesville, VA: University of Virginia Press, 2002.

Goddard, Stephen B. *Getting There: The Epic Struggle between Road and Rail in the American Century.* New York: Basic Books, 1994.

Goodman, Jordan. *The Devil and Mr. Casement: One Man's Battle for Human Rights in South America's Heart of Darkness.* New York: Farrar, Strauss, and Giroux, 2009.

Gordon, Linda. *The Moral Property of Women: A History of Birth Control Politics in America.* Urbana, IL: University of Illinois Press, 2002.

Gouda, Frances. *Dutch Culture Overseas: Colonial Practice in the Netherlands Indies, 1900–1942.* Amsterdam: Amsterdam University Press, 1995.

Gould, James W. *Americans in Sumatra.* The Hague: Martinus Nijhoff, 1961.

Grandin, Greg. *Fordlandia: The Rise and Fall of Henry Ford's Forgotten Jungle City.* New York: Metropolitan Books/Henry Holt, 2009.

Grant, Kevin. *A Civilised Savagery: Britain and the New Slaveries in Africa, 1884–1926.* New York: Routledge, 2005.

Greenhalgh, Paul. *Ephemeral Vistas: The Expositions Universelles, Great Exhibitions and World's Fairs, 1851–1939.* Manchester: Manchester University Press, 1988.

Grossmann, Atina. *Reforming Sex: The German Movement for Birth Control and Abortion Reform, 1920–1950.* New York: Oxford University Press, 1995.

Gueslin, André, ed. *Michelin, Les hommes du pneu: Les ouvriers Michelin, à Clermont-Ferrand, de 1889 à 1940.* Paris: Les Editions de l'Atelier/Editions Ouvrières, 1993.

Gueslin, André, ed. *Les hommes du pneu: Les ouvriers Michelin à Clermont-Ferrand de 1940 à 1980.* Paris: Les Editions de l'Atelier/Editions Ouvrières, 1999.

Harms, Robert W. "The End of Red Rubber: A Reassessment." *Journal of African History* 16 (1975): 73–88.

Harp, Stephen L. *Marketing Michelin: Advertising and Cultural Identity in Twentieth-Century France*. Baltimore, MD: Johns Hopkins University Press, 2001.

Harper, T.N. *The End of Empire and the Making of Malaya*. Cambridge: Cambridge University Press, 1999.

Headrick, Daniel R. *The Tools of Empire: Technology and European Imperialism in the Nineteenth Century*. New York: Oxford University Press, 1981.

Headrick, Daniel R. *The Tentacles of Progress: Technology Transfer in the Age of Imperialism, 1850–1940*. New York: Oxford University Press, 1988.

Hochschild, Adam. *King Leopold's Ghost: A Story of Greed, Terror, and Heroism in Colonial Africa*. Boston, MA: Houghton Mifflin, 1998.

Hodeir, Catherine, and Michel Pierre. *1931: L'exposition coloniale*, Paris: Editions Complexe, 1991.

Hodeir, Catherine. *Stratégies d'empire: Le grand patronat colonial face à la décolonisation*. Paris: Belin, 2003.

Hoff Wilson, Joan. *Herbert Hoover: Forgotten Progressive*. Boston, MA: Little, Brown, 1975.

Hoganson, Kristin. "Cosmopolitan Domesticity: Importing the American Dream, 1865–1920." *AHR* 107, no. 1 (February 2002): 55–83.

Hokanson, Drake. *The Lincoln Highway: Main Street across America*. Iowa City, IA: University of Iowa Press, 1988.

Horowitz, Roger, ed. *Boys and Their Toys? Masculinity, Technology, and Class in America*. New York: Routledge, 2001.

Horowitz, Roger, and Arwen Mohun, eds. *His and Hers: Gender, Consumption, and Technology*. Charlottesville, VA: University Press of Virginia, 1998.

Houben, Vincent J.H., and J. Thomas Lindblad et al. *Coolie Labour in Colonial Indonesia: A Study of Labour Relations in the Outer Islands*. Wiesbaden: Harrassowitz Verlag, 1999.

Hounshell, David A. *From the American System to Mass Production, 1800–1932: The Development of Manufacturing Technology in the United States*. Baltimore, MD: Johns Hopkins University Press, 1984.

Jackson, James C. *Planters and Speculators: Chinese and European Agricultural Enterprise in Malaya, 1786–1921*. Kuala Lumpur: University of Malaya Press, 1968.

Jackson, Joe. *The Thief at the End of the World: Rubber, Power and the Seeds of Empire*. New York: Viking, 2009.

Jain, Ravindra K. *South Indians on the Plantation Frontier in Malaya*. New Haven, CT: Yale University Press, 1970.

Jennings, Eric. *Imperial Heights: Dalat and the Making and Undoing of French Indochina*. Berkeley, CA: University of California Press, 2011.

Jennings, Eric. *Free French Africa in World War II: The African Resistance*. Cambridge: Cambridge University Press, 2015.

Jeffreys, Diarmuid. *Hell's Cartel: IG Farben and the Making of Hitler's War Machine*. New York: Metropolitan Books/Henry Holt, 2008.

Jewell, K. Sue. *From Mammy to Miss America and Beyond: Cultural Images and the Shaping of US Social Policy*. London: Routledge, 1993.

Johnson, Charles S. *Bitter Canaan: The Story of the Negro Republic*. New Brunswick, NJ: Transaction Books, 1987.

Suggested Readings

Johnston, Louise. "Tuskegee in Liberia: The Politics of Industrial Education, 1927–1935." *Liberian Studies Journal* 9, no. 2 (1980–81): 61–68.

Jones, E.L. *The European Miracle: Environments, Economies, and Geopolitics in the History of Europe and Asia.* Cambridge: Cambridge University Press, 1981.

Jones, Geoffrey. "The Multinational Expansion of Dunlop, 1890–1939." In *British Multinationals: Origins, Management and Performance.* Edited by Geoffrey Jones. Aldershot: Gower, 1986, pp. 24–42.

Jones, Geoffrey. *Merchants to Multinationals: British Trading Companies in the Nineteenth and Twentieth Centuries.* Oxford: Oxford University Press, 2000.

Jones, Geoffrey, and Judith Wale. "Merchants as Business Groups: British Trading Companies in Asia before 1945." *Business History Review* 72 (Autumn 1998): 367–408.

Kaur, Amarjit. *Wage Labour in Southeast Asia since 1840: Globalisation, the International Division of Labour and Labour Transformation.* New York: Palgrave Macmillan, 2004.

Kidd, Alan, and David Nicholls, eds. *Gender, Civic Culture, and Consumerism: Middle-Class Identity in Britain, 1800–1940.* Manchester: Manchester University Press, 1999.

Kirsch, David A. *The Electric Vehicle and the Burden of History.* New Brunswick, NJ: Rutgers University Press, 2000.

Klippert, Walter E. *Reflections of a Rubber Planter: The Autobiography of an Inquisitive Person.* New York: Vantage Press, 1972.

Knoll, Arthur J. "Harvey S. Firestone's Liberian Investment (1922–1932)." *Liberian Studies Journal* 14, no. 1 (1989): 13–33.

Knoll, Arthur J. "Firestone's Labor Policy, 1924–1939." *Liberian Studies Journal* 16, no. 2 (1991): 49–75.

Krasner, Stephen D. *Defending the National Interest: Raw Materials Investments and U.S. Foreign Policy.* Princeton, NJ: Princeton University Press, 1978.

Lai, Walton Look. *Indentured Labor, Caribbean Sugar: Chinese and Indian Migrants to the British West Indies, 1838–1918.* Baltimore, MD: Johns Hopkins University Press, 1993.

Laird, Pamela Walker. *Advertising Progress: American Business and the Rise of Consumer Marketing.* Baltimore, MD: Johns Hopkins University Press, 1998.

Lamy, Christian, and Jean-Pierre Fornaro. *Michelin-Ville: Le logement ouvrier de l'entreprise Michelin, 1911–1987.* Nonette: Créer, 1990.

Leach, William. *Land of Desire: Merchants, Power, and the Rise of a New American Culture.* New York: Pantheon Books, 1993.

Lears, T.J. Jackson. *Fables of Abundance: A Cultural History of Advertising in America.* New York: Basic Books, 1994.

Leathard, Audrey. *The Fight for Family Planning: The Development of Family Planning Services in Britain, 1921–74.* London: Macmillan, 1980.

Lemire, Beverly. *Fashion's Favourite: The Cotton Trade and the Consumer in Britain, 1660–1800.* Oxford: Oxford University Press, 1991.

Lerman, Nina E., Arwen Palmer Mohun, and Ruth Oldenziel. "Versatile Tools: Gender Analysis and the History of Technology." *Technology and Culture* 38 (1997): 1–8.

Lewis, Martin W., and Kären E. Wigan. *The Myth of Continents: A Critique of Metageography.* Berkeley, CA: University of California Press, 1997.

Lewis, William Roger. *Imperialism at Bay: The United States and the Decolonization of the British Empire, 1941–1945.* New York: Oxford University Press, 1978.

Liauzu, Claude. *Aux origines des tiers-mondismes: Colonisés et anticolonialistes en France (1919–1939).* Paris: L'Harmattan, 1982.

Lief, Alfred. *The Firestone Story: A History of the Firestone Tire and Rubber Company.* New York: McGraw-Hill, 1951.

Lief, Alfred. *Harvey Firestone: Free Man of Enterprise.* New York: McGraw-Hill, 1951.

Lim Teck Ghee. *Peasants and Their Agricultural Economy in Colonial Malaya, 1874–1941.* Kuala Lumpur: Oxford University Press, 1977.

Litchfield, P.W. *Industrial Voyage: My Life as an Industrial Lieutenant.* Garden City, NY: Doubleday, 1954.

Loadman, John. *Tears of the Tree: The Story of Rubber, A Modern Marvel.* Oxford: Oxford University Press, 2005.

Loadman, John, and Francis James. *The Hancocks of Marlborough: Rubber, Art, and the Industrial Revolution, A Family of Inventive Genius.* Oxford: Oxford University Press, 2010.

Long, Ngo Vinh. *Before the Revolution: The Vietnamese Peasants under the French.* Cambridge, MA: MIT Press, 1973.

Look Lai, Walton. *Indentured Labor, Caribbean Sugar: Chinese and Indian Migrants to the British West Indies, 1838–1918.* Baltimore, MD: Johns Hopkins University Press, 1993.

Lorcin, Patricia M.E. *Historicizing Colonial Nostalgia: European Women's Narratives of Algeria and Kenya, 1900–Present.* New York: Palgrave Macmillan, 2012.

Louis, William Roger, and Jean Stengers. *E.D. Morel's History of the Congo Reform Movement.* Oxford: Clarendon Press, 1968.

Love, Steve, and David Giffels. *Wheels of Fortune: The Story of Rubber in Akron.* Akron, OH: University of Akron Press, 1999.

Lulofs, Madelon H. *Rubber: A Romance of the Dutch East Indies.* Trans. by G. J. Renier and Irene Clephane. London: Cassell, 1933.

Lulofs, Madelon. *Coolie.* Trans. by F.J. Renier and Irene Clephane. New York: Viking Press, 1936.

MacDonald, Robert H. *The Language of Empire: Myths and Metaphors of Popular Imperialism, 1880–1918.* Manchester: Manchester University Press, 1994.

Mansvelt, W.M.F., and P. Creutzberg. *Changing Economy in Indonesia: A Selection of Statistical Source Material from the Early 19th Century up to 1940. Vol. 1, Indonesia's Export Crops 1816–1940.* The Hague: Nijhoff, 1975.

Marchal, Jules. *E.D. Morel contre Léopold II: L'histoire du Congo, 1900–1910.* 2 vols. Paris: Editions L'Harmattan, 1996.

Marchal, Jules. *L'état libre du Congo, paradis perdu: L'histoire du Congo, 1876–1900.* 2 vols. Borgloon, Belgium: Editions Paula Bellings, 1996.

Marchand, Roland. *Advertising the American Dream: Making Way for Modernity, 1920–1940.* Berkeley, CA: University of California Press, 1985.

Marshall, Jonathan. *To Have and Have Not: Southeast Asian Raw Materials and the Origins of the Pacific War.* Berkeley, CA: University of California Press, 1995.

Suggested Readings

Mason, Peter. *Cauchu, the Weeping Wood: A History of Rubber.* Sydney: Australian Broadcasting Commission, 1979.

McClintock, Anne. *Imperial Leather: Race, Gender, and Sexuality in the Colonial Contest.* New York: Routledge, 1995.

McConnell, Curt. *Coast to Coast by Automobile: The Pioneering Trips, 1899–1908.* Stanford, CA: Stanford University Press, 2000.

McFadyean, Andrew, ed. *The History of Rubber Regulation, 1934–1943.* London: International Rubber Regulation Committee, 1944.

McMillan, James. *The Dunlop Story: The Life, Death and Re-Birth of a Multinational.* London: Weidenfeld and Nicolson, 1989.

McShane, Clay. *Down the Asphalt Path: The Automobile in the American City.* New York: Columbia University Press, 1994.

Meikle, Jeffrey L. *American Plastic: A Cultural History.* New Brunswick, NJ: Rutgers University Press, 1995.

Michon, Michel-Maurice. *Souvenirs d'un monde disparu: Les plantations de caoutchouc (Viet-Nam, Cambodge, 1956-1972).* Paris: La Pensée Universelle, 1987.

Miller, Michael B. *Europe and the Maritime World: A Twentieth-Century History.* Cambridge: Cambridge University Press, 2012.

Mills, Charles W. *The Racial Contract.* Ithaca, NY: Cornell, 1997.

Mintz, Sidney W. *Sweetness and Power: The Place of Sugar in Modern History.* New York: Penguin, 1985.

Morel, E.D. *The Scandal of the Congo: Britain's Duty.* Liverpool: J. Richardson, 1904.

Morel, E.D. *Red Rubber: The Story of the Rubber Slave Trade Flourishing on the Congo in the Year of Grace 1906.* New York: Haskell House, 1970 [1906].

Morris, Peter J.T. *The American Synthetic Rubber Research Program.* Philadelphia, PA: University of Pennsylvania Press, 1989.

Moulin-Bourret, Annie. *Guerre et industrie: Clermont-Ferrand (1912–1922): La victoire du pneu.* 2 vols. Clermont-Ferrand: Publications de l'Institut d'Etudes du Massif Central, 1997.

Moutet, Aimée. *Les logiques de l'entreprise: La rationalisation dans l'industrie française de l'entre-deux-guerres.* Paris: Editions de l'EHESS, 1997.

Moyn, Samuel. *The Last Utopia: Human Rights in History.* Cambridge, MA: Harvard University Press, 2010.

Murray, Martin J. *The Development of Capitalism in Colonial Indochina (1870–1940).* Berkeley, CA: University of California Press, 1980.

Musgrave, Toby and Will Musgrave. *An Empire of Plants: People and Plants That Changed the World.* London: Cassell, 2000.

Nelson, Samuel H. *Colonialism in the Congo Basin, 1880–1940.* Athens, OH: Ohio University Center for International Studies, 1994.

Northrup, David. *Indentured Labor in the Age of Imperialism, 1834–1922.* Cambridge: Cambridge University Press, 1995.

O'Connell, Sean. *The Car and British Society: Class, Gender, and Motoring, 1896–1939.* Manchester: Manchester University Press, 1998.

Oldenziel, Ruth. *Making Technology Masculine: Men, Women, and Modern Machines in America, 1870–1945.* Amsterdam: Amsterdam University Press, 1999.

de Padirac, Raymond. *L'Institut de Recherches sur le Caoutchouc, 1936–1984.* Paris: CIRAD, 1993.

Panthou, Eric. *Les plantations Michelin au Viêt-Nam: Le particularisme des plantations Michelin.* Clermont-Ferrand: Editions La Galipote, 2013.

Pelley, Patricia M. *Postcolonial Vietnam: New Histories of the National Past.* Durham, NC: Duke University Press, 2002.

Pelzer, Karl J. *Planters against Peasants: The Agrarian Struggle in East Sumatra, 1947–1958.* S'-Gravenhage: Martinus Nijhoff, 1982.

Pendergast, Tom. *Creating Modern Man: American Advertising and Consumer Culture, 1900–1950.* Columbia, MO: University of Missouri Press, 2000.

Pomeranz, Kenneth, and Steven Topik. *The World That Trade Created: Society, Culture, and the World Economy, 1400–the Present.* Armonk, NY: M.E. Sharpe, 1999.

Pratt, Mary Louise. *Imperial Eyes: Travel Writing and Transculturation.* London: Routledge, 1992.

Pugh, Peter et al. Edited by Guy Nickalls. *Great Enterprise: A History of Harrisons & Crosfield.* London: Harrisons & Crosfield, 1990.

Raitz, Karl, ed. *The National Road.* Baltimore, MD: Johns Hopkins University Press, 1996.

Ramamurthy, Anandi. *Imperial Persuaders: Images of Africa and Asia in British Advertising.* Manchester: Manchester University Press, 2003.

Ramasamy, P. *Plantation Labour, Unions, Capital, and the State in Peninsular Malaysia.* Kuala Lumpur: Oxford University Press, 1994.

Reed, James. *The Birth Control Movement and American Society: From Private Vice to Public Virtue.* Princeton, NJ: Princeton University Press, 1984 [1978].

Riello, Giorgio. *Cotton: The Fabric That Made the Modern World.* Cambridge: Cambridge University Press, 2013.

Rimmer, Peter J., and Lisa M. Allen, eds. *The Underside of Malaysian History: Pullers, Prostitutes, Plantation Workers.* Singapore: Singapore University Press (for the Malaysia Society of the Asian Studies Association of Australia), 1990.

Rosenberg, Emily S. *Financial Missionaries to the World: The Politics and Culture of Dollar Diplomacy, 1900–1930.* Cambridge, MA: Harvard University Press, 1999.

Rosenberg, Emily S., ed. *A World Connecting, 1870–1945.* Cambridge, MA: Harvard University Press, 2012.

Rydell, Robert W. *All the World's a Fair: Visions of Empire at American International Expositions, 1876–1916.* Chicago, IL: University of Chicago Press, 1984.

Rydell, Robert W. *World of Fairs: The Century-of-Progress Expositions.* Chicago, IL: University of Chicago Press, 1993.

Scharff, Virginia. *Taking the Wheel: Women and the Coming of the Motor Age.* New York: Free Press, 1991.

Schidrowitz, P., and T.R. Dawson, eds. *History of the Rubber Industry (Compiled under the auspices of the Institution of the Rubber Industry).* Cambridge: W. Heffer & Sons, 1952.

Serier, Jean-Baptiste. *Histoire du caoutchouc.* Paris: Editions Desjonquères, 1993.

Shaffer, Marguerite S. *See America First: Tourism and National Identity, 1880–1940.* Washington, DC: Smithsonian Institution Press, 2001.

Suggested Readings

Shennan, Margaret. *Out in the Midday Sun: The British in Malaya, 1880–1960*. London: John Murray, 2000.

Sinha, Mrinalini. *Colonial Masculinity: The "Manly Englishman" and the "Effeminate Bengali" in the Late Nineteenth Century*. Manchester: Manchester University Press, 1995.

Slack, Charles. *Noble Obsession: Charles Goodyear, Thomas Hancock, and the Race to Unlock the Greatest Industrial Secret of the Nineteenth Century*. New York: Hyperion, 2002.

Stanfield, Michael Edward. *Red Rubber, Bleeding Trees: Violence, Slavery, and Empire in Northwest Amazonia, 1850–1933*. Albuquerque, NM: University of New Mexico Press, 1998.

Stepan, Nancy Leys. *Picturing Tropical Nature*. Ithaca, NY: Cornell University Press, 2001.

Stoler, Ann Laura. *Capitalism and Confrontation in Sumatra's Plantation Belt, 1870–1979*. New Haven, CT: Yale University Press, 1985.

Stoler, Ann Laura. *Carnal Knowledge and Imperial Power: Race and the Intimate in Colonial Rule*. Berkeley, CA: University of California Press, 2002.

Strasser, Susan, Charles McGovern, and Matthias Judt, eds., *Getting and Spending: European and American Consumer Societies in the Twentieth Century*. Washington, DC: German Historical Institute/Cambridge: Cambridge University Press, 1998.

Sundiata, I.K. *Black Scandal: America and the Liberian Labor Crisis, 1929–1936*. Philadelphia, PA: Institute for the Study of Human Issues, 1980.

Sundiata, Ibrahim. *Brothers and Strangers: Black Zion, Black Slavery, 1914–1940*. Durham, NC: Duke University Press, 2003.

de Syon, Guillaume. *Zeppelin! Germany and the Airship, 1900–1939*. Baltimore, MD: Johns Hopkins University Press, 2002.

Taladoire, Eric. *Les terrains de jeu de balle (Mésoamérique et Sud-ouest des Etats-Unis)*. Mexico City: Etudes Mésoaméricaines, 1981.

Tarling, Nicholas. *Southeast Asia: A Modern History*. South Melbourne: Oxford University Press, 2001.

Tate, D.J.M. *The RGA History of the Plantation Industry in the Malay Peninsula* (Commissioned by the Rubber Growers' Association (Malaysia) Berhad). Kuala Lumpur: Oxford University Press, 1996.

Thee, Kian-wie. *Plantation Agriculture and Export Growth: An Economic History of East Sumatra, 1863–1942*. Jakarta: National Institute of Economic and Social Research, 1977.

Thomas, Martin. "Fighting 'Communist Banditry' in French Vietnam: The Rhetoric of Repression after the Yen Bay Uprising, 1930–1932." *French Historical Studies* 34, no. 4 (Fall 2011): 611–648.

Thomas, Martin. *Violence and Colonial Order: Police, Workers and Protest in the European Colonial Empires, 1918–1940*. Cambridge: Cambridge University Press, 2012.

Thoms, David, Len Holden, and Tim Claydon, eds. *The Motor Car and Popular Culture in the 20th Century*. Aldershot: Ashgate, 1998.

Tone, Andrea. *Devices and Desires: A History of Contraceptives in America*. New York: Hill and Wang, 2001.

Topik, Steven C., and Allen Wells. *Global Markets Transformed, 1870–1945*. Cambridge, MA: Harvard University Press, 2012.

Trachtenberg, Alan. *The Incorporation of America: Culture and Society in the Gilded Age*. New York: Hill and Wang, 1982.

Treue, Wilhelm. *Gummi in Deutschland: Die deutsche Kautschukversorgung und Gummi-Industrie im Rahmen weltwirtschaftlicher Entwicklung* (Issued on behalf of Continental Gummi-Werke AG Hannover). Munich: F. Bruckmann, 1955.

Tucker, Richard P. *Insatiable Appetite: The United States and the Economic Degradation of the Tropical World*. Berkeley, CA: University of California Press, 2000.

Tully, John. "A Victorian Ecological Disaster: Imperialism, the Telegraph, and Gutta-Percha." *Journal of World History* 20, no. 4 (2009): 559–579.

Tully, John. *Devil's Milk: A Social History of Rubber*. New York: Monthly Review Press, 2011.

Vanthemsche, Guy. *Belgium and the Congo, 1885–1980*. Trans. by Alice Cameron and Stephen Windross. Cambridge: Cambridge University Press, 2012.

Verney, Sébastien. "Le nécessaire compromis colonial: Le cas de la plantation Michelin de Dau Tieng (Cochinchine) de 1932 à 1937." In *Les administrations coloniales, XIXe–XXe siècles: Esquisse d'une histoire comparée*. Edited by Sania El Mechat. Rennes: Presses Universitaires de Rennes, 2009, pp. 163–173.

Verney, Sébastien. *L'Indochine sous Vichy: Entre révolution nationale, collaboration et identités nationales 1940–1945*. Paris: Riveneuve, 2012.

Vidal, Vincent. *La petite histoire du préservatif*. Paris: Syros Alternatives, 1993.

Vidal, Vincent. *Le préservatif*. Paris: Editions Alternatives, 1996.

Vigna, Xavier. *Histoire des ouvriers en France au XXe siècle*. Paris: Perrin, 2012.

de Vogüé, Arnaud. *Ainsi vint au monde: La S.I.P.H. (1905–1939)*. Vichères: Amicale des Anciens Planteurs d'Hévéa, 1993.

Voon, Phin Keong. *Western Rubber Planting Enterprise in Southeast Asia, 1876–1921*. Kuala Lumpur: University of Malaya, 1976.

Vos, Jelmer. "The Economics of the Kwango Rubber Trade, c. 1900." In *Angola on the Move: Transport Routes, Communication and History*. Edited by Beatrix Heintze and Achim von Oppen. Frankfurt: Verlag Otto Lembeck, 2008, pp. 85–98.

Wallerstein, Immanuel. *The Modern World-System: Capitalist Agriculture and the Origins of the European World-Economy in the Sixteenth Century*. New York: Academic Press, 1974.

Wallerstein, Immanuel. *The Modern World-System II: Mercantilism and the Consolidation of the European World-Economy, 1600–1750*. New York: Academic Press, 1980.

Webster, C.C., and W.J. Baulkwill. *Rubber*. London: Longman Scientific and Technical, 1989.

Weinstein, Barbara. *The Amazon Rubber Boom, 1850–1920*. Stanford, CA: Stanford University Press, 1983.

Wells, W.G.B. *Coolly Tamil as Understood by Labourers on Tea and Rubber Estates, Specially Arranged for Planters and Planting Students*. Colombo: Ceylon Observer, 1915.

Westoff, Charles F., and Norman B. Ryder. *The Contraceptive Revolution*. Princeton, NJ: Princeton University Press, 1977.

White, Nicholas J. *Business, Government, and the End of Empire: Malaya, 1942–1957*. Kuala Lumpur: Oxford University Press, 1996.

Whittington, E. Michael, ed. *The Sport of Life and Death: The Mesoamerican Ballgame*. New York: Thames & Hudson, 2001.

Whittlesey, Charles R. *Governmental Control of Crude Rubber: The Stevenson Plan*. Princeton, NJ: Princeton University Press, 1931.

Wilkins, Mira. *The Emergence of Multinational Enterprise: American Business Abroad from the Colonial Era to 1914*. Cambridge, MA: Harvard University Press, 1970.

Wilkins, Mira. *The Maturing of Multinational Enterprise: American Business Abroad from 1914 to 1970*. Cambridge, MA: Harvard University Press, 1974.

Wilkins, Mira, and Harm Schröter, eds. *The Free-Standing Company in the World Economy, 1830–1996*. Oxford: Oxford University Press, 1998.

Wolf, Eric R. *Europe and the People without History*. Berkeley, CA: University of California Press, 1982.

Woshner, Mike. *India-Rubber and Gutta-Percha in the Civil War Era: An Illustrated History of Rubber and Pre-Plastic Antiques and Militaria*. Alexandria, VA: O'Donnell Publications, 1999.

Woycke, James. *Birth Control in Germany, 1871–1933*. London: Routledge, 1988.

Wynants, Maurits. *Des ducs de Brabant aux villages congolais: Tervuren et l'exposition coloniale 1897*. Tervuren: Musée Royal de l'Afrique Centrale, 1997.

Yacob, Shakila. "Model of Welfare Capitalism? The United States Rubber Company in Southeast Asia, 1910–1942." *Enterprise and Society* 8, no. 1 (March 2007): 136–174.

Yacob, Shakila. *The United States and the Malaysian Economy*. London: Routledge, 2008.

Yee Fong, Leong. *Labour and Trade Unionism in Colonial Malaya: A Study of the Socio-Economic and Political Bases of the Malayan Labour Movement, 1930–1957*. Pulau Pinang: Penerbit Universitii Malaysia, 1999.

Yergin, Daniel. *The Prize: The Epic Quest for Oil, Money, and Power*. New York: Simon and Schuster, 1992.

Index

Index

Index